Exports and technology

Exports and Technology

Kirsty Hughes
University of Manchester

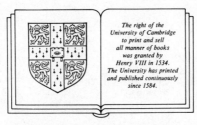

The right of the
University of Cambridge
to print and sell
all manner of books
was granted by
Henry VIII in 1534.
The University has printed
and published continuously
since 1584.

CAMBRIDGE UNIVERSITY PRESS
Cambridge
London   New York   New Rochelle
Melbourne   Sydney

Published by the Press Syndicate of the University of Cambridge
The Pitt Building, Trumpington Street, Cambridge CB2 1RP
32 East 57th Street, New York, NY 10022, USA
10 Stamford Road, Oakleigh, Melbourne 3166, Australia

First published 1986

Printed in Great Britain at the University Press, Cambridge

British Library Cataloguing in Publication Data

Hughes, Kirsty
Exports and technology
1. Export marketing   2. Technological innovations
I. Title
382'.6   HF1009.5

Library of Congress Cataloguing in Publication Data

Hughes, Kirsty
Exports and technology.
Bibliography; p.
Includes index.
1. Commerce. 2. Technology. 3. Research,
Industrial. 4. Great Britain — Commerce.
5. Technological innovations — Great Britain. I. Title.
HF1008.H84 1986   382'.6   85-30920
ISBN 0 521 32036 4

AN

To Nicola

Contents

Figures and tables

Acknowledgements

This book is based on my Ph.D. thesis carried out in the Department of Economics, University of Bristol. I have benefited from the help and advice of a number of people in the Bristol Economics Department. In particular, I would like to thank my supervisor, Alan Winters, for his advice and encouragement throughout my research. I am also grateful to Stephen Davies for advice on certain parts of this work. I am grateful for permission from the Controller of Her Majesty's Stationery Office to reproduce tables 2.14, 2.15 and 2.16. I would also like to thank the University of Bristol scholarship fund for financial support during my research.

CHAPTER 1

Introduction

1.1 Technology and competitiveness

This study aims to analyse the role of technological ability and the role of skilled labour in determining trade performance. Both in the economic literature, and more widely, there has been an emphasis on the contribution of technology and skill to countries' relative competitiveness. The importance to the advanced industrial economies of maintaining a technological lead has been stressed increasingly as the newly industrialising countries compete in an ever wider range of markets. Technological differences are, therefore, likely to be central in explanations of the changing relative positions and performance of the different OECD countries.

This contemporary emphasis on skill and technology has also been a major theoretical and empirical concern of the international trade literature. More recent theoretical developments have stressed, in addition, the effects of various aspects of industrial structure – in particular, monopoly power, product differentiation and scale economies – on trade levels and trade performance. An analysis of these different factors and their interconnections can contribute to an explanation of trade patterns, of variations in the performances of different countries and of changes in relative performance over time. In terms of policy, such an analysis may also have implications for the ability of a country to change its relative competitiveness over time – for example, through changing its endowment of skilled labour or changing its industrial structure. By analysing and developing existing theoretical and empirical studies of these issues, the current work aims to throw further light not only on the roles of technology and skill in determining trade performance, but also on the question of the determinants of technological effort and technological success. Thus, this work argues that the various possible interconnections between trade success and technological success are a crucial part of the analysis.

1

In terms of technological intensity and competitiveness, the U.S. economy is clearly of major importance and many studies have analysed the relationship between technology and trade, in particular in manufactured goods, for the U.S. (discussed further in Chapter 3). These studies have emphasised the advantages the U.S. gains from its technological leadership in many fields and from its relative abundance of highly skilled labour. However, the position of the U.S. in a world of changing technology has, inevitably, not been static. The U.S. has been challenged technologically in a number of areas, most notably by Japan but also by other countries. Furthermore, even where it has not been overtaken, there has been a reduction of the gap, in technological terms, between the U.S. and its major competitors. Theoretical analysis of the determinants of technological change, and empirical analysis of the trade and technological performance of countries other than the U.S., can contribute to an explanation both of the dominance of the U.S. and of the nature of the challenge to it by other countries. Such an analysis can also contribute to explanations of differences in performance across countries − for example, the success of the Japanese economy, and the continued relative decline of the U.K. economy.

It has been suggested that different economies may get caught in virtuous or vicious circles, of growth or decline respectively. Thus, in the current context, the possibility arises that interaction between export success and technological success may result in virtuous circles of cumulative causation (Myrdal 1957) − a possibility not allowed for in traditional trade theory. This could contribute to an explanation both of the exceptional performance of Japan and of the poor performance of the U.K. Various explanations of the so-called 'de-industrialisation' of the U.K. have argued that the U.K. has been caught in a vicious circle, in which trade and technology play important roles. Thus, Matthews (1973) suggests that the U.K. has become trapped in a process of cumulative causation in which slow domestic growth (whatever its initial cause) leads to trade difficulties, since relatively faster foreign growth results in both higher productivity and higher quality of products. A weak foreign trade position may then reduce aggregate demand, both because of lower export demand and by limiting the government's ability to sustain demand. This results in lower investment, which reduces technical progress and productivity and leads to a weaker competitive trade position (Singh 1977). Schott (1981) stresses very clearly the crucial role of innovation in this vicious circle ⊢ 'poor economic performance . . . inhibits innovation and declining growth in innovative activity in turn inhibits economic performance' (pp. 1–2).

As international markets become more intensely competitive, technological ability is likely to be increasingly important to the advanced industrial countries. An OECD report (1980) concludes that there has been an intensification of high technology competition in particular, and that the major asset of the industrialised countries lies in their aptitude for technological innovation. However, it has also been found that in the more uncertain climate of the 1970s, research and development (R&D) expenditure was increasingly directed to the short-run and safe (OECD 1980; Schott 1981). This may have serious implications for future competitiveness.

Given the stress on technology of studies such as that of the OECD (1980), it is important to consider whether this emphasis is appropriate. By analysing theoretical and empirical explanations of trade flows and trade performance, the differing roles of technology, skill and other variables can be assessed. In carrying out such an analysis, it is also important to consider the determinants of technological activity.

1.2 An overview

Before considering the analysis and extension of existing theoretical and empirical work, Chapter 2 presents some general descriptive evidence on the technology, skill and trade performance of the five main OECD countries. Chapter 3 then considers developments of traditional trade theory, with particular reference to the neo-technology and neo-factor endowment theories of trade. The chapter goes on to summarise and assess some of the existing empirical literature with respect to these theories. In the light of the analysis in Chapter 3, Chapter 4 considers in more depth the expected relationship between technology and exports, and then establishes the specification of an estimating equation for manufactured exports. Chapter 5 proceeds to analyse the various theories of the determinants of technological effort — focusing in particular on R&D expenditures — and then assesses the empirical evidence on the determinants of R&D. Chapter 6 sets out a model of R&D expenditure, derived from the analysis of advertising, and goes on to establish the specification of an estimating equation for R&D. The chapter puts forward the hypothesis of a simultaneous relationship between exports and R&D. Chapters 7 and 8 present the results of estimating the export and R&D equations as a simultaneous system for the U.K. Chapter 9 presents results for estimating changes in U.K. trade performance. To give a broader empirical picture, Chapter 10 presents results of estimating the export and R&D equations, at a higher aggregation level, for the U.K. relative to West Germany, and for each country separately. Chapter 11 presents a general summary and conclusions.

CHAPTER 2

Technological competitiveness and export performance in the U.S., Japan, West Germany, the U.K. and France

The main aim of this study is to analyse and develop theoretical and empirical explanations both of the roles of technology and skilled labour in trade performance, and of the determinants of technological activity. However, prior to developing this in depth, the current chapter provides some general descriptive evidence on countries' relative performance over time. While a descriptive (or an econometric) study cannot fully assess all relevant factors and their dynamics and interactions, the evidence presented here provides a backdrop of relevant information. This may help to place in context evidence and results from econometric work and from other more detailed studies. The chapter focuses on the U.S., Japan, West Germany, the U.K. and France as the largest OECD countries, who between them account for over 85 per cent of R&D spending in the OECD. The evidence presented here gives some indication of the relative importance of technological effort in these countries, of its variation by industry and of the role of government in encouraging innovation. The chapter then assesses trends in trade performance across industries, and by industries classified according to technological intensity. Finally, some general evidence is briefly considered on the level and distribution of skills in the workforces of these countries.

2.1 Technological competitiveness

Chapter 1 stressed the crucial importance of technological ability to the competitiveness of the advanced capitalist countries. However, technological ability is a multi-faceted concept and there is not a simple or unique link between technological ability — however defined — and economic performance. There are various possible ways of attempting to measure the technological activity of a particular country or industry, of which R&D expenditures and patents are frequently used. There are well known difficulties

4

in using these and other measures precisely, because of the complex nature of technological effort and innovation.

The focus here is on R&D expenditures, because of the relative ease of comparison across industries and countries and the availability of detailed data. R&D data suffer nevertheless from various drawbacks. In particular, they are an input measure – they do not account, therefore, for variations in effectiveness of R&D, or for duplication of R&D. The effects of R&D are also cumulative and so, ideally, a stock measure should be used, but there are inevitably major measurement problems (Schott 1978). Furthermore, data on R&D give no indication of the amount of subsequent expenditure necessary to translate an innovation fully into production.[1] Neither R&D nor patent data provide information on the speed or extent of diffusion of innovations, which will vary by both industry and country (see, for example, Davies 1979; Stoneman 1983). In the light of these points, it is clear that the information presented below cannot give a complete picture of technological competitiveness. It nevertheless provides evidence on one major aspect of technological activity, and so contributes to an understanding of differences between countries and between industries, and of their relative development over time.

The five main R&D-performing nations are – in order of importance – the U.S., Japan, Germany, the U.K. and France. Table 2.1 indicates the importance of their R&D expenditure relative to total OECD R&D, and the rate of growth of R&D expenditures from 1969 to 1981. The U.S. dominates

Table 2.1. *Gross expenditure on R&D as proportions of total OECD R&D*

	1971	1975	1981	Average annual real growth rates 1969–81 (%)
United States	50.37	47.22	46.33	1.8[a]
Japan	11.90	14.11	17.04	8.1
Germany	9.60	9.84	9.87	5.4
United Kingdom	7.54[a]	7.52	6.97[a]	2.0
France	6.64	6.79	6.82	3.5
OECD total	100.00	100.00	100.00	3.4[a]

[a]OECD estimate.
Sources: OECD 1984a; OECD 1984b.

R&D spending, accounting for almost a half of OECD R&D in 1981. However, it is Japan, in particular, that has improved its position, partly at the expense of the U.S. By 1981 it accounted for 17 per cent of OECD R&D. Germany and France maintained their relative positions over this period, while the U.K. slipped back slightly. Of the five countries, the U.K. and the U.S. exhibited the slowest rates of growth during the 1970s.

Table 2.2 shows total expenditure on R&D as a proportion of gross domestic product (GDP), and government R&D as a proportion of GDP. This presents information on R&D effort relative to size. However, to the extent that R&D leads to growth, and vice versa, absolute figures, and not only R&D data deflated for size, are important. Table 2.2 shows that the five countries are quite similar in their R&D/GDP ratios − and more so in 1981 than 1970. There are differences however in governments' contributions, Japan having a notably low ratio. This difference is, in large part, due to the importance of defence R&D in the U.S., the U.K. and France (OECD 1984c).

This is highlighted in Table 2.3, which shows defence R&D and non-defence R&D as proportions of GDP. Japan's defence R&D is negligible; Germany's is relatively low. The other three countries, however, maintain a large defence input. By 1984 the U.S. defence R&D spending relative to total government R&D had risen from 55 per cent in 1981 to 66 per cent. In terms of non-defence R&D, Japan and Germany have clearly become the most R&D-intensive countries of the five. In absolute terms, Japan has moved from

Table 2.2. *Gross expenditure and government expenditure on R&D as proportions of GDP*

	Gross expenditure		Government expenditure	
	1970	1981	1970	1981
United States	2.77	2.52	1.55	1.15
Japan	1.85	2.38	0.55[b]	0.64
Germany	2.06	2.49	0.96	1.15
United Kingdom	2.29[a]	2.46	1.19	1.43
France	1.91	2.01	1.14[c]	1.31

[a]1969. [b]1971. [c]1974.
Source: OECD/STIU data bank.

Table 2.3. *Defence R&D and non-defence R&D as proportions of GDP*

	Defence R&D		Non-defence R&D	
	1970	1981	1970	1981
United States	0.81[a]	0.63	1.96[a]	1.89
Japan	0.01[b]	0.01	1.84[b]	2.37
Germany	0.17	0.10	1.89	2.39
United Kingdom	0.51[c]	0.70	1.78[c]	1.76
France	0.36[d]	0.50	1.55[d]	1.51

[a]1971 figure used to calculate defence proportion.
[b]1975 figure used to calculate defence proportion.
[c]1970 figure used to calculate defence proportion; rest of data, 1969.
[d]1974 figure used to calculate defence proportion.
Source: OECD/STIU data bank.

spending less than a third of total U.S. non-defence R&D, in 1970, to spending nearly a half in 1981. For smaller countries like the U.K. and France, the large amounts spent on defence R&D may absorb scientific resources and inhibit R&D in other areas (M. Kaldor 1980). Even for the U.S., its allocation of R&D resources is likely to make it more susceptible to Japanese competition. While there may be 'spin-off' effects from defence R&D, these are inevitably less than the benefits of direct application of R&D to non-defence purposes.

Japanese industry has notably less direct government funding of industry's R&D (even taking account of differences in defence spending). In 1981 the proportions of business expenditure on R&D financed by industry were: Japan, 98 per cent; Germany, 82 per cent; the U.S. and France, 68 per cent; and the U.K., 61 per cent. The U.S. proportion rose markedly over the 1970s. Japan's position does not reflect lack of government interest in, or support for, R&D, but rather the fact that the Government tends to play a long-run planning and co-ordinating role. It does this through MITI (Ministry of International Trade and Industry). MITI, through in-depth analysis and collection of information, and discussion and collaboration with industry, determines which fields are promising technologically. It may then launch or support certain projects in their initial stages, subsequently providing advice, industrial co-ordination, tax incentives, etc. (OECD 1984a). However, there is some concern that Japanese industry does not undertake sufficient basic research and, therefore, that the Government should undertake more research in this field (*Journal of Japanese Trade and Industry*, no. 1, 1985, p. 21). It is clear, though, that the Government plays an active role in Japan, and that its scope and importance is not adequately reflected in data on its direct R&D spending.

One complement to R&D data at an aggregate level is data on technological receipts and payments. These both give some indication of countries' relative dependence on technology performed abroad, and show the extent to which domestic R&D efforts are being supplemented by other sources. Table 2.4 shows technological receipts and payments as a proportion of business expenditure on R&D in 1979, and the net technological balance of payments in 1980. The U.S. stands out particularly clearly as having a very low payments ratio and a large surplus. While the U.K. also has a positive surplus this is a result of low absolute payments, not of high receipts. Japan and Germany by contrast have relatively low receipts.

Technological effort at a national or aggregate level does not present a complete picture. In the case of the U.K., for example, it has been suggested that, even in the 1950s and 1960s when its research effort was relatively high, its R&D was completely misdirected to a few high technology areas (Freeman 1978). These were areas where the U.S. was also concentrated, but

Table 2.4. *Technological receipts and payments as a proportion of business expenditure on R&D, and the net technological balance of payments*

| | 1979 | | 1980 Net balance (million $ purchasing power parities, 1975 prices) |
	Payments	Receipts	
United States	0.02	0.17	+ 4321
Japan	0.08	0.05	− 238
Germany	0.11	0.04	− 420
United Kingdom	0.14[a]	0.17[a]	+ 114
France	0.16	0.14	− 96

[a]1978.
Source: OECD 1984b.

the U.S. was much better placed to benefit from associated scale economies and to achieve the high sales necessary to recoup the large R&D costs. Thus, it is relevant to consider the industrial distribution of R&D in the five countries focused on here.

Table 2.5 shows manufacturing industry disaggregated into twenty-one industries and categorised into high, medium and low technology groups (OECD 1984d). The definition of high, medium and low technological intensity is not simple, as this may vary over time and by country (Soete 1980). Also in Table 2.5 intensities are calculated as R&D/sales. This may reduce the apparent intensity of industries with relatively low value-added/ sales ratios. Nevertheless, table 2.5 does give some overview of average research intensity across industries. There have been some changes in ranking during the 1970s, but these are not major (OECD 1984a). The high R&D intensity industries have experienced the fastest growth in the OECD area, in particular electronics and computers, though chemicals and automobiles also grew relatively fast in the 1970s (OECD 1984d). In contrast to the other countries, Japan devotes only 40 per cent of its R&D to high technology intensity industries. The other four devote over 50 per cent. This reflects, in part, the diversified and highly flexible nature of Japanese R&D (OECD 1984d).

Table 2.6 shows R&D shares of the U.S., Japan, Germany and France by seven main industry groups. This confirms the overall dominance of the U.S. but also indicates variation by industry field. Japan, for example, is relatively strong in the basic metal industries group and the chemically linked groups. The U.S. dominates − as would be expected − in the aerospace group.

A more detailed picture is given in Table 2.7. This shows the distribution of R&D spending across manufacturing industry for each of the five countries.

Table 2.5. *Average^a R&D intensity by industry*

1980		Intensities
High intensity		
1 Aerospace		22.7
2 Office machines, computers		17.5
3 Electronic equipment & components		10.4
4 Drugs		8.7
5 Instruments		4.8
6 Electrical machinery		4.4
	Average	11.4
Medium intensity		
7 Motor vehicles		2.7
8 Chemicals		2.3
9 Other manufacturing industries		1.8
10 Non-electrical machinery		1.6
11 Rubber, plastics		1.2
12 Non-ferrous metals		1.0
	Average	1.8
Low intensity		
13 Stone, clay, glass		0.9
14 Food, beverages, tobacco		0.8
15 Shipbuilding		0.6
16 Petroleum refineries		0.6
17 Ferrous metals		0.6
18 Fabricated metal products		0.4
19 Paper, printing		0.3
20 Wood, cork, furniture		0.3
21 Textiles, footwear, leather		0.2
	Average	0.5

^{a}Weighted average of the eleven main OECD countries – R&D expenditure/output.
Source: OECD 1984d.

As noted above, the U.S., the U.K. and France have a particularly high concentration of their R&D in aerospace. The U.K. has also increased its R&D effort in electronic equipment and components, from 16.6 per cent in 1969 to 30 per cent in 1981. It also has a notably lower motor vehicles weight. Germany continues to maintain its particular emphasis in chemicals and drugs. The U.S. appears to put relatively more of its research effort into instruments and into office machinery and computers, though Japan also has a relatively strong emphasis on instruments. It is interesting to note, however, that Japan also has a relatively large emphasis on ferrous metals, and on stone, clay and glass. This reflects the less narrow focus in Japan on high technology products, and its aim to keep abreast of potential developments in a number of fields, such as fine ceramics and other new materials (*Japanese Journal of Trade and Industry*, no. 1, 1985).

Table 2.6. *Shares in OECD[a] industrial R&D, 1981 (percentages)*

	U.S.	Japan	Germany	France	Total
Electrical group	49.9	19.6	12.5	7.7	100.0[b]
Chemical group	44.7[b]	18.5	15.5	7.5	100.0[b]
Aerospace	83.7	0.0	4.7	7.9	100.0[b]
Other transport	48.9[b]	24.8	13.2	6.6	100.0[b]
Basic metal group	37.3	34.1	12.2	5.3	100.0
Machinery group	61.3	13.8	10.9	3.7	100.0
Chemically linked group	41.1[b]	30.4	8.8	8.7	100.0[b]
Other manufacturing group	53.2[b]	22.4	6.8	4.3	100.0[b]
Total services	41.0	23.2	5.5	8.0	100.0
Total	54.8[b]	17.5	11.5	6.8	100.0[b]

[a]Data have been calculated for thirteen countries only, which represent some nine-tenths of total industrial R&D in the OECD area. Missing countries are, by economic importance (GDP): the U.K., Spain, Australia, the Netherlands, Turkey, Belgium, Yugoslavia, Greece, Portugal and New Zealand.
[b]Including elements estimated by OECD.
Source: OECD 1984a.

Table 2.8 presents OECD calculations of R&D relative to output, for the same industries as table 2.7. This tells a similar but not identical story in terms of R&D effort across countries. The high U.S. and U.K. aerospace intensities reflect again their R&D emphasis in this area, while the German figure reflects its relatively low aerospace output. The U.K. motor vehicle effort now looks similar to those of its competitiors. It is necessary, however, to be cautious in interpreting these figures since any sudden changes in output will alter the ratios. Thus, for example, the relatively high R&D intensities of the U.K. may reflect sharp falls in output in 1980.

2.2 Trade performance

The potential links between technological effort and trade performance are discussed in subsequent chapters. Technological effort is only one of a number of potential influences on trade and simple correlations cannot, therefore, provide much insight into the problem. In this section, evidence is presented on the relative trade performances of the five countries by industry and in aggregate, with some reference to technology groups but without attempting to draw direct links with the evidence of the previous section.

Table 2.9 presents market shares of exports of the seven main OECD countries. Since the 1960s the U.S. and the U.K. have both lost market shares, while Japan has experienced a dramatic increase in its share, and both France and Germany a small increase.

Table 2.10 presents market shares of manufacturing industry for exports and for import penetration. There is little change in average export shares

Table 2.7. *Business enterprise total R&D expenditure, 1981 (percentage distribution)*

	U.S.[a]	Japan	Germany	U.K.	France
Electrical machinery	7.1	8.4	25.7	3.4	3.7
Electronic equipment and components	14.4	18.0		29.9	22.5
Chemicals ✓	6.7	11.8	24.0	7.9	9.9
Drugs	4.2	6.5		8.3	6.5
Petroleum refineries	3.6	1.2	0.9	1.1	3.6
Aerospace	21.6	0.0	6.7	21.5	18.6
Motor vehicles	11.6	15.5	14.8	5.1	12.1
Ships	0.4	2.8	0.2	0.3	0.1
Other transport		0.2	0.1	–[b]	0.3
Ferrous metals	1.0	5.1	1.9	0.9	1.2
Non-ferrous metals	0.6	2.0	0.5	0.6	1.1
Fabricated metal products	1.3	1.9	2.4	1.1	1.2
Instruments	7.1	3.8	2.0	1.7	1.4
Office machinery & computers	9.3	3.4	15.2	4.9	4.9
Machinery n.e.c.	4.6	7.2		6.2	3.4
Food, drink & tobacco	1.5	2.9	1.2	2.6	1.3
Textiles & clothing	0.3	1.9	0.5	0.4	0.6
Rubber & plastics	1.6	2.9	1.6	2.0	3.7
Stone, clay & glass	1.0	2.5	1.1	1.0	1.3
Paper & printing	1.1	0.6	0.4	0.5	0.3
Wood, cork & furniture	0.3	0.3	0.3	0.1	0.1
Other manufacturing	0.8	1.0	0.1	0.6[b]	0.5
Total manufacturing[c]	100.0	100.0	100.0	100.0	100.0

[a] 1980 data.
[b] Other transport included in other manufacturing.
[c] Totals may not add precisely due to rounding errors.
Source: OECD/STIU data bank.

in the 1970s, with Japan showing the largest gain, and Germany remaining the largest exporter. In terms of import penetration more marked changes can be observed. The U.S. is the only country not to show an increase in import penetration, while the three European countries show very marked increases, and from much higher levels than those of the U.S. and Japan.

Table 2.11 presents more detailed information on trade performance by industry. As would be expected given the aggregate trade performance of these countries, Japan shows a general improvement in its net trade balance in many industries. Germany, France and the U.K. have a more varied experience. The U.K., in particular, experienced a fall in the net trade balance of the vast majority of its industries. The U.S. also had a varied experience but with no very marked changes.

Tables 2.12 and 2.13 give further information on export and import

Table 2.8. R&D intensity^a by industry and country, 1980

	U.S.	Japan	Germany	U.K.	France
Electrical machinery	5.81	3.94	⎫ 9.48	2.79	1.66
Electronic equipment & components	12.38	6.24	⎭	20.48	11.13
Chemicals	1.72	3.15	⎫ 4.69	3.16	1.85
Drugs	8.78	8.66	⎭	16.48	4.89
Petroleum refineries	0.74	0.50	0.35	0.42	0.48
Aerospace	29.04	1.53	21.21	28.71	14.56
Motor vehicles	2.96	2.56	2.85	2.66	2.26
Ships	n/a	4.13	0.66	2.07	n/a
Other transport group	2.65	2.51	2.63	2.46	2.00
Ferrous metals	0.33	1.11	0.57	0.48	n/a
Non-ferrous metals	0.78	2.08	0.58	0.66	1.36
Fabricated metal products	0.52	0.45	0.83	0.65	0.46
Instruments	6.92	2.48	2.42	2.50	2.42
Office machinery & computers	18.00	n/a	⎫ 3.70	23.29	10.11
Machinery n.e.c.	1.32	1.69	⎭	1.49	0.58
Machinery group	4.33	1.70	3.22	3.47	1.39
Food, drink & tobacco	0.18	0.40	0.17	0.52	0.12
Textiles & clothing	0.10	0.33	0.25	0.46	0.13
Rubber & plastics	1.17	1.30	1.77	0.66	1.55
Stone, clay & glass	0.91	1.28	0.89	0.91	0.55
Paper & printing	0.36	0.22	0.24	0.29	n/a
Wood, cork & furniture	0.32	0.16	0.32	0.10	n/a
Other manufacturing	2.14	1.39	0.56	5.42	1.41
Total manufacturing	2.26	1.64	2.30	2.66	1.42

^{a}R&D expenditure/output (approximate value). n/a = not available. n.e.c. = not elsewhere classified.
Source: OECD 1983.

Table 2.9. Market shares of total exports of goods and services (current dollars)

	1963	1973	1977	1980	1982
United States	30.50	25.46	23.56	23.72	24.73
Japan	6.51	11.72	14.17	13.19	16.13
Germany	17.79	21.18	20.99	20.47	20.30
France	11.26	12.86	12.81	13.29	10.69
United Kingdom	17.83	12.26	12.07	13.50	11.37
Canada	8.44	8.33	7.49	6.75	8.26
Italy	7.58	8.15	8.86	9.04	8.49
Total (7 countries)	100.00	100.00	100.00	100.00	100.00

Source: OECD 1983.

performance, at the industry level, classified into technology groups (table 2.5 above), in the early 1970s and early 1980s.

The U.S. has lost markets in particular in aerospace, and also in many areas of electronics — due to Japanese competition. Japan increased its large

Table 2.10. *Market shares (volume) of OECD^a exports and the rate of import penetration for manufacturing industry (average of annual values)*

	Exports		Imports	
	1970–4	1975–80	1970–4	1975–80
United States	16.8	17.6	8.3	8.2
Japan	11.4	13.5	4.3	5.6
Germany	20.8	19.6	21.4	28.7
United Kingdom	9.4	8.6	19.4	25.7
France	10.3	10.9	16.6	21.8
Total^a	100.0	100.0		

^{a}OECD here means the eleven main OECD countries.
Source: OECD 1983.

market share in electronics and also doubled its export market share of motor vehicles. Only in some low intensity industries has it been losing market share, reflecting its aim of moving away from any reliance on traditional industries. Germany lost market share in computers and electronics. It also experienced a large increase in import penetration in instruments and electrical machinery – as did France and the U.K. Taking the EEC as a whole, its competitiveness in manufactured products has been declining since 1975 in both high and medium R&D intensity industries (OECD 1984d).

Taking the overall trade balances of the three technology categories, the five countries focused on here are the only ones with positive trade balances in the high intensity industries throughout the period 1970–82. This could reflect, in part, the importance of absolute levels of R&D spending and of domestic market size, though without further analysis this can only be speculative. The U.S. is the only country where the high intensity surpluses are higher than those for medium intensity industries, although in absolute terms Japan has a larger surplus. However, the U.S. is also the only country whose share in OECD output of high technology industries is falling sharply, reflecting, in part, the catching-up process of other countries. Japan is the only country with a surplus in all three categories (OECD 1984d).

Thus, while the five countries focused on here have favourable trade balances in high technology products relative to other OECD countries, their performance relative to each other has varied considerably. Taking the period between 1971 and 1979, Japan not only showed the best performance, in terms of the net trade ratio, in the high technology category, but also strongly improved its position in the 1970s. The U.S. was in second position, but had experienced the most important relative loss. Germany and the U.K. also experienced some deterioration while France improved its position, enabling it to move into fourth position ahead of the U.K. (OECD 1984b).

Table 2.11. *Net trade balances^a of manufacturing industry*

	U.S.		Japan		Germany		U.K.		France	
	1970	1980	1970	1980	1970	1980	1970	1980	1970	1980
Electrical machinery	1.6	1.5	3.9	7.3	2.5	2.2	2.1	1.6	1.5	1.7
Electronic equipment and components	0.8	0.6	9.7	10.7	1.7	1.1	1.3	0.8	1.0	0.8
Electrical & Electronic group	1.0	0.8	7.0	9.4	2.1	1.6	1.6	1.1	1.2	1.1
Industrial chemicals	2.5	2.4	1.7	1.5	2.0	1.7	1.3	1.5	1.0	1.0
Drugs and medicines	4.7	2.4	0.2	0.2	2.8	1.7	3.9	3.2	1.5	2.1
Petroleum refineries	0.4	0.2	0.07	0.07	0.8	0.3	0.7	1.0	1.1	0.8
Chemical group	1.5	1.2	0.8	0.6	1.7	1.1	1.2	1.4	1.0	1.0
Aerospace	9.8	4.1	0.1	0.07	0.5	0.8	1.6	1.1	1.0	1.3
Motor vehicles	0.6	0.5	13.7	38.5	3.6	3.4	4.7	1.0	2.0	1.7
Shipbuilding, repairing	1.8	2.6	24.6	8.9	2.2	4.0	3.0	2.2	1.8	2.0
Other transport	0.7	1.0	0.4	4.5	1.7	0.9	7.5	4.2	0.5	1.2
Transport group	0.6	0.6	19.8	25.8	3.4	3.2	4.4	1.1	2.1	1.7
Iron & steel basic industries	0.6	0.3	10.3	16.9	1.4	1.7	1.6	0.7	1.1	1.3
Non-ferrous metals basic industries	0.5	0.6	0.2	0.4	0.3	0.7	0.5	0.7	0.4	0.6
Fabricated metal products	1.1	1.2	5.9	8.0	2.8	2.0	2.9	1.6	1.0	1.2
Basic metals group	0.6	0.6	2.7	3.4	1.1	1.4	1.0	0.8	0.9	1.0
Instruments	2.1	1.5	2.9	4.3	2.3	1.4	1.4	1.1	0.8	0.8
Office machines, computers	3.0	3.3	1.0	2.2	1.2	0.9	0.6	0.8	0.6	0.7
Other machinery & equipment except electrical	3.2	4.4	1.8	6.0	3.5	3.2	2.2	1.7	0.8	1.0
Machinery group	3.0	2.8	1.8	6.9	2.9	2.3	1.7	1.4	0.8	0.9
Food, drink & tobacco	0.5	0.8	0.4	4.7	0.3	0.6	0.3	0.6	0.9	1.1
Clothing, footwear, leather	0.3	0.4	4.6	1.4	0.7	0.5	1.3	0.7	1.7	0.8

Table 2.11 (continued)

	U.S.		Japan		Germany		U.K.		France	
	1970	1980	1970	1980	1970	1980	1970	1980	1970	1980
Rubber, plastics	0.5	0.5	15.5	5.1	1.3	1.1	1.8	1.1	1.6	1.2
Chemically linked group	0.4	0.6	2.0	0.8	0.5	0.6	0.6	0.7	1.2	1.0
Stone, clay, glass	0.7	0.7	6.2	4.9	1.4	1.2	2.1	1.6	1.1	1.0
Paper, printing	0.8	0.9	0.8	0.5	0.6	0.8	0.3	0.4	0.5	0.6
Wood, cork, furniture	0.3	0.5	0.5	0.1	0.6	0.6	0.1	0.2	0.4	0.4
Other manufacturing industries n.e.c.	0.4	0.5	2.1	1.8	1.3	1.6	1.0	0.9	1.1	0.7
Other manufacturing industries group	0.6	0.7	1.4	0.9	0.8	0.8	0.5	0.7	0.7	0.7

[a]Exports/imports.
Source: OECD 1983.

Table 2.12. Export market shares[a] (current dollars)

	U.S.		Japan		Germany		U.K.		France	
	1972	1982	1972	1982	1972	1982	1972	1982	1972	1982
High intensity										
Aerospace	58.1	44.9	0.6	0.6	2.6	16.3	15.5	16.1	7.3	9.8
Computers	31.4	40.4	9.5	13.2	20.3	12.8	10.0	9.7	9.2	6.8
Electronic equipment & components	17.6	21.5	31.1	39.4	15.9	12.7	6.9	6.1	5.3	5.2
Drugs & medicines	17.8	20.2	3.1	2.7	23.7	18.0	16.8	14.5	11.8	23.2
Instruments	24.2	26.7	17.4	23.8	23.6	18.1	11.2	10.9	7.8	6.8
Electrical machinery	18.3	20.0	13.6	19.6	25.1	21.4	10.4	9.4	10.6	10.2
Medium intensity										
Motor vehicles	16.9	12.9	11.3	23.8	22.9	24.8	8.4	5.0	10.0	8.6
Chemicals	18.9	20.7	9.5	8.0	23.6	21.4	10.2	10.2	9.8	10.5
Other manufacturing industries	14.9	18.9	14.4	28.3	12.6	15.8	24.5	8.7	6.7	10.0
Non-electrical machinery	22.6	25.5	7.5	14.0	28.0	22.6	11.7	9.7	7.5	7.5
Rubber & plastics	11.4	10.9	13.8	19.5	19.1	17.9	9.4	8.8	16.0	16.3
Non-ferrous metals	10.1	13.3	4.0	6.6	12.6	16.9	13.2	11.8	6.7	8.9
Low intensity										
Stone, clay, glass	10.3	11.3	11.0	13.7	20.6	19.8	9.8	7.8	12.4	12.5
Food & drink	17.6	17.7	2.7	1.9	8.3	14.2	8.9	8.5	16.1	15.8
Shipbuilding	8.6	16.9	37.1	42.5	15.4	11.2	7.4	5.6	6.0	7.6
Petroleum refineries	10.1	14.3	1.4	1.2	15.8	8.9	10.1	9.8	9.1	8.0
Ferrous metals	5.5	4.5	23.3	31.6	19.4	20.0	6.2	4.7	11.7	11.5
Fabricated metal products	13.5	14.6	12.5	14.2	24.2	22.3	11.8	9.0	9.3	10.3
Paper & printing	17.2	16.3	3.2	3.6	10.2	13.5	6.4	6.4	6.6	7.1
Wood, cork & furniture	11.8	13.1	4.7	2.1	11.5	15.1	2.3	3.5	6.5	7.0
Footwear, clothing & leather	6.5	7.5	14.7	11.9	16.1	18.1	9.6	8.4	13.6	11.4

[a]Shares of eleven main OECD countries' exports.
Source: OECD 1984d.

Table 2.13. *The rate of import penetration (imports/domestic sales)*

	U.S.		Japan		Germany		U.K.		France	
	1970	1980	1970	1980	1970	1980	1970	1980	1970	1980
High intensity										
Aerospace	1.8	15.1	60.6	72.8	41.0	93.4	1.6[a]	—	29.9	18.1
Computers	8.3	14.1	22.5	14.8	43.4	62.6	52.5	86.1	58.0	69.8
Electronic equipment & components	7.8	21.7	2.4	5.1	22.6	45.6	10.8	28.8	18.3	26.0
Drugs & medicines	1.4	4.5	7.8	9.2	12.6	17.5	11.7	15.2	9.9	9.9
Instruments	6.9	14.7	7.6	11.2	28.7	52.2	33.2	60.8	51.3	78.3
Electrical machinery	3.4	9.0	2.2	2.9	12.0	26.6	9.0	19.7	12.5	21.9
Medium intensity										
Motor vehicles	10.8	15.5	0.9	1.3	18.8	23.4	8.7	41.5	19.0	27.1
Chemicals	3.9	6.1	6.9	9.9	20.5	32.9	19.9	31.7	27.9	41.7
Other manufacturing industries	11.9	23.0	10.6	10.8	31.3	61.6	9.0[a]	—	18.9	41.1
Non-electrical machinery	4.3	10.2	4.9	4.9	20.4	32.7	21.4	37.0	25.1	29.5
Rubber & plastics	4.5	6.4	0.6	1.3	16.2	31.3	5.7	15.4	10.9	15.8
Non-ferrous metals	10.3	15.8	16.7	31.7	38.4	56.5	49.9	69.6	31.7	37.5
Low intensity										
Stone, clay, glass	3.2	5.3	0.9	1.3	9.9	19.2	5.5	9.7	12.4	13.9
Food & drink	4.8	5.3	5.0	5.8	18.1	21.1	15.6	15.3	9.5	13.1
Shipbuilding	6.4	5.2	2.9	12.1	32.5	37.1	15.8	39.0	18.7	24.3
Petroleum refineries	5.9	5.6	13.1	10.1	17.8	50.2	14.9	14.2	4.8	12.1
Ferrous metals	7.0	8.5	1.9	1.9	18.3	25.6	9.8	15.8	21.0	28.3
Fabricated metal products	2.3	3.4	0.8	1.0	6.3	12.8	4.0	15.6	14.9	22.6
Paper & printing	3.5	4.4	2.6	3.7	17.0	23.0	15.1	19.0	14.0	17.3
Wood, cork & furniture	6.3	9.1	3.7	7.5	14.9	20.5	25.3	27.4	12.2	20.9
Footwear, clothing & leather	6.1	11.5	4.1	8.7	22.8	45.7	14.0	35.4	12.0	28.2

[a] *Economic trends* 1980.
Source: OECD 1984d.

2.3 Skilled labour

The potential relationships between skilled labour, technology and trade are analysed in subsequent chapters. It is of interest here to try to compare skilled labour in the countries under consideration. This is important for many reasons; at the least, it is reasonable to expect a relationship between quality and productivity and skilled labour — regardless of an industry's technological intensity. Given the numerous different types and levels of skills, and given the differences in countries' training and educational systems, only a general comparison is attempted here.

Of the five countries being looked at, many studies have commented on the relatively poor training and educational standards of the U.K. in terms of teaching workers skills and abilities relevant to contemporary economic life. One study of engineering concluded that U.K. engineering education is generally worse than that of France, Germany and Sweden (Ahlström 1982). Since 1963, the number of skilled workers in U.K. engineering and construction has fallen absolutely and relative to the total workforce (Thatcher 1978). Adverse attitudes in the U.K. to engineering and to scientists and engineers in management have frequently been commented on. Freeman concludes that 'Perhaps the biggest, single, long-term contrast between British and German industry has been in the number and quality of engineers deployed in all managerial functions' (Freeman 1978, p. 62). Prais (1981), in a detailed comparison of the U.K. and German labour forces, found the German labour force to be better qualified at all levels.

Similar conclusions were drawn in a joint study by the National Economic Development Council and Manpower Services Commission (NEDC/MSC 1984). This undertook a detailed survey of training and education in Germany, the U.S. and Japan, and used the results to draw implications and policy conclusions for the U.K. In terms of training and skills the report concluded that there was a major resource gap between the U.K. and its major competitors. They found that 'all three countries see education and work competence as a key to their economic success; they are devoting effort to it with the will which has earned them their present position' (NEDC/MSC 1984, p. 1). The report considered that the U.K. needed to recognise flexibility and self-reliance as major educational and training objectives. An adequate supply of professional engineers was also seen as crucial. The U.K.'s output of such engineers was generally low relative to those of the U.S. and Japan. In contrast, Germany — acknowledging belatedly its relative shortfall in engineers — was found to have responded fast and dramatically to reverse this. The report also stressed that the U.K.'s problems were not ones that could or should be solved by the Government alone.

Table 2.14 shows educational participation of 16–24 year olds in the four countries. The U.K.'s total figure is the lowest of the four. The figure for U.K. 16–18 year olds is particularly low.

Table 2.14. *Percentage of population in age ranges 16–24 participating in education, 1981*

	16–18	19–20	21–24	16–24
Germany (1980)	86	36	17	45
United States	n/a	n/a	n/a	73
Japan (1982)[a]	96	40	30	54
United Kingdom	52–60[b]	28–36[c]	18–26[c]	32–40

[a] Japan's official minimum school-leaving age is 15; data therefore refer to ages 15–23.
[b] Higher figure in range includes the Department of Education and Science (DES) estimate for education element in the Youth Opportunities Programme, etc. (see *DES Statistical Bulletin*, 2/83, Feb. 1983).
[c] Higher figure in range includes DES estimate for those studying for professional qualifications, but for whom data are not collected nationally.
Source: NEDC/MSC 1984.

Table 2.15. *Workers with a recognised qualification as a proportion of the population*[a]

	Proportion	Nature of minimum qualification
Germany (1980)	66% of labour force	Vocational qualifications
United States (1981)	78% of civilian labour force	High school diploma
Japan (1982)	60% of population 21 +	Lower secondary school diploma
Great Britain (1981)	50% of working population	1 CSE pass

[a] Note that what constitutes a 'recognised qualification' differs from one country to another. No attempt is made here to put them on a comparable footing. One attempt to do so was made by S.J. Prais (1981) for Germany and Great Britain. On his assumptions (and using 1974–8 data for Britain, and 1978 data for Germany), the proportions of the labour force with stated vocational qualification levels were 67% (Germany) and 36% (Great Britain).
Source: NEDC/MSC 1984.

Table 2.16. *Percentage of relevant age group in population*[a] *gaining higher education qualifications, 1979*

	Below degree standard	At degree standard	At both standards	At postgraduate level
Germany	12	8	20	1
United States (1981)	10	22	32	9
Japan	12	25	37	1
United Kingdom (1981)	4	14	18	4

[a] DES estimates (unpublished) based on normal age range of new entrants to higher education.
Source: NEDC/MSC 1984.

Table 2.15 presents evidence on the proportion of workers with at least minimal qualifications. Even though the minimum qualifications are not directly comparable, the relatively poor performance of the U.K. is clear.

Table 2.16 presents information on higher education qualifications. The U.K. in particular has a very low proportion gaining below degree standard qualifications, while in overall terms both the U.K. and Germany perform considerably worse than do the U.S. and Japan.

2.4 Conclusions

This chapter has presented evidence on technological effort (as proxied by R&D expenditure), trade performance and human capital of the U.S., Japan, Germany, U.K. and France. All five countries have relatively large R&D inputs and export market shares in comparison with other OECD countries. However, their R&D efforts, skill levels and trade performance are varied and have changed over time. Both theory and empirical evidence would suggest that these three factors are interconnected. An understanding of these interconnections is crucial in answering a number of major questions, ranging from the determinants of trade shares and trade compositions over time to the causes of relatively poor U.K. economic performance. The following chapters aim to assess some of these issues at both a theoretical and an empirical level.

CHAPTER 3

___

Neo-factor endowment and neo-technology theories of trade

This chapter analyses the role of skill, technology and industry structure in different theories of international trade, and considers some of the empirical evidence.

The traditional factor endowment theory of international trade became increasingly questioned the more that evidence suggested it was contrary to the experience of the twentieth century (Hufbauer 1966). The restrictive nature and inaccuracies of this theory and the need for its development or replacement became clear and acute following the results of the Leontief paradox (Leontief 1953, 1956). Many analyses of international trade, both theoretical and empirical, have subsequently considered alternative explanations of trade flows to the traditional factor endowment approach. These have included extension of the latter theory to include human capital – the neo-factor endowment theories – and the development of the neo-technology theories of trade which stress the role of changes in technology and innovation. Both sets of theories stress the importance of productive knowledge, whether through its embodiment in skilled labour or its creation in the innovation process. The neo-technology theories also complement those analyses of trade that stress the structural characteristics of industries.

3.1 Skill, technology and industry structure
Human skills and technology

The neo-factor endowment, or human skills, theory of trade aims to explain observed trade patterns by recognising the importance of human capital as one part of a country's capital endowment. The Leontief paradox, that the U.S. appears not to be capital-abundant, is therefore attributed 'to a misspecification, based on the identification . . . of "capital" with capital equipment and "labour" with human bodies regardless of skill' (Johnson 1970,

21

p. 14). Johnson suggests that a full solution to the paradox could be made 'by extending the concept of capital to include the capitalised value of productive knowledge created by research and development expenditure' (Johnson 1970, p. 14). He argues that the human skills theory may cover or include the neo-technology theories which add the notion of dynamic diffusion to differences in human capital endowments (Johnson 1975). This is discussed further in Chapter 4. As in the traditional factor endowment theory, the neo-factor endowment theory assumes that techniques of production are the same across countries and that there are no skill-intensity reversals. Thus the country with the larger endowment of skilled labour will have a comparative advantage in the production of skill-intensive goods (see, for example, Hufbauer 1970; Keesing 1971).

Assuming that slightly different varieties of a good have similar factor requirements, the human skills theory can therefore offer no explanation of intra-industry trade, although this has become an increasingly important component of trade in many countries (Grubel and Lloyd 1975; Acquino 1978). The human skills theory does not take into account rapidly changing technology and assumes away differences in technological knowledge across countries. Production location is determined by relative amounts of capital and of skilled and non-skilled labour in different countries. It does not predict shifts in production from one country to another; to explain these it would have to appeal to a change in technology making a different type of labour or capital appropriate (for example, Vernon 1966), or to a change in relative endowments. Endowments are usually treated as fixed and there is little discussion of how, or how fast, they may change over time, or whether a country may act to alter its endowment. The essentially static nature of the theory means such factors are treated as external to the model. The inadequacies of the human skills theory lie, therefore, in the failure to allow for the dynamic implications of differences in technology and the failure to recognise that there will not be a one-to-one correspondence between skill endowments and a country's innovative capacities and abilities.

The neo-technology theories of trade, by contrast, stress the roles of changes in technology and of differences in technological knowledge in leading to trade. The neo-technology theory aims to establish a framework that will explain how product and process innovation may lead to trade. Product and process innovation may result in reduced costs and better performance, and different or improved combinations of characteristics in a product. Innovation does not fall manna-like, or uniformly, on all countries, but is largely the result of consciously directed innovation effort — reflected in R&D expenditures — within firms and industries (determined by conditions that will vary across industries and countries). Development of new products and processes will therefore not occur simultaneously in all countries (Posner

1961). Furthermore, since technological change is not necessarily or mostly disembodied, many other factors will influence the speed at which, and the extent to which, innovation is incorporated into production, notably the rate of investment.

Time and costs are involved in imitating an innovation, and during this time lag the innovating industry will have an advantage in production, raising home and export demand for its product. Posner stresses the role of the imitation lag in creating trade. The lag in imitation of a new product or process depends on the time necessary to start production and on how large a learning gap there is. The demand lag depends on the time it takes consumers in other countries to demand the new product. If this is long it will reduce the effects of the imitation lag. The literature on the timing of innovation suggests that market structure will also be important in determining the speed of imitation (Kamien and Schwartz 1982). The trade created from an innovation will be impermanent, unless there is a continuing sequence of innovations or there are associated scale economies in production.

However, if there are sufficient dynamic learning effects, it could be a considerable period before knowledge is identical across countries and trade depends on comparative costs again. The existence of an uneven flow of innovations across countries will mean some trade is always due to technology gaps to which some industries will be more prone than others, reflected in differences between industries in their investment in innovation. Posner suggests that there may be clusters of innovations, connected technically, or through demand effects, to the original innovation. The ability to imitate an innovation may also depend on the imitator having a stock of R&D knowledge, in which case, whilst the initial technology gap trade between the innovator and countries with R&D stocks will not persist, it may remain for a much longer period with respect to countries without R&D stocks. It has also been suggested that there may be a feedback loop of causality running from trade success to R&D (Keesing 1967; Mansfield, Romeo and Wagner 1979; Walker 1979).

A development of the technology gap theory of trade, which in fact minimised some of its more interesting implications, notably that of a continuing sequence of innovations, was the product life cycle theory (Hirsch 1965; Vernon 1966). Its development can be seen in part as a consequence of the technology gap theory's 'rather naive view of the mechanisms behind the transfer of production from one country to another; imitation was over-emphasised, capital mobility (and monopoly powers) under-emphasised. As a consequence, the theory lacks precision in its prediction of the timing and direction (to which countries) of production transfers' (Walker 1979, p. 18). In the product life cycle theory, location of production depends on the stage of its lifetime, or of standardisation, that the product has reached.

The product life cycle theory was developed with particular reference to the U.S. market. In the early stages of production of a new product or new variety of product, it was argued, production would remain in the home market of the advanced nation. This was due both to the existence of a sophisticated, high income consumer group that might more rapidly and easily accept or demand certain products, and also to the existence of skilled labour and specialist scientific and engineering knowledge. Vernon (1966) stresses the importance, initially, of flexibility in changing inputs, together with the advantage of a low initial price elasticity of the product, making relative costs less crucial, and the importance of effective, close communication between the (potential) market and the (potential) supplier of the market. As demand expands and the product matures, with less need for flexibility, there may be a shift in location to take advantage of lower input costs and production may start by competitors. However, if production requires an advanced industrial environment, it is not likely to shift to the less developed countries. While the technological gap theory emphasises imitation lags, the product life cycle 'emphasises the transition from product differentiation to product standardisation' (Hufbauer 1970, p. 190). It is with such a distinction made clear that Hufbauer tests the technological gap theory by taking first trade dates and the product life cycle by developing a product differentiation variable – the coefficient of variation in unit export values to different countries. A further development of the two theories suggests it is the rate of product turnover, not the newness of the technology, which is central, and results in another different measure – the rate of product turnover for a specific period relative to a base year (Finger 1975). A high rate of product turnover ensures that a continuing advantage remains with producers in the advanced countries and that there is no shift in production or return to factor proportions trade. This is similar to the effects of a continuing sequence of innovations.

A more recent model combines transfer of production between countries with continuing innovation (Krugman 1979a). Krugman develops a simple general equilibrium model of trade with two countries, the innovating North and the non-innovating South. After a lag, new products from the North are able to be produced in the South. This lag gives rise to trade. North has to innovate continually to gain its quasi-rents from its monopoly of new products and so to maintain its relative and absolute income levels. The simple specification of the diffusion process as a given lag means that continuing innovation is vital for the developed country to maintain its real income. Technology transfer shifts demand (and so capital) to the South.

Criticism of the product life cycle theory has focused on its lack of generality. Its description may apply to some goods, or some phases of the development of some goods, but not to all, nor is it possible to predict in advance which products it may be more applicable to. Within industries some technologies may standardise, others do not; capital mobility may have little to do with trends to product standardisation (Walker 1979). The structure of an industry may also affect product development, and whether phases of the product life cycle are observed. Oligopolistic competition, for instance, may lead to a stress on product development and innovation and shifts in production will not then be observed.

The neo-technology theory does not, therefore, provide a comprehensive explanation for the persistence or otherwise of the technology gap, but the product life cycle theory does not address this question adequately either. The explanation must lie with the determinants of innovation and, in particular, of diffusion both within and between countries. In a world of oligopolistic competition first mover advantages may be crucial (Spencer and Brander 1983), and the rents derived from specific assets, such as R&D, by firms operating in imperfect markets may be vital in allowing further innovation advantages in the next period.

Industry structure

It has frequently been suggested that there may be a positive relation between exports and scale economies. The larger that scale economies are, the greater benefit there may be to be gained from expanding into export markets — though this raises the possibility of the direction of causation running from exports to scale. The ability to expand into export markets may depend on having a large domestic market initially, allowing scale economies to be exploited at home first. It is usually assumed that this results in large countries specialising in production of scale economy goods (Hufbauer 1970). However, the degree of product differentiation may intervene here, such that smaller countries may reap scale economies if they specialise in goods manufactured to some standard international specification (Drèze 1960).

Various models have used scale economies to explain trade between similar countries in conjunction with product differentiation and variety. If R&D output leads to different varieties of a product being available, and there are scale economies associated with the production of these varieties, then there will be permanent intra-industry trade between countries with similar technological knowledge, as well as technology gap trade with countries with different levels of technological knowledge. Thus, the level of innovative output as well as gaps in technology may lead to trade.

Krugman has developed a model where there are gains from trade even if the two economies have identical tastes, technology and factor endowments (Krugman 1979b, 1980, 1981). On the demand side an industry consists of a number of products which are imperfect substitutes; on the supply side they are perfect substitutes. There are scale economies and equilibrium takes the form of Chamberlinian monopolistic competition. Given his 'extremely restrictive assumptions' on cost and utility, Krugman shows that there will be gains from intra-industry trade. If scale economies are sufficiently important, or if factor endowments are sufficiently similar, both factors gain from trade. He further shows that the index of intra-industry trade equals the index of similarity in factor proportions. Another two-country model (Markusen 1981) has shown that imperfect competition can form a basis for trade: assuming Cournot—Nash behaviour there will be a bilateral welfare improvement, when countries are identical, as a result of trade. Ethier (1979) highlights the two alternative means by which an expanded market through trade produces gains — either through expanding the scale of production or by increasing the number of varieties. In general, it may be expected that both will occur. Many of these models use an imperfect competition framework. In the context of advanced country trade and R&D expenditures, it may be argued, or observed, that oligopolistic competition is a more appropriate framework. Oligopolistic interaction may have various effects on factors such as foreign direct investment in competitors' countries, the number of varieties produced, attempts to produce new varieties and to influence consumers, the exploitation of scale economies and developments of production, given productive knowledge, over time. As Krugman points out, he achieves a determinate equilibrium in all essential respects 'because the special nature of demand rules out strategic inter-dependence among firms' (Krugman 1980, p. 951). However, some models with few sellers have been developed (for example, Dixit and Norman 1980).

An emphasis on variety of goods leading to trade was made by Barker (1977) who pointed out that the initial technology gap theory could not explain the post-war phenomenon that trade grew faster than production and income growth. Barker assumes that there are transport costs and scale economies. The variety hypothesis is then proposed that, as real income increases, consumers as a group can buy more varieties of a product (which they wish to do because of variety of tastes). A greater number of varieties are available abroad, so imports grow more than proportionately to real income per head. Economies of scale are not independent causes of trade, but are necessary in addition to product differentiation and demand for variety. The emphasis of this theory is different from that of Krugman's, which focuses on the pattern of trade between identical countries, while Barker is stressing the relation between real income growth and trade. However, the underlying factors moving the two models are the same — scale and variety. Barker's model might be brought closer to the neo-technology theories, if investment in R&D makes more varieties available in some countries, and these are then exported. To the extent that innovation leads to product differentiation, these scale economy models can be linked to the technology gap theory to explain permanent trade flows between similar countries.

The degree of concentration in an industry may also affect both exports and imports. If more concentrated market structures reflect entry limitations based on efficiency and/or scale factors, these may be associated with, or contribute to, an industry's comparative advantage, again leading to a positive relation to exports (Das 1982). Concentration, reflecting monopoly power, may have positive or negative effects on exports. Higher concentration may enable greater co-ordination or joint ventures in exporting strategies to different markets. If oligopolistic strategies in creating domestic barriers to entry require excess capacity, this capacity may be used for exports, if it can be switched back to the domestic market if necessary. A monopolised industry may export relatively less than does a competitive industry. For example, where the export price is lower than the domestic price, and it is not possible to discriminate between markets, if it is possible not to participate in the export market, the monopolist may supply only the home market (L.J. White 1974). More concentrated industries are also likely to be associated with higher import levels; thus the overall effect of concentration on net trade may be ambiguous.

There are, therefore, potential roles for skill, technology, investment, scale and concentration in determining trade. These factors may provide alternative explanations of trade flows or they may be complementary. Thus R&D and skilled labour may be complementary in the process of carrying innovation through to production, or they may explain the trading patterns of different industries and between different countries. However, they may provide competing explanations of trade. Similarly, it is possible to explain trade by combining the roles of R&D and scale, or by taking each separately. These potential inter-dependencies need further empirical and theoretical consideration. However, it is clear that once some role is allowed for technology differences, a more dynamic theory is required than is provided by the human skills theory.

Thus, as discussed above, the central difference between the neo-technology and neo-factor endowment theories is that the latter takes the technology of an industry as fixed, whereas the technology gap and product life cycle theories emphasise changing technology and changing products. In neo-factor proportions theory production location is determined, essentially, by the relative amounts of skilled and non-skilled labour, and of capital, in different countries. The theory does not explain trade between similar countries or intra-industry trade, and also fails to explain shifts in production from one country to another. This is due to the essentially static nature of the theory – not only are technology changes not incorporated, but there is little analysis of what the endowment is and how it may change. This results from the use of the concept of an endowment itself – it is treated as given whereas, though it changes relatively slowly, skilled labour depends on economic, social and political factors and does change. The neo-technology theories, by contrast, do not take the rate of technological change as given. It is dependent on current and previous innovative effort determining inter-industry and inter-country differences in technology.

Innovative effort itself will depend, among other factors, on industry structure and conduct, while industry structure may in addition have a separate, direct influence on trade. The technology theories not only explain advanced countries' trade, but also provide some framework within which to consider changes and developments in trade and location of production.

If variety is changing, the variety and scale theories may be linked to the neo-technology theories. There is no clear link between variety theory and the neo-factor endowment theory – this would require the assumption that the level of skill and the number of varieties in an industry are closely correlated. It is not clear why this should be so. It may be the case that the technology gap and human skills theory are complementary in that they explain different parts of international trade, such as that within advanced industrial countries and that between these countries and less developed countries respectively. The above discussion suggests that the technology theories can explain trade flows between both similar and dissimilar countries, and thus offer a more comprehensive explanation of trade flows. The two sets of theories may compete if they equally well explain trade between dissimilar countries; hence a choice between the two may depend on which performs best overall.

3.2 Empirical evidence

This section focuses on empirical tests of the neo-factor endowment and neo-technology theories and of the influence of scale and other structural factors on trade. The studies discussed have used various different variables and data, and refer to different years. For example, there have been various approaches to measuring human capital, such as using inter-industry wage differentials or inter-industry employment of different kinds of labour (Keesing 1965; Hufbauer 1970) or attempting to combine human skills and physical capital into a single measure (Lary 1968). Direct comparisons are not therefore possible. However, they can indicate whether certain theories receive strong support, whether different conclusions have been drawn in tests of the same theory, and where weak results have been found.

Much of the work testing the neo-technology and neo-factor endowment theories has been done across a number of countries. As shown in Chapter 2, technology and skill levels of different countries are not static, though less analysis has been carried out of causes of changes over time. Changes in countries' relative and absolute technology and skill levels suggest that results of studies done at different points in time or for different countries will vary. For example, between 1963 and 1977, seven of the OECD countries increased the relative proportion of their exports going to high technology products; these were the U.S., the U.K., Japan, France, West Germany, Belgium and Sweden. Of these, four (the U.S., the U.K., Germany and Sweden) increased their exports and imports together. In general, the most specialised countries increased in varying proportions their needs of imported goods in the same sector (Hatzichronoglou 1980). The U.S. had the greatest technology content in its exports, but in 1977 its export share in these products was second to West Germany (Aho and Rosen 1980). This study also found that the gap was closing between high technology exports and imports, although from 1962 to 1977 the five 'technology-rich' countries had a trade surplus in technology-intensive products (defined as industries with greater than average R&D intensity). In this same period the U.K. lost over half its market share in these products.

One of the best known cross-country studies is that of Hufbauer (1970). He categorises seven different trade theories and tests these in relation to the manufactured goods trade of twenty-four countries. He finds that the physical and human capital/skill theories together produce very good results (whether skill is measured by skilled employment or by wage rates). However, a combination of scale economies, product life cycle and technology gap measures also provides a strong explanation of trade. In conclusion he suggests that 'Linder — perhaps supplemented by product cycle and scale economy theory — works best in accounting for trade within the rich country zone' (p. 205). This suggests that no one theory of trade will necessarily explain all trade flows, but different theories may be appropriate for different types of trade or trade between similar or dissimilar countries.

The importance of differences between areas is highlighted in an analysis of manufactured exports in 1964, which looked at exports from ten exporting areas to each of twelve importing areas (Gruber and Vernon 1970). The eight industries classified as technology-intensive are found to be major contributors to world trade and their importance declines in moving from highly to less developed countries. Areas which are prominent exporters of technology-intensive products tend to be the most important or prominent exporters of other manufactured products, implying the existence of other aspects of comparative advantage relevant to all manufactured goods. A separate variable — the distance factor — is found to have strong explanatory power. Ranked by income level, any exporting area when selling to a lower income area has a greater stress on technology-intensive goods than when selling to areas of similar or higher income. As opposed to Hufbauer's conclusion, Gruber and Vernon's results suggest that the technology theories might better explain trade between dissimilar areas. However, Gruber and Vernon also find that export profiles of countries at similar development levels were not necessarily close. The U.S. export profile is found to be negatively related to all other countries except Canada and the U.K., while the U.K.'s profile was close to that of West Germany, suggesting other factors may be operating here.

In another cross-country analysis, Baldwin (1979) finds that the only industrialised country for which R&D has a positive relation to exports was the U.S. However, human capital variables did play a significant role for many countries. His results, therefore, offer some support for the human skills theory, and less for the neo-technology theory.

It has been suggested that factor endowments could play a role in influencing innovation (Vernon 1966). Davidson (1979) found, for the U.K. the U.S., Japan and Europe, a statistically significant correlation between factor cost and innovation frequency. A study of the electronic calculato industry also found a relation between technological leadership and cos competitiveness. U.S. advances were imitated by Japan, which had a cos advantage until the U.S. moved ahead again with a new innovation (Majumda 1979).

Balassa (1979) obtains statistically significant results in using human and physical capital intensity to explain the revealed comparative advantage of eighteen developed and eighteen developing countries. He does not include a direct technology measure such as R&D, since these expenditures would be very low for most developing countries. A country's relative export performance in industrial product categories is taken to reflect its 'revealed comparative advantage in the manufacturing sector.

There are drawbacks in the use of revealed comparative advantage indices The index reflects comparative advantage across one country's industries not relative to other countries. It does not raise the question of what determines the average market share. Such indices do remove general tradeabilit which may lead to differences in absolute export levels or exports relativ to sales.

Many tests of the theories considered here just rely on simple correlatio measures or procedures. Hirsch (1974) uses Balassa's comparative advantag measure in a study of twenty-five industries and twenty-nine countries similar to that of Hufbauer (1970). He ranks industries by those whos comparative advantage is positively related to value-added (since this highly correlated with capital, skill and R&D) and then considers whic of the three factor variables performs best in explaining the ranking. R&D is found to have the superior performance. Physical capital does not perform well without the presence of human capital, though human capital performs quite well on its own. Hirsch concludes that his findings are consistent with a two-factor model in which capital is mobile but labour and technology are not, which therefore suggests that the neo-technology approach may be more useful in analysing trade flows.

Another simple correlation has been carried out for forty industries, for most of the OECD countries except the U.S., relating exports per head, 1974, to cumulative U.S. patents (by foreign industries) 1963–76 (Pavitt and Soete 1980). The results imply a significant relationship in capital goods, most chemicals and some transport equipment, and for the larger countries in consumer durables. The U.K.'s position is 'nowhere near' the leading countries in capital goods, chemicals or durables. Trying to relate exports to a revealed technology comparative advantage index produces poor results especially for the six major OECD countries (Soete 1980). Relating various trade measures not only to patents in the U.S. (including a proxy for the U.S. itself) but to capital intensity, population (to capture scale effects) and distance, results in significant positive relations for most industries, except the natural resource-intensive industries, organic chemicals and what are termed a number of 'typical factor proportions' industries (Soete 1981). Distance is important in many industries, and scale in some – notably those where the advantages of scale economies are particularly high.

Walker (1979) estimates a simple correlation between technology and exports. His analysis also looks at changes over time in relation to these variables. Walker first applies the product life cycle model to manufacturing industry with the result that some, but by no means all, industries may be said to conform to this. He then goes on to consider which industries show a positive relation to R&D in their exports, in the ten major OECD countries, for seventeen product groups, in the periods 1963–5 and 1971–3. He uses a revealed comparative advantage index similar to that of Balassa (1979). As he stresses, this gives a purely static view of the structure of trade; it does not indicate how trade may change over time or whether different levels of innovative activity in different countries in the same industry will change trade shares. The rank correlations suggest, across countries, that in the U.S., the U.K. and West Germany comparative advantage was relatively strong in R&D-intensive goods, in contrast to Canada, the rest of the EEC and Japan. The differences between the periods 1963–5 and 1971–3 also suggest that Japanese, and to a lesser extent, the U.K. and Swedish export compositions were becoming more R&D-intensive, while the EEC (not Germany) and Canada moved in the opposite direction.

Assessing changes between 1963 and 1973, innovative effort in each industry (for fifteen industries) is ranked across countries and correlated with the relative changes in trade shares. He finds three distinct groups of industries: those that are positively correlated, poorly correlated and negatively correlated (the latter group being motor vehicles, and stone, clay and glass). It is noted that the direction of causation is not necessarily one-way. The results show a positive correlation for four R&D-intensive industries (chemicals, aircraft, drugs and instruments) and one 'traditional' industry (ferrous metals), and a poor correlation for eight industries. The varying results underline his conclusions in relation to the product life cycle: that one general model may not be able nor should be expected to explain all industries' trading patterns.

Another test of the product life cycle ranked countries by their technology endowments, and calculated technology elasticities across countries for individual products (Acquino 1981). He found that technological intensity of products declined as they got older, though the strength of these results also varied by product. He also finds that some, but not all, products have significant, positive or negative relations to scale effects.

Whether the technology or skills theory could explain differences between a pair of advanced countries has been tested for the U.S. and the U.K. in 1962 (Katrak 1973). This was again done through simple correlation – of relative R&D, skill and scale, separately, and then together – across fourteen industries. The scale variable performs best, with partial success for the skills variable, while the R&D variable did not perform well, in either of the alternative relative R&D measures used. Taken together, their overall explanatory power was high. Katrak comments that the poor performance of R&D may in part be a result of the aggregation level and of different industry diffusion rates between the countries and, finally, that R&D data might not be a good indicator of new product output. It might also be the case that there are more important gaps in resources devoted to later stages of the innovation process, not captured in the R&D variable.

The studies discussed above give varying support to both the neo-technology and the neo-factor endowment theories, with some slight preference for the neo-technology theory. However, given the preceding theoretical discussion it may be argued that many of these studies have omitted relevant variables, and have failed to distinguish between causation and correlation. This problem arises again in many studies of individual countries.

A large proportion of the tests of the human skills and neo-technology theories have been done for the U.S. Results of these studies may not necessarily be directly generalised to the experience of other countries, given the specific characteristics of the U.S. such as its size, different industry structure and its closeness to technological frontiers, though in fact it is no longer the technological leader in many fields.

Studies of the U.S. have confirmed the expectation that the U.S. has a comparative advantage in technology-intensive or skill-intensive goods. U.S. export shares in the early 1960s were positively related to scientists and engineers in R&D (Keesing 1967). Keesing found that the R&D skilled workers variable performed considerably better than one for general skill requirements. Baldwin (1971), looking at net trade in 1962, concluded that the U.S. had a relative abundance of engineers and scientists and that this was an important source of its comparative advantage, in particular with respect to manufactures. Baldwin suggests that the fact that a proportion of this labour group is engaged in R&D activities is probably particularly important. However, this is not directly tested, and so his results do not allow a distinction to be drawn between skill and technology theories. Harkness (1978) finds similar results in 1958 for scientists and engineers, but again it is not possible to distinguish the two theories. Baldwin stresses the importance of splitting skilled labour into a number of distinct groups. He finds no significant effects of scale or concentration in accounting for the U.S. trade pattern, although both concentration and the engineers—scientists variable had a positive and significant effect on export growth.

Weiser and Jay (1972) repeat Baldwin's study, using the scale economies variable from Hufbauer's study (1970), and taking the U.S. share of world exports as the dependent variable. They confirm Baldwin's results, except that they find a positive and significant effect of scale. Baldwin (1972) suggests that this stresses the importance of the choice of dependent variable, since Weiser and Jay do not find scale significant when using net trade.

Baldwin's results (1971) also confirm the Leontief paradox. Leamer (1980) argues that the Leontief paradox arises from a conceptual misunderstanding. He shows that, when the net exports of capital and labour services are both positive, in order to reveal if a country is well endowed with capital, it is necessary to compare capital per person embodied in net exports with the capital per person embodied in consumption. Following this method, he shows, using Leontief's data, that the paradox no longer holds. However, with Baldwin's data the paradox persists, suggesting that the importance of considering human capital, in its widest sense, remains. Sveikauskas (1983) uses Leamer's methodology to examine U.S. trade in 1967, and concludes that it is technology rather than human skills or capital intensity that differentiates the U.S. from other countries.[1]

Gruber, Mehta and Vernon (1967) also find the U.S. had the strongest position in foreign markets in industries with the largest R&D effort. This is linked to these industries' new product orientation. Their general conclusion is that the export trade of the U.S. is heavily weighted with products that require large scientific and technological inputs in the selling process. In the same study, it is found that almost all the significant relations disappear if U.S. exports are normalised by U.K. or West German exports, but reappear using French exports. This implies that the U.K. and West Germany derive their export strength from characteristics similar to those of U.S. exports.

Another 'U.S. only' study finds that a combined technology variable of R&D and scientists and engineers is positively related to export shares and growth (taken as a geometric average) in both 'old' and 'new' industries into which U.S. industry had been categorised. Combining a time-series and cross-section analysis, the technology variables, including concentration, are the most important (Goodman and Ceyhun 1976). A firm level study of thirty U.S. manufacturing firms also observes an important link between R&D and U.S. exports, though this study suggests that exports may determine R&D: on average the firms expected 30 per cent of R&D returns to come from trade (Mansfield, Romeo and Wagner 1979). A Heckscher–Ohlin model with three factor inputs (skilled and unskilled labour, and capital) is found to provide a good model for the structure of U.S. trade in crosssection analyses from 1958 to 1976. Using more detailed skilled labour variables and R&D relative to value-added, both are positively related to exports in 1960 and 1970 and significant in 1970 (Stern and Maskus 1981). One test of the product cycle theory was done for the U.S. for consumer durables (Wells 1969). A strong correlation between U.S. export performance and the income nature of the product is found, and it is concluded that U.S. export performance between 1952 and 1963 was consistent with the predictions of the product life cycle model.

The Leontief paradox has been found to hold for West Germany also. West German exports in 1954 were labour-intensive, and human capital was the most abundant factor (Roskamp and McMeekin 1968). West Germany lagged behind the U.S., the U.K., Sweden and other countries in its R&D relative to its manufacturing output up to the early 1970s. By 1974 West Germany was second to the U.S. (OECD 1979). There is some support for the technology theory for West Germany. Taking fifty-five single products, at four- or five-digit level, chosen as research-intensive products, there is a strong connection between R&D efforts and trade performance (Horn 1977). Comparing market share and comparative advantage indices for twenty-six industries in 1970, for West Germany and the U.S., Horn finds they are quite similar. This suggests that Freeman's argument (1978), that the U.K. has been too similar to the U.S. in its R&D efforts, cannot be the only explanation of relatively poor U.K. performance in this field. Horn's study concludes that the R&D variable performs better than other variables in relation to trade with industrial countries. Looking at West Germany's structure of comparative advantage in 1972–3 and its change from 1963–4, the skill and technology theories are both supported (Wolter 1977).

Scale economies are also important. Separate measure of R&D/sales and human capital are used, and it is concluded that the neo-technology and neo-factor endowment theories mostly compete in explaining trade performance. The results also indicate that in trade with the world and with the developed countries, the competitiveness of West German industry fell as physical capital intensity increased.

For Canada, Caves *et al.* (1980) show R&D intensities to be positively related to net exports, and some evidence of scale economies raising exports and imports. A study of Denmark (Hansen, Moller and Strandskov 1983) observes a positive and significant effect of R&D on exports in 1971 and 1978, and for a human capital variable in 1971. Looking at net trade, the variables are no longer significant.

There have been few studies of changes over time in comparative advantage, although R&D expenditures and skill levels have changed. From the mid-1950s to the late 1960s, Japan's endowment of human capital increased and converged to that of the developed countries (Heller 1976). Heller finds Japan was rich in human capital. From 1955 to 1968 its capital and skill intensity increased. It exported more capital- and skill-intensive goods to the less developed countries, but over this period there was a strong convergence in the pattern of its exports to the less developed and developed countries. By the end of the period there had been a strong alteration of Japan's comparative advantage, emphasising the inadequacy of trade theories that treat endowments as static.

There have been few tests of the neo-technology and human skills theory for the U.K. alone. There have been some industry case studies, particularly of engineering (Saunders 1978; Rothwell 1979, 1980) that have suggested that the U.K. tends to have lower export unit values than its main competitors, and that continuing technical change is necessary for competitive success.

Four recent studies have included measures of technology and skill in cross-industry studies (Cable and Rebelo 1980; Katrak 1982; Smith *et al.* 1982; Lyons 1983). The results of these studies have varied but show some role either for skill or for technology in the U.K.'s export composition. These analyses are considered in detail here to aid comparison with the econometric results for the U.K. presented in Chapters 7 to 9.

Katrak (1982) differs from the other three studies in that he does not use a regression framework, nor does he look at export shares or other measures of trade performance. Katrak focuses on the skill, R&D and capital intensities of exports, imports and foreign investment inflows and outflows. He begins with the premise that the U.K. does suffer from a low technology syndrome. This implies that increasing skill and R&D intensities of imports to exports should be observed. The R&D intensity of exports may also increase due to 'the increasing technological complexity of product innovation' (p. 39), though no evidence is offered to support this statement. Due to the low technology syndrome, Katrak suggests that the U.K.'s exports to the advanced countries will be intensive in unskilled labour. This assumes the U.K. has already fallen considerably behind its competitors. This hypothesis is not tested. Katrak also predicts that the capital intensity of exports relative to imports will increase. Further, due to the U.K.'s assumed low technology level, inward investment is expected to be R&D-intensive relative to outward investment, and vice versa for capital-intensive investment. If this were true for R&D investment, it would suggest that the U.K. does have a relatively high level of skilled labour – assuming that this is necessary in R&D-intensive industries.

Katrak's basic hypotheses receive some confirmation. The skill intensity of exports exceeds that of imports in 1968 and 1972, but the ratio is smaller in 1972. Similar results are found for R&D in 1972 and 1978. Capital intensity is found to have risen in both exports and imports, but by more in exports. Katrak's predictions for direct investment also receive support. Most of the changes in the ratios reported are small and there is no test of their significance. Since in other countries, including West Germany, the gap between technology-intensive exports and imports has narrowed, especially where industries are most specialised (Hatzichronoglou 1980), it is not clear that these results can be said to confirm the low technology syndrome for the U.K. Katrak quotes Japan as an example of intensities moving in the other direction, but Japan was catching up from a very different position, relative to countries such as the U.K. or West Germany. Katrak's data, therefore, suggest that the skill and R&D content of exports may be important in indicating sources of U.K. comparative advantage, and that these might be changing over time, but there are no direct tests of these hypotheses. In that Katrak does consider changing competitiveness he is not adopting the completely static neo-factor endowment view, but is stressing that endowments, whether of skilled labour or R&D, may change.

A more comprehensive study has been carried out by Cable and Rebelo (1980). They analyse U.K. trade patterns at a point in time, and over time, with the world as a whole and with different groups of countries. They aim to explain the pattern of U.K. manufacturing trade by combinations of factor endowments, industrial structure characteristics and the regional concentration of manufacturing. Their analysis covers eighty-seven non-food manufacturing industries in 1970 and 1978, for trade with developed and developing countries, various individual countries and groups of countries.

Their results show some support for the neo-technology theories. The R&D/sales ratio is used to represent the technology variable, and R&D data for thirty-two industries is applied to the eighty-seven industries. R&D

has a positive and significant relation to the export sales ratio for the world as a whole, and for less developed countries, Japan, the U.S. and the EEC. However, R&D is not significant in the world export equation when a measure of the proportion of unskilled and semi-skilled workers in the labour force was included. This latter variable was significant. R&D also has a significant positive relation with imports except, surprisingly, with imports from Japan. A human skill measure of the proportion of operatives in the workforce is negative and significant in both the world and Japan export equations. Using measures of revealed comparative advantage, R&D was not significant.

Cable and Rebelo found very weak results for their industry structure variables – average firm size and concentration – though some effect of their regional variable. Looking at changes over time, their results are also quite weak. The equations for the change in exports between 1970 and 1978 and for revealed comparative advantage are not significant. The change in imports equations perform better. They show a negative relation to capital intensity and to value-added per head, and positive relations to three skill variables: the share of operatives, the share of women in the labour force and the average annual wage. Their overall results indicate some support for both technology and skill variables, though with the latter dominating the former in some equations.

A similar study, with different results, relates different measures of trade to various factor endowment and structure variables for ninety-seven U.K. non-food manufacturing industries (Smith *et al.* 1982). The skill theory is tested by taking three different skilled labour variables – managerial, professional and technical, and skilled manual – and a measure of average weekly manual earnings. The technology theory is tested by taking R&D expenditures relative to net output. The R&D data is disaggregated by guesswork from thirty-two sectors to the ninety-seven used. Other variables are capital intensity, concentration, average plant size, plants unaffected by disputes, and the proportion of foreign-owned firms. The last-named variable is excluded from the principal equations reported because of the difficulty in distinguishing whether it is making a separate contribution or merely reflecting the pattern of competitiveness. The preferred dependent variable is the ratio of the trade balance to consumption $[(X - M)/C]$ but various alternative measures are also used: net trade measures, exports/sales and imports/consumption, all for 1979. Contrary to the results of Cable and Rebelo, the R&D variable performs badly. It is significant in only one equation, when the professional and technical labour variable is excluded. Clear positive and significant effects of the professional and technical staff and average earnings variables are found in the net trade equations – though the latter measure may reflect other factors including competitiveness leading to higher earnings. Neither managerial or skilled manual labour is significant in net trade or export or import equations. Professional and technical staff (PT) performs well in both the export and import equations, but average earnings is insignificant in the former and negative in the latter. The capital/ labour ratio is usually negative though not always significant. Plant size is positively related to net trade and, when included, foreign ownership is positive and significant in the export and import equations but not net trade.

Due to the poor overall performance of the equations, they are re-estimated for trade with the less developed countries (LDCs) and with the EEC. In the LDC results, manual skill becomes more significant as well as PT and average earnings. Capital intensity is negative and significant. R&D is insignificant.

In estimating U.K./EEC trade the net trade variable performs badly, probably due to high intra-industry trade. Good industrial relations is the only variable to reach significance. In the export and import equations PT is again strongly positive and significant, as is foreign ownership. Manual earnings is negative and sometimes significant.

The overall conclusion of the study suggests that PT, average earnings and, possibly, capital intensity are the most clear influences on trade, and that R&D does not appear to have an influence. Smith *et al.* suggest various reasons for the poor performance of the R&D variable: the disaggregation is poor, nor are the initial data collected on a precise minimum list heading basis; the estimation does not consider technology levels in other countries; the variable is an input not output measure; multinationals, using technology from elsewhere, may mean the industry technology level is not correctly reflected in U.K. R&D; and R&D is highly correlated with PT. These arguments do not give a clear indication of why the results of Smith *et al.* differ from that of Cable and Rebelo. This may be due to the use of different and more detailed skilled labour variables in Smith *et al.* leading to superior performance of these variables. In that case, the results of Smith *et al.* may be influenced by the fact that the data for PT is available at the level of disaggregation of their study, while the R&D data is not. R&D was also insignificant in Cable and Rebelo's work when certain skilled labour variables were included.

Lyons (1983) finds a positive role for the R&D variable. He suggests that product and market characteristics may be more important in determining trade levels than factor endowment characteristics, which assumes that the two sets of characteristics are not related. He estimates import and export sales ratios in 1963 and 1980 for trade with the world and with EEC and non-EEC countries. He reports the use of two measures of skill: those with 'A'-level and post 'A'-level qualifications as a proportion of the workforce, and average wages and salaries per employee. As mentioned above, average earnings may reflect, not determine, competitiveness, while 'A'-level qualifications may not have any very clear relation to production skills of the workforce.

Lyons finds that the variable reflecting 'A'-level qualifications has a positive effect on both exports and imports. R&D also has a positive influence on exports and imports. Of the other variables employed, transport costs are consistently significant and negative, and minimum efficient scale is consistently positive in both export and import equations. Concentration has a negative effect on imports but no significant effect on exports. Lyons finds the concentration effect very sensitive to specification of the equation. A durable goods dummy had a positive effect on exports and sometimes on imports. Capital intensity was positively related to imports, and also to exports for 1980. Both the average wages and advertising variables were usually insignificant. When looking at non-EEC exports, R&D was no longer significant, nor was it significant for EEC imports. Concentration had a significant negative effect on EEC exports. As in Cable and Rebelo's results, the equation for the change in exports between 1968 and 1980 was not significant. Lyons concludes that scale economies, transport costs and, through various proxies, product differentiation are major influences on trade.

The work done for the U.K. suggests that some role exists for skill and/or technology variables and, possibly, for industry structure variables, particularly scale. The results suggest that R&D and skill variables provide partly competing explanations of U.K. exports. The contrasting results presented here suggest that the proxies used and the specification of equations may have an important influence on the results, as may the initial degree of aggregation of different variables.

3.3 Conclusions

This chapter has discussed both theoretical and empirical analyses of neo-factor endowment and neo-technology theories of trade. It was suggested that, in combination with industrial structure variables, the technology theories may provide a more comprehensive explanation of trade. While human skills and technology could be complementary, the acknowledgement of the role of technology undermines the static nature of the neo-factor endowment theories.

The chapter considered empirical evidence on the determinants of export composition and trade performance. The studies discussed did not support a traditional factor endowment approach, though some found combinations of physical and human capital variables had good explanatory power. Some support was found for both the neo-technology and neo-factor endowment theories, the evidence being sometimes complementary, sometimes competing. Various other factors were found in some studies to have significance, such as distance measures and industrial structure variables. However, it is difficult to make any general conclusions on the role of these additional variables, since different studies include different sub-sets, with varying results. The results highlight the importance of obtaining precise definitions and measures of variables, and indicate the differing results — in particular on skill or technology theories — that can occur due to different measurement. The U.K. results also indicated difficulty in measuring or assessing the causes of changes in exports over time.

The varying results obtained therefore indicate the importance of clear theoretical specification of the underlying relationships and the application of this to empirical estimation, rather than just using simple correlation measures. Overall, these studies give support to the explanation of trade using skill and technology variables, while suggesting that these variables may be either complementary or competing and may play different roles in different industries and countries and in explaining trade between different groups of countries.

CHAPTER 4

Technology and export composition

This chapter draws on the theories analysed in Chapter 3 to develop the specification of an equation to estimate export composition. First the potential role of technological intensity in determining trade flows is analysed in more depth, then the role of other factors is considered.

4.1 Technology, exports and endowments

The discussion in Chapter 3 stressed that the neo-technology theories emphasise differences in technology, while for human skills theories technology is the same across countries and so skill requirements will be the same in a given industry in different countries. It is, therefore, differences in skill endowments that result in some countries having a comparative advantage in more skill-intensive industries. This section considers why there may be trade when a given industry in two different countries has the same level of R&D expenditure in both countries, and goes on to consider whether there is any meaning in the concept of an R&D 'endowment'.

Technological gaps have been shown to lead to impermanent trade due to different products being available in different countries, and because innovation may affect both costs and prices. If there is an uneven, continuing flow of innovations some trade will always be due to technology gaps. However, countries with similar levels of technological effort or R&D expenditures may also trade; R&D expenditures may result in trade even though there are no measured technological gaps. If country A spends the same amount on R&D in industry j as country B does, country A may still export some of its products from industry j to B (and to the rest of the world) if its R&D output is different from that of country B or if there are scale economies. For similar reasons, if country B spends more on R&D in industry j than A does, A may still export some new products to B. In addition, even if R&D output were identical for a given R&D input, if R&D output results in increased differentiation of products, in conjunction with scale economies, there will again be trade between A and B in industry j. Thus if R&D results in higher levels of product differentiation, and if scale economies are not more extensive in low R&D industries, more trade will be observed in R&D-intensive industries, and countries with high levels of R&D expenditure will trade more in those industries, *ceteris paribus*. Both exports and imports may, therefore, be higher in R&D-intensive industries, contrary to standard comparative advantage predictions. Where there is a clear technological gap, the country with an R&D advantage may export and not import R&D-intensive products; however, in this case, trade may rest on absolute not comparative advantages (Dosi and Soete 1983).

Various other market imperfections or characteristics may be added to this explanation of different countries exporting similar R&D-intensive goods and trading between themselves, and countries, not in the highest R&D spending group, having an advantage in exports of some R&D-intensive goods. These imperfections might include: deliberate restriction and control of information and knowledge; consumers' imperfect access to information on the range of products available or on their characteristics and 'quality adjusted' price (for example, Cowling and Cubbin 1971); oligopolistic co-ordination across countries; and general uncertainties relating to supply and future product developments and competitiveness. Thus, in addition to the effect of technological gaps on trade, the level of R&D expenditure can lead to two-way trade between countries at a similar technological level, and to intra-industry trade.

If trade can occur between countries at similar or even identical technological levels, then it may be asked whether the suggestion that technological knowledge can, in part, be treated as an endowment in the same way as skilled labour (Johnson 1970, 1975) is appropriate. It may still have relevance to explaining trade flows between dissimilar countries, though even then the concept of an R&D endowment cannot be analysed in the same way as a skill endowment.

If technology were treated as an endowment, and if the U.K., for example, were assumed to be relatively well endowed with technology, then, following traditional comparative advantage theory, the U.K. would be expected to export the more technology-intensive products. Assuming that the technological endowment is proxied by R&D expenditures, then industries may be ranked by the input of R&D required, which will be the same across countries. R&D expenditure below the required input level will result in no production in that industry, while expenditure above that level will be superfluous. The U.K. will then export R&D-intensive products.

Even in this restrictive scenario, it is not possible to treat R&D as identical to other endowments. Trade shares are not expected to change if relative endowments are stable. However, the output from a certain input of R&D is uncertain both in terms of the expected quantity and its characteristics. As Walker states: 'In this respect, R&D, if regarded as a factor of production, behaves quite differently. By generating new opportunities for expanding production (opportunities that are uniquely held by the innovating country), innovation can bring about an increase in the parent country's trade share, and a corresponding decrease in the share of competitors' (Walker 1979, p. 64). Furthermore, there are not precise R&D input coefficients. Firms have some discretion over their R&D expenditure (in any one period, firms could choose not to carry out R&D expenditure, and in this sense R&D is like investment, not like other inputs into the production process) and there can be trade between similarly 'endowed' countries. Thus, even including R&D in a comparative advantage framework, its effects on trade are not necessarily equilibrium or static ones and so are not directly comparable to the effects of other endowments. These and other aspects of the nature of R&D suggest that it is not appropriate to treat it as an endowment in a strict sense.

It could still be argued, however, that the economy as a whole has a potential R&D 'endowment' which will vary according to decisions of firms and government. The maximum size of this potential endowment, at any point in time, will vary across countries and depend, among other factors, on previous R&D expenditure. While there are not given R&D input coefficients, there may be some minimum point of R&D expenditure which must be spent over time in order to produce in an industry. If this minimum varies by industry, it would then be possible to rank industries. Exports would be greater in industries with a higher minimum R&D point, in countries well endowed with R&D. The existence of fixed costs and product differentiation would still mean no one firm or one country's industry dominated world markets completely.

As there are not precise R&D input coefficients, above the minimum R&D point there may be a band over which R&D expenditure is observed. The precise level of R&D within the band will depend on the determinants of R&D (as discussed in Chapters 5 and 6 below). If these determinants vary across industries and countries, there will be gaps between competitors' R&D which will affect exports, in addition to the effect of 'endowments'. The band or range over which R&D is spread may be determined by the technological opportunity level of the industry. The technological opportunity level of an industry represents its underlying scientific base and the potential for exploiting this in the industry's production processes and products. This varies across industries and so can determine the level and width of the bands. The end points of each band may be such that beyond

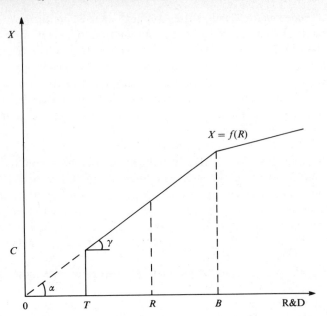

Figure 4.1 *The relation between exports, R&D and technological opportunity*

them there is no effect of R&D on exports or output, or there may be diminishing returns. For estimation purposes, it must be assumed that the relation of exports to R&D over the band is the same across industries, though end points will vary.

However, if there are bands of R&D for separate industries, these may overlap. Consider two industries with overlapping bands: if actual R&D expenditure is higher in the lower R&D band industry, its exports will be higher. If industries were ranked by their minimum R&D point, the endowment theory would be disproved. If actual R&D expenditures, not an independent measure, were used, it would not be disproved, but the need to use actual R&D expenditures itself disproves the strict endowment theory. Alternatively, if industries were ranked by the minimum point of their bands, point T — representing the minimum necessary level of R&D as determined by technological opportunity — the expected effect on exports would depend on both T and $(R - T)$, where R is R&D. The relationship for one industry can be represented diagrammatically as in Figure 4.1, where X = export revenue.

In this diagram, it is assumed R&D has no effect until amount OT is spent, while after point B there are sharply diminishing returns. Alternative assumptions might be that after point B there is no effect of R&D, and that exports up to point C can be achieved without any R&D input. The effect of

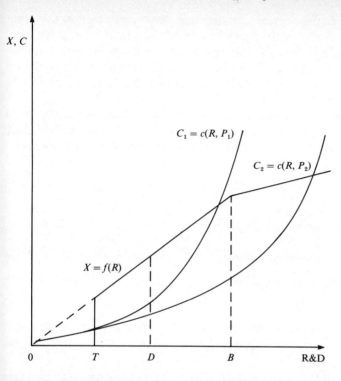

X, C

$C_1 = c(R, P_1)$

$C_2 = c(R, P_2)$

$X = f(R)$

0   T   D   B   R&D

Figure 4.2. *Exports, R&D costs and the choice of R&D level*

R&D on exports is measured by $\alpha T + \gamma(R - T)$. As presented here, α equals γ, hence the overall effect is captured by αR, i.e. the effect of actual R&D expenditure. To predict an effect αT would be correct only in the case where $R = T$. It has already been assumed that γ is constant across industries. Given this assumption, for a cross-section analysis, it is also necessary to assume $\alpha = \gamma$, otherwise α will vary across industries. There is, anyway, no presumption that the effect, rather than the level, of T (or technological opportunity) should vary by industry.

It is expected that profit maximisation will ensure that actual R&D is in the band *TB*, not beyond *B*. If costs of R&D vary for different firms, industries within and across countries will not be observed at the same point on their bands. This can be demonstrated using, as an example, the availability of internal funds. If the cost of internal finance of R&D is relatively less than the cost of external finance, varying availability of internal funds across firms will alter the profit-maximising level of R&D. This is shown in Figure 4.2, where $C =$ costs, $P =$ internal funds. It is assumed that the proportion of external funds has an increasing effect on costs. If internal funds are at level P_1, C_1 is the relevant cost function. With cost function C_1, profit maximisation results in R&D expenditure at point D. If internal funds are at level P_2, greater than P_1, R&D expenditure will then be at point B, the end point of the band. Costs would have to be sharply decreasing for expenditure to be beyond B. R&D expenditure is therefore expected to lie within the band TB.

The technological opportunity level of an industry, the deviation of actual R&D from the technological opportunity level and the technology gap between countries can, therefore, affect exports. This can be expressed as follows:

$$X = \alpha T + \gamma(R - T) + \delta(R - FR) \text{ for } R \geqslant T, \text{ if } R < T, X = 0 \qquad (4.1)$$

where: X = exports
T = technological opportunity
R = U.K. R&D
FR = competitors' R&D

If, as argued above, $\alpha = \gamma$, this reduces to:

$$X = \alpha R + \delta(R - FR) \qquad (4.2)$$

Exports depend on actual R&D expenditure and the gap between U.K. and competitors' R&D. A strict endowment approach would not be compatible with this analysis.

An approach that allows some flexible role for endowments can therefore be combined with the approach previously stressed of the level of R&D working through both technology gaps and variety and scale effects. Countries' overall 'endowments' of R&D may have an influence on which industries are specialised in and which goods are exported. These industries cannot, however, be ranked by technological opportunity alone. Within a country, actual R&D expenditures may not be ranked in the same order as technological opportunity. Across countries, R&D expenditures in a particular industry may vary. This will lead to trade. In addition, the same level of R&D across countries can also lead to trade. Furthermore, R&D endowments are not static, and will not result in equilibrium patterns of trade. Thus, to the extent that it is possible to rank countries in terms of R&D expenditures or endowments, this is not sufficient to enable precise predictions on trade flows. These will depend on the distribution as well as the level of domestic and foreign R&D across industries and on the level of product differentiation and scale economies.

These arguments reinforce the importance of trying to distinguish the effects of R&D and skilled labour on trade, and of trying to assess whether they are competing or complementary as explanations of trade. This is done in specifying an estimating equation below.

4.2 Specification of an estimating equation for determinants of manufactured exports

This section sets out the specification of the export equation and analyses the expected determinants of exports other than technology. The equation is intended to be generally appropriate for estimating the export composition of an industrialised country. However, since the equation is estimated for the U.K. below, the U.K. is referred to here, without intending to indicate that the equation is U.K.-specific.

It has been argued that both domestic and foreign R&D may affect exports. In addition, skilled labour may have a complementary role or may provide an alternative explanation of exports. The existence of scale economies is expected to affect trade and other industry structure variables may also be relevant. The full export equation specifying the determinants of the exports of manufacturing industry is expressed as follows:

$$X = f[R, FR, C, I, SM, HS, PT, K] \tag{4.3}$$

where:
X = exports
R = U.K. R&D
FR = foreign R&D
C = concentration ratio
I = investment
SM = scale economies
HS = skilled manual labour
PT = technical and professional staff
K = capital/labour ratio

As previously discussed, R is expected to have a positive effect on exports, FR a negative effect. The expected role of the remaining variables is now considered.

Concentration

The concentration variable reflects structural differences across industries that may affect exports. As discussed in Chapter 3, the extent of monopoly power in an industry may have positive or negative effects on exports. In addition, concentration may have a positive relation to exports due to its probable correlation with firm size. Firm size may be positively related to exports if there are fixed costs of exporting, such as those associated with gathering information about overseas markets or costs of uncertainty (Caves and Khalilzadeh-Shirazi 1977). Firm size may also be positively associated with scale economies; this effect might thus operate through the scale variable.

Investment

Since the neo-technology theories stress that technological progress is not purely exogenous, but arises due to explicit innovation effort, in particular through R&D expenditure, then it is apparent that the introduction of new products or new processes will, in general, require new investment to incorporate these developments. Investment levels may thus affect exports positively since higher investment indicates that more modern equipment and processes are being used, which may incorporate technological developments and/or result in higher productivity or improved quality (which would affect demand also). If investment is measured relative to the capital stock, it will reflect the modernity of the capital stock and may also reflect the general dynamism of the industry (N. Kaldor 1957, 1961).

Scale

As discussed above, the existence of scale economies can explain permanent, and intra-industry, trade flows due to technological developments or the existence of differentiated goods (Krugman 1979b). Thus, scale may have a positive effect on exports. It may have a separate effect from this due to the potential relationships between country size, product differentiation, scale and exports (Drèze 1960). The effect of scale economies on U.K. exports will then depend in part on the ability of U.K. industry to achieve available scale economies relative to its competitors. In a direct comparison with the U.S., for example, it may not be surprising to find negative effects of scale (Katrak 1973); in relation to competition on world markets, the U.K. might have a relative advantage in scale economy industries.

Skilled labour

As discussed above, skilled labour may contribute to an explanation of trade between dissimilar countries, even though it cannot directly explain trade between similar countries.

Countries' endowments of skilled labour may vary not only in their levels, but in the types of skilled labour present. It is potentially important to distinguish different types of skilled labour. There are various characteristics on which this distinction can be based, in particular production skills and education levels. The former are possibly more relevant since there will not necessarily be a direct relation between educational qualifications and particular skills used in production. A clear distinction can be drawn between skilled manual and non-manual labour. It may be expected that, as countries develop, assuming that their education systems improve and that technical and professional staff require a higher level of education, any human capital advantage may shift from manual to non-manual skilled labour. This does not imply that skilled labour is no longer needed; depending on other countries' stage of development, a country may have a comparative advantage in both types of skilled labour. Alternatively, if, in the U.K.'s case, its competitors have increased their skilled non-manual labour at a greater rate, then the U.K. may have lost, or be losing, any advantage in non-manual labour, though in skilled manual labour it may come increasingly into competition with developing countries.

Some, though not all, studies of the human skills theory have adopted the approach of looking at more than one category of skilled labour (for example, Keesing 1967; Smith *et al.* 1982). The neo-factor endowment theory stresses the role of skilled labour in production, not innovation. However, skilled labour may be necessary to undertake R&D. Thus the endowment of skilled labour may limit potential R&D activity, although it does not provide information on where within that limit R&D activity will lie, nor does its potential limiting effect alter the analysis of the differences between R&D and skilled labour. There may nevertheless be some overlap between the technology and human skill theories since, in particular, non-manual professional and technical staff will be necessary both in R&D, and to put R&D results into practice and to extend an innovation into production. While the existing technology will be the main determinant of the number of professional and technical staff employed, there may be some flexibility which, as well as being related to R&D, may affect factors such as quality. This may make it difficult to distinguish whether R&D or human skills are the main influence on trade and could represent a serious problem in trying to differentiate the two theories.

Capital intensity

Finally, a capital intensity variable is included to test the traditional factor endowment theory. However, this is not expected to play a significant role in determining the U.K.'s export composition. The determinants of the U.K.'s exports, relative competitiveness or comparative advantage are expected to lie in those factors already discussed, in particular in those highlighted by the neo-technology theory. Thus, for example, Baldwin (1971) finds capital intensity to be insignificant for the U.S. once natural resource industries are excluded.

Simultaneity

Some of the determinants of R&D expenditure have been discussed above, in particular the role of technological opportunity. Given the stress laid on the role of technology in this analysis, it is of interest to consider in more detail the potential determinants of R&D. However, in addition to this, it may be necessary to consider these determinants if, as has been suggested in the literature, there is a two-way or simultaneous relationship between exports and technology (Keesing 1967; Mansfield, Romeo and Wagner 1979; Walker 1979). Prior to empirical estimation of the export equation, therefore, the theoretical determinants of R&D must be analysed. This is done in Chapters 5 and 6.

4.3 Conclusions

This chapter has considered the different channels by which technology can affect exports and the possibility of interpreting R&D expenditure as an endowment. It was argued that R&D cannot be analysed as an endowment in the traditional sense, even though the level of R&D as well as the technology gap may positively affect trade. Finally, an estimating equation was specified for exports, drawing on the analysis of the theoretical determinants of trade flows previously considered.

CHAPTER 5

Research and development spending – theories and evidence

This chapter considers the various explanations of the determinants of research and development spending proposed in the literature, and the empirical tests of these theories. Chapter 6 sets out some possible extensions to these explanations. The determinants of R&D expenditure are of interest not only because of the expected role of R&D in determining trade patterns and international competitiveness, but also because of the potential effects of R&D on various other aspects of industrial structure and performance – ranging from its effect on productivity growth to its possible role as a barrier to entry.

5.1 Theories of R&D expenditure

The theoretical and empirical determinants of invention and innovation have been considered in many studies and summarised in surveys (Blaug 1963; Kennedy and Thirlwall 1972; Kamien and Schwartz 1975, 1982). A major part of the literature has focused on R&D expenditures in industry as proxying invention and innovation for both products and processes.[1] Once analysing R&D within industry, the starting point for many studies is the work of Schumpeter (1976) with its emphasis on firm size and market structure. Other major determinants of R&D proposed in the literature include the scientific base of industries, and the level of, and growth in, demand in user industries. A contrast can be drawn between those theories of R&D that stress the influence of supply side factors – both industry structure and scientific opportunity – and those that stress the influence of demand. However, these factors are not necessarily competing, and are not always treated as such. No consensus has been reached on the role of firm size and market structure, and there is a lack of evidence for the U.K. Here the Schumpeterian theories are considered first, then the other determinants of R&D proposed in the literature.

51

Firm size and industry structure

Schumpeter (1976) considers the causes of innovation of products and processes in the context of his analysis of the evolutionary processes of capitalism, in particular of the dynamics of competition and monopoly. Thus he considers theoretical analysis focusing on equilibria to be inappropriate. Furthermore, if firms and industries were in a stable equilibrium at any point in time, this would be likely to impede the progress that may come from 'the perennial gale of creative destruction' (Schumpeter 1976, p. 84). Innovations are developed in response to the pressures of oligopolistic competition, as firms attempt to achieve a dominant position in the industry through product and process competition. In addition to this competitive effect, large firm size may promote innovation both because of fixed costs of R&D and the uncertainty of R&D, and also because larger firm size may interact with market structure to allow some monopoly protection, and reward, in the initial phases of developing new products and processes. Schumpeter's analysis of the determinants of innovation thus points to three main factors: the effect of the competitive processes within an industry, the appropriability of the results of innovation as affected by the degree of monopoly, and the effect of scale. Given the variety of potential reactions or strategies of oligopolists, it is clearly not possible in general to specify a unique effect of a particular industry structure on innovation, nor to suggest that a particular structure is optimal. However, oligopoly theory can provide some basis for analysing possible outcomes. Leffler (1981) specifies a model of new product R&D where there is only one Nash equilibrium that is the industry equilibrium, which is where firms have equal R&D expenditures and equal probabilities of success in R&D. He also shows that if the fixed costs of R&D increase, firm size increases, while the equilibrium number of firms fall, but the level of industry R&D may rise. Parker (1978) argues that if expected profit from an input of R&D is low, concentration may be important. Markham (1965) makes the suggestion that oligopolistic reactions may lead to R&D expenditures that are not systematically related to firm size at all. It has also been suggested that whether competition or oligopoly leads to more R&D depends on the speed and costs of imitation. Where imitation is immediate, the competitive industry will not innovate, but the oligopoly may (Shrieves 1978).

Arrow (1962) has shown that the return to the inventor is greatest when the invention is used in a competitive market, which thus provides the stronger incentive to undertake R&D. This is in relation to process innovation and assumes that the monopolist can choose not to innovate, i.e., that there is no entry threat. In the case of product innovation the opposite may hold (Needham 1975). Demsetz (1969) drew the opposite conclusion from

Arrow's by assuming the same output level of the two industry types pre-invention; the increase in profit is then greater for a monopoly. Arrow's analysis is limited, however, in its focus on the profitability of a single invention, directly controlled by the inventor. Thus he ignores the effects of market structure on the costs of invention and the possibility of competing inventions (Stoneman 1983). An oligopolistic industry may be able to absorb the risks associated with R&D — given that its output is uncertain — where a perfectly competitive industry could not. It has been suggested — in part following empirical results — that an intermediate degree of rivalry may be most effective in encouraging R&D whereas higher and lower levels of concentration will have weaker effects (Kamien and Schwartz 1976), or that there may be some threshold effect (Markham 1965).

The various factors that affect the influence of market structure on R&D underline the problem that the degree of concentration may be a poor proxy for the intensity and nature of competition in an industry (Markham 1965). There is a similar lack of consensus in the various theoretical and empirical analyses of the relationship between quality and market structure (Schmalensee 1979). This may be relevant to R&D theory since similar effects may apply in, for example, the decisions of monopolists on supplying new products. The conclusions of the studies tend to vary according to the precise industry structure and market elasticities assumed. In general, the price and quality choices of a monopolist will not be optimal (Spence 1975) but the firm may over- or under-supply quality (Sheshinski 1976). Relative to a competitive industry a monopoly may delay introduction of new products that compete with or are substitutes for its products (Swan 1970). In a monopolistic competition structure, high fixed costs will tend to reduce product variety, while high cross-elasticities will increase variety, and vice versa (Spence 1976). These studies offer varied conclusions, but do not clearly support the concept that more monopolistic industries will introduce more new products or do more R&D. They also raise the possibility, not always taken into account in the R&D literature, that certain industry structures could result in too much R&D, though the uncertain nature of R&D makes a definition of excessive R&D difficult.

Some studies have suggested that there may be a difference between the environment most conducive to innovation and the organisation that can use it (Kennedy and Thirlwall 1972). It has often been proposed that the organisational structure and size of the research laboratories of large oligopolistic corporations may be conducive only to relatively minor inventions (for example, Hamberg 1966; Jewkes, Sawers and Stillerman 1960). Pressures for high output and productivity may result in a change from flexibility and innovation to standardisation (Utterback 1979a). Thus, smaller firms and individuals may be better at producing inventions but are likely to be inefficient with respect to their subsequent development and marketing.

In addition to the problems inherent in attempting to predict the effects of market structure on R&D, the influences and interactions involved are clearly not static. The outcome of Schumpeterian competition could result in forces that increase or decrease concentration. It has been argued that while concentration may lead to innovation, innovation – if successful over time – may lead to increased concentration (Nelson and Winter 1978). Alternatively, the nature of an innovation may make it easier for other firms to enter an industry or provide a means to enter; new entry may occur around new products (Utterback 1979b). High concentration on the buyers' side may also reduce the effect of sellers' concentration on R&D (Farber 1981). It can be argued that the relationship is not two-way, but goes in the opposite direction to that proposed by Schumpeter. Thus the basic technological environment of an industry could lead to scale economies and concentration, not vice versa (Nordhaus 1969). Whether innovation differences depend on innate or structural differences between industries is not only important theoretically, but will also have different policy implications (Nelson and Winter 1977). The two are not automatically exclusive of each other, however.

R&D expenditure may increase or maintain concentration by acting as a barrier to entry. While market shares of firms within the industry may vary according to R&D expenditure and R&D output, those expenditures will also tend to make entry more difficult (Sylos-Labini 1969). The effect of the barrier will in part depend on whether there has been product or process innovation. A series of product innovations may raise consumer goodwill and loyalty. Innovation and R&D intensity may vary with the life cycle of the product or the stage of development of the industry, and barriers to entry will therefore also vary (Parker 1978; Mueller and Tilton 1969). Mueller and Tilton suggest there are four stages in the development of an industry: innovation, imitation, technical competition and standardisation. They argue that entry will be most difficult at the technical competition stage, since firms already in the industry will have a stock of knowledge and of learning developed during the earlier stages. R&D expenditures, like advertising, may have a stock effect. Firms build up their stocks of R&D by annual expenditure, and these will depreciate, in similar fashion to capital goods (Bosworth 1978). The R&D barrier to entry of an industry will depend, therefore, on current and past expenditure of firms. It is likely that entry will be easier for existing firms in industries with similar technologies, in particular since R&D carried out in one industry may be applicable to other industries. R&D may therefore encourage diversification. Alternatively, diversification may encourage R&D since there may be a higher probability of being able to use R&D results if a firm has various market openings (Scherer 1965; Bosworth 1981).

Technological opportunity and demand

There is disagreement — both theoretically and empirically — as to whether the direction and intensity of inventive and innovative effort will depend on market demand, on the underlying scientific opportunities of the industry or on structural factors. N. Rosenberg (1974) has argued that to establish the independence of the supply side argument, it is necessary to show that scientific knowledge is partly independent of economic need, that this constrains the direction of innovation and that it leads to different costs by industry of R&D. Related to the technological opportunity argument is the view that ease of changing physical characteristics of the product and the underlying differentiability of products will affect R&D (Wilson 1977; Comanor 1967).

It may be argued that inventive activity is mainly correlated with, and responds more to, external factors, in particular demand and investment demand — a view that is associated with Schmookler (1962, 1966). This has been supported by others, suggesting that R&D is done mostly in relation to recognition of production and marketing needs (Norris and Vaizey 1973), or depends on expected prices of factors of production, expected output and expected price of R&D (Nelson 1980). The expected price of R&D may, though, depend on the scientific opportunity level of the industry. Related to the demand theories, various writers have suggested that expected profit or cash flow may be important in determining R&D (for example, Smyth, Samuels and Tzoannos 1972; Bosworth 1981). Many studies have also tried to assess the contribution of R&D or technical change to productivity growth, though recognising the problems of lag structures, R&D depreciation, and links with other sectors (Griliches 1979; Terleckyj 1980). Griliches also notes the potential problem of simultaneity between past and future output, expected output and R&D.

Multinational enterprises

Most studies of R&D have not considered the potential influence of foreign trade other than through the effects of multinational enterprises (MNEs). Multinational enterprises tend to be based in high trade, research-intensive industries (Hood and Young 1979; Parker 1978). This has implications for their subsidiaries, which may carry out R&D as well as the parent company, or to which the parent company may transfer technology. Some studies have looked at the determinants of technology transfer, in particular to subsidiaries in less developed countries (Solo 1966; Mansfield and Romeo 1980). Others have considered the amount and type of R&D the subsidiaries may do. MNEs may carry out R&D overseas both because technology transfer is not costless and also because overseas R&D may concentrate on factors connected with the market being served, such as product modification (Hirschey and Caves 1981). If MNEs are research-intensive they may stimulate domestic host country firms to do more R&D. They may also carry out R&D overseas if R&D costs are cheaper – until the late 1970s this was particularly likely, for U.S. MNEs (OECD 1979). The existence of MNEs in a host country may therefore have positive effects on R&D, or could have a negative relation with R&D if research results are transferred from abroad.

The effects of trade on R&D have not been considered in detail. However, references to potential effects may be found in the technology and trade literature. It has been suggested that there may be a positive 'feedback loop of causality' (Keesing 1967) or 'reverse causation' (Mansfield, Romeo and Wagner 1979) from exports or trade success to R&D (Walker 1979). By contrast, in a study of the Canadian economy (Caves *et al.* 1980) it is suggested that exports and imports may have a negative effect on R&D since, for a relatively small economy, the presence of foreign trade may be associated with greater ease, or lower costs, of adapting to or imitating innovation. However, this link is vague and not clearly specified.

Government influence

Government expenditure and policies may affect R&D both through direct government R&D expenditure, which may in part substitute for private R&D expenditure, and through incentives or regulation. Since many studies suggest that there is a gap between private and social rates of return to innovation, which may be higher for major projects, there is a positive role for government (Mansfield *et al.* 1977; Shonfield 1981; G.M. White 1981). However, government regulations (for instance, on pollution or safety) may both distort and redirect R&D if resources are limited (Eads 1980), though this will obviously depend on the costs and benefits associated with such regulations. Government expenditure on R&D may not always have, or only have, its intended effects, since private industry may respond in various ways to government funding or to direct government R&D activity. In particular, it has been suggested that defence R&D may have negative effects on other R&D expenditure (Horwitz 1979; M. Kaldor 1980). In contrast, as discussed in Chapter 2, the actions of the Japanese Government, through MITI, suggest that major positive effects can be had on technological effort and success without large direct government spending.

This section has considered the determinants of R&D spending that have been raised in different theoretical analyses. Three main potential determinants of R&D expenditure have been outlined: the effect of firm size and industry structure, the effect of technological opportunity, and the effect of demand. While some analyses have argued for the sole importance of only one of these influences, the three are not necessarily incompatible and may interact. Various other factors may also affect R&D. These include the effects of cash flow, MNEs, exports and government expenditure and policy. These potential determinants operate mainly at the level of the firm, though some operate via industry level effects or industry level interaction, and some, such as the potential negative effect of MNEs, will only be observed at industry level. The second half of this chapter considers some of the existing empirical evidence.

5.2 Empirical evidence

There has been a considerable amount of empirical work on the determinants of innovation, using both data on samples of firms for a number of industries and industry level data. Most of the work uses R&D expenditure or employment data, though some uses patent data. Patents have the advantage of being an output measure, though the available evidence suggests that in most, but not in all, cases it may be reasonable to assume a linear relationship between R&D input and product innovation (McLean and Round 1978). The comparability of patents, and of tendencies to patent, within and across industries and countries, and over time, may be considerably less than the comparability of R&D expenditures, though this will also be inexact. While there do exist standard international definitions of R&D (OECD 1976), not only may these be difficult to apply at firm level and, moreover, applied inconsistently across firms and industries, but they do not cover the complete innovation process. R&D costs may only account for a half or less of the costs of the innovation process (Mansfield *et al.* 1971; ACARD 1978; Kamin, Bijaoui and Horesh 1982). Evidence shows that R&D expenditures in the industrialised countries grew more slowly in the 1970s; in particular, basic research has fallen, and the emphasis of R&D projects has been on the short run and safe, and on improvement of existing products and processes (OECD 1975, 1979, 1980; Schott 1976, 1981). This may affect any relationships that exist or have existed between market structure, or other variables, and R&D. Much of the existing empirical work has focused on the relations between R&D, firm size and market structure, for the U.S. in particular. There has been a lack of results for the U.K. (Cowling *et al.* 1980).

Firm size, market structure and R&D

Results of empirical tests of the relations between firm size, market structure and R&D have been varied, allowing no definite conclusions on the validity of these relations to be drawn. In a survey of the literature, it was concluded that, while early studies suggested at most a weak positive association between R&D input intensity and firm size, on an overall assessment there did not appear to be any significant relationship (Kamien and Schwartz 1975, 1982). This is subject to qualification: there do exist inter-industry differences in this relationship; much of the evidence failed to take into account other factors that may be important in explaining firm size; and the evidence relates to firms that do have a sustained R&D effort. As discussed below, Soete (1979) questions this conclusion. In addition, to test that R&D increases with firm size is only an indirect test of the existence of scale economies in R&D (Fisher and Temin 1973). Furthermore, smaller firms undertaking R&D may have to do relatively more R&D to begin to compete with the larger firms. Kamien and Schwartz also concluded that there was little support for the view that R&D increases with monopoly power, although rivalry in R&D might have a non-linear relation to concentration.

In a well known study of the U.S. petroleum, coal and steel industries, it was found that the largest firms accounted for the larger share of innovations in the first two industries but not in steel (Mansfield 1968). Looking at inter-firm differences in chemicals, petroleum and drugs, the same study found that the larger firms in the industries seemed to spend no more on R&D relative to sales than the smaller firms. Inventive output per unit of R&D seemed lower in the larger firms, possibly indicating diminishing returns to R&D after some size is reached. Scherer (1965), for a sample of large U.S. firms, found that inventive output increased with sales, but less than proportionately. For the smaller firms, R&D employment increased faster than firm size. A more recent study of 2600 U.S. manufacturing firms concluded that both small and large firms do relatively more R&D and that there was no significant size threshold (Bound *et al.* 1982). Other evidence suggested where firms were typically small, the smaller firms might do more R&D, while when the typical firm was large, large and small firms spent equal amounts relative to output (Comanor 1967). A U.K. study of eighty-six firms in chemicals, electrical engineering, electronics and machine tools, 1963–6, found that larger firms were more likely to participate in patenting, and that number of patents increased more than proportionately with firm size in the chemicals industry and (for all but the largest firms) in electrical engineering and electronics, but fell in machine tools (Smyth, Samuels and Tzoannos 1972). Shrieves (1978) found, for a sample of forty-one U.S. firms in 1965 that smaller firms performing R&D allocated more resources to it. Looking at the largest four firms in an industry, it was found that the relative share of innovations, for iron and steel, petroleum and coal, of the largest firm fell as concentration increased (Williamson 1965). However, it is not clear whether this was because the largest firm was increasing its market share relative to the other firms, or vice versa. Another U.K. study suggested that small firms contributed little to innovation in industries with high capital intensity (Freeman 1971).

A study of the relation between firm size and inventive activity by Soete (1979) casts doubts on the results of many of the previous studies. He argues that R&D expenditure is a more neutral measure than the more frequently used R&D employment and patent data, because expenditure on other R&D inputs increases with size at a faster rate than employment does, and because larger firms tend to patent inventions less than small firms do (Taylor and Silberston 1973). Using R&D expenditure he finds R&D activity increases more than proportionately with size for U.S. firms in 1975 and 1976. He also points out that many other studies use much earlier data, subsequent to which there have been major changes in firm size distributions and in R&D activity. At the industry level Soete finds it less easy to draw general conclusions, but the evidence certainly does not suggest that inventive inputs increase less than proportionately with size.

There is more substantive evidence of some positive effect of concentration on R&D, though again the results are varied. In a study of 448 U.S. firms, Scherer (1965) found no role for market power. However, in a different study of fifty-six industry groups he found concentration was significant, though its explanatory power fell with the introduction of dummy variables representing four technological opportunity classes (Scherer 1967). His results also offered some support for a 50–55 per cent threshold for the effect of concentration. Kelly's (1970) results for 181 U.S. firms supported Scherer's finding of a threshold for maximum R&D intensity at concentration levels of about 55 per cent. Varying results according to industry class were noted by Comanor (1967). He found a stronger positive effect of concentration in industries where prospects for product differentiation were relatively weak, in particular in non-durables and material inputs. He concluded that intermediate technical barriers to entry may be most conducive to innovation. The importance of product market factors was shown in Shrieves' study of forty-one U.S. firms taken from fifty-six industries (Shrieves 1978). Concentration levels were significantly associated with R&D performance for material inputs and consumer goods.

Grabowski and Baxter (1973) analysed firms in the U.S. chemical industry and found that an individual firm's R&D was sensitive to the level of other firms' R&D. In a cross-section of twenty-nine industries they found higher concentration led to greater conformity in research expenditures. This is an interesting finding, since it suggests the existence and potential importance of firms acting as 'R&D leaders' or as barometric firms with respect to R&D. Thus, new entry may be important in shifting pre-existing patterns of R&D spending – for example, if a technologically dynamic MNE or conglomerate entered an industry.

J.B. Rosenberg (1976) considered the effect of market share, in addition to that of market concentration, on research intensity, to test the hypothesis that market share might have a negative effect, given concentration, due to leading firms having a preference for the status quo. In a study of 100 companies, there was a negative relation between market share and research intensity, and positive effects of concentration, technological opportunity and sales growth. In contrast, a Canadian study found R&D varied inversely with concentration in industries with greater technological opportunity (Globerman 1973). In a comparison of the U.S. and France it was found that for the high technology industries, there was lower R&D intensity in the industry with higher concentration. For lower technology industries the results were mixed (Adams 1970). It may be the case that, where concentration is higher, there is less duplication of R&D results, in which case the implied adverse effects of higher concentration do not necessarily hold. A study of eleven U.K. manufacturing industries for the period 1956–65 found that R&D was not related to any particular type of industrial structure (Buxton 1975). Another U.K. study for 1968, using the Herfindahl index of concentration, for sixteen manufacturing industries also failed to find any positive relationship between R&D and concentration (Leech and Stoneman 1976). In an analysis of the diffusion of process innovations, for twenty-two innovations in the U.K., it was found that concentration could have both positive and negative effects on diffusion and that the ideal industry structure would be one of a few equally sized firms (Davies 1979).

In conclusion, the evidence on the role of market power, proxied by concentration, in determining R&D spending is unclear. Some results do show a positive effect of concentration on R&D, but others fail to find this, especially where technological opportunity or other industry characteristics are taken into account. There is also evidence that, if there is a positive concentration/R&D relationship, it may be non-linear.

Technological opportunity and demand

As discussed above, different theories have given varying or competing emphasis to technological opportunity relative to growth or demand variables. Empirical studies have produced varied results.

In Scherer's study (1965) of 448 U.S. firms, technological opportunity differences across industries, proxied by dummy variables for different industries, were found to be very important whereas profit and liquidity variables were not. Doubt was also thrown on a pure demand theory of innovation by Davidson (1979). Using data on individual innovations, a significant correlation was observed between factor cost and innovation, especially for process innovations. Using data on 350 U.S. firms, two important dimensions of an industry in determining R&D were found to be the complexity of the product and technological opportunity (Wilson 1977). Wilson defined high and low technological opportunity categories as those containing products likely, respectively, to have high or low opportunities for new product breakthroughs. As with most studies, the categorisation of technological opportunity groups is arbitrary and inevitably subjective. One non-subjective proxy was used in a Canadian study. U.S. R&D was used as a proxy for technological opportunity and was clearly significant in determining Canadian R&D (Caves *et al.* 1980). Although their results for concentration were not strong, it had a positive effect which appeared to be non-linear. Contrary to other studies, the non-linear effect seemed to reflect higher, not weaker, R&D intensity in the more highly concentrated industries.

Schmookler, in particular, stressed the chronic tendency of technology to lag behind demand. He tested this hypothesis for railroads, petroleum and the building industry and found it was supported (Schmookler 1962). Extending this to twenty-four U.S. industries, inventive activity responded more to common external factors than to differing industry characteristics, with a particularly strong correlation between investment and capital goods invention. These results depended critically on investment being classified according to the industry that used the invention (Schmookler 1966). This demand-pull hypothesis is also supported in an earlier, well known work, where it was found that hybrid corn strains were developed for different regions in a time sequence largely determined by the relative profitability of developing appropriate strains for each region (Griliches 1958).

Schmookler's hypothesis was re-tested by Scherer (1982) using a sample of 443 U.S. companies with 1976–7 patent data. Support for Schmookler was 'equivocal'. There was a positive, significant relation between demand flows and patents, but the relation of capital goods invention with investment in user industries was much stronger than that of industrial materials invention. In general, original industry sales performed better than user industry investment did. Adding seven technological opportunity slope dummies – groups categorised by the perceived richness of their knowledge base – raised the R^2 of one of the estimating equations from 0.243 to 0.809. Stoneman (1979) carried out an analysis of the influence of demand pressures for the U.K. Technological opportunity was measured as the R&D cost per patent, to avoid the subjectivity inherent in other measures. The analysis was done for fourteen industries, both time-series and cross-section. The technological opportunity and demand factors were both significant, and output performed better as a demand indicator than did investment. Both Scherer's and Stoneman's results therefore refute the strong version of Schmookler's hypothesis and attribute importance to the level of technological opportunity. However, to the extent that demand does positively affect R&D output, the additional R&D output may increase the perceived technological opportunity level of industries in future periods.

The level of internal funds or cash flow has been found to have a positive effect on innovation, both in U.S. studies (Grabowski 1968; Grabowski and Baxter 1973) and in a U.K. study (Smyth, Samuels and Tzoannos 1972). The U.K. results found that prior profits were not significant but prior cash flow was. However, in a study of U.K. machine tools it was suggested that shortage of technical expertise was the main problem, and that shortage of risk capital was only a symptom (Daly 1981). Analysing individual innovations, their success was found to depend on how clear a market already exists as well as on awareness of users' needs, marketing performance and strength of management (Rothwell and Teubal 1977). Technologically new products have also been found to have a worse initial market performance compared with new products with technology similar to that of existing products (Little 1979).

In analysing the links between R&D and output, the direction of causation is not necessarily one-way. Various attempts have been made to assess the effects of R&D on productivity growth and, more recently, to see if it may have contributed to the U.S. productivity slowdown. The studies are mostly for the U.S. Positive relations between productivity and R&D have been found (Shaw and Leet 1973), though it may also be that if R&D leads to new products initially offered at a relatively high price then this may distort these studies (Gustafson 1962). A Canadian study found no significant relation between R&D and industrial growth (Globerman 1972). Mansfield found a significant relation between basic R&D and increases in total factor productivity, and suggested that basic R&D may be proxying long-term productivity growth (Mansfield 1980). Griliches (1980) suggested that lower R&D is not the cause of the U.S. productivity slowdown, while another study suggested that, though varying in time periods and industry groups, R&D had made some contribution (Nadiri and Schankerman 1981).

In general, studies that have included measures of technological opportunity have found these to be positive and significant. Measures of demand, expected profit and cash flow have received support, although it is not clear which may be the best measure of demand side effects. The hypothesis that demand influences alone are relevant in determining R&D is not supported.

Other influences on R&D

Other potential influences on R&D have received less attention in the literature. Some of the results are summarised here.

Multinational enterprises (MNEs) might affect the level and the nature of R&D. Looking at R&D by MNEs' subsidiaries, from a sample of fifty-five

U.S. firms, it was found that three-quarters of their overseas R&D was aimed at modifications and improvements (Mansfield, Teece and Romeo 1979). A sample of seventy large U.K. firms assessed whether U.S. technology transfer affected them. Two-thirds considered that their technological capabilities had been increased, although only 20 per cent thought this significant. Over half the firms had introduced products and processes more quickly in response to U.S. firms introducing products (Mansfield and Romeo 1980). Thus MNEs may act to improve innovation and diffusion in the host country, but this does not imply that there will be any direct positive effect on R&D expenditures. The positive effect of diversification on R&D has been tested for but received little support. It is also possible that any relationship would operate in the other direction (Kamien and Schwartz 1982).

Considering the effects of U.S. exports on R&D, for a sample of thirty firms from a variety of manufacturing industries, it was expected that on average 30 per cent of the returns to R&D would come from foreign sales (Mansfield, Romeo and Wagner 1979). This proportion varied considerably across firms, and it is not made clear to what degree expected returns to R&D were higher than exports as a proportion of sales. In a study of Canadian R&D, trade is predicted to have a negative effect on R&D since it may be easier for Canadian firms to license or imitate the necessary innovations (Caves *et al.* 1980). However, imports were not always negative, and exports, though negative, were not quite significant.

The case for government support of R&D has frequently been on the basis of the risks involved and the problems of allowing a reward to the innovator versus the desirability of diffusion of knowledge. Governments have, in different ways, subsidised R&D or taken some of the risk (Stout 1981; Stroetmann 1979; Allen 1981). The case for government involvement was supported by the results of seventeen individual case studies, where it was found that the median social rate of return was 56 per cent, the private rate of return 25 per cent (Mansfield *et al.* 1977). A different study suggested that type of ownership control might affect the willingness to take risks as represented by R&D. In chemicals and drugs, but not in petroleum, it was found that firms with external control had higher R&D intensity (McEachern and Romeo 1978). Whether government R&D positively or negatively affects private R&D is unclear; some evidence suggests a potential positive effect (Caves *et al.* 1980), other evidence a negative relation (Shrieves 1978). It has been suggested, in particular, that defence R&D may adversely allocate resources away from other more commercial projects that would have more potential applications or lead on to more connected innovations. Negative correlations have been observed between defence R&D spending and economic growth (Freeman 1978; Horwitz 1979; M. Kaldor 1980). A U.K. government study suggested that public corporations did too much R&D in support of their purchasing decisions, as the results of the R&D did not then tend to be applied to other uses (ACARD 1980).

5.3 Conclusions

This chapter has considered theoretical and empirical analyses of the determinants of R&D expenditure. The most consistent positive influence on R&D is found to be technological opportunity, though there are measurement problems with this variable. Results on the role of firm size are inconclusive. Market structure may have a positive, non-linear effect on R&D, but again the evidence is inconclusive. Positive effects of different demand variables have been found, though the most appropriate measure is not clear, various different measures having been used. Other influences have been considered – MNEs, diversification, trade and the role of government – but yet again empirical results are not consistent or conclusive. Various simultaneities may be involved in the relationships considered, but these have been rarely mentioned or tested for. The empirical evidence shows that further work is necessary – on the basis of results obtained so far – to test the determinants of R&D at firm and at industry level. This work needs to be based on clear theoretical predictions of the expected influences on R&D and their direction of effect, and precise measurement of these influences.

CHAPTER 6

A model of the determinants of R&D intensity

This chapter extends the analysis of advertising expenditure to R&D expenditure, to derive the determinants of optimal R&D intensity. The chapter then considers the limitations of this approach, and goes on to establish an estimating equation for R&D expenditure drawing on both the model developed here and the theories discussed in Chapter 5.

6.1 Modelling R&D expenditure

Advertising and R&D have certain similarities in that they both act, in part, as selling costs and may also act as barriers to entry into an industry. They represent non-price aspects of competitive behaviour and, as such, may be more attractive to firms operating in oligopolistic market structures as they do not have the 'joint disaster properties of the Prisonner's Dilemma' (Shubik with Levitan 1980). Theoretical analyses of advertising decisions may therefore have some relevance for, or be applicable to, the R&D decisions of firms and the level of industries' R&D expenditure. However, the differences between R&D and advertising may require extension of advertising models or mean they have only a limited usefulness. This section briefly considers the theoretical determinants of optimal advertising intensity and then uses this framework to develop a model of the determinants of optimal R&D intensity.

Dorfman and Steiner (1954) formulated the static conditions for optimal advertising intensity. Taking a monopoly with both price and advertising as decision variables, they derived the optimal advertising/sales ratio, which can be shown to equal the ratio of the industry advertising elasticity to the industry price elasticity. The model has been extended to include dynamic conditions, assuming that advertising may also have a stock effect, as a stock of goodwill. The optimal advertising/sales ratio then also depends on

65

the rate at which the stock of goodwill depreciates, and the rate at which the firm discounts the future (Nerlove and Arrow 1962).

The Dorfman—Steiner conditions can be extended to a situation of oligopoly to consider the effects of interaction among firms. If there is no collusion, the advertising/sales ratio will depend not only on the two elasticities but also on the expected reaction of other firms. If Cournot behaviour is assumed no extension is necessary, since each firm assumes other firms will not react to its decisions. If advertising by one firm provokes an increase in advertising by a competitor with negative effects on the initial firm's output, the optimal ratio is reduced (Cowling *et al.* 1975).

There are, of course, difficulties with formalising the expected reactions of firms under oligopoly. Shubik comments on the difficulties of constructing models of product differentiation under oligopoly, and in particular on the inability to supply a general analysis of the non-symmetric market (Shubik with Levitan 1980). He argues, furthermore, that although product differentiation appears to have some fundamental differences from advertising, connected in particular with the nature of the investment, the length of time involved and the associated uncertainty, no satisfactory operational distinction can be made, at least in his models, unless it was possible to be explicit about the dynamics and uncertainty associated with product variation and advertising.

Various analyses of the effects of uncertainty on advertising have been carried out. It may be shown that, at a given price, the risk-evading firm will advertise more; once advertising and price are jointly determined it is not possible to predict the outcome (Horowitz 1970). Uncertainty will not alter the actions of a risk-neutral firm, but may cause a risk-adverse firm to advertise less (more) if advertising has an aggressive (defensive) character (Dehez and Jacquemin 1975). Dehez and Jacquemin also conclude that 'it does not seem workable to derive unambiguous comparisons between the risk-averse firm's optimal price and advertising policies and the corresponding policies in the case of certainty or risk neutrality' (p. 78). Given the difficulties in deriving clear predictions of the effects of uncertainty on advertising, this suggests that greater difficulties may be encountered in trying to differentiate between the effects of uncertainty on advertising and on product differentiation.

Following the approach of Dorfman and Steiner (1954), the analysis of advertising can be directly applied to R&D expenditure (Needham 1975). If demand depends on price and R&D, and costs depend on output and R&D, then the following demand and cost functions of a firm in a monopoly position can be specified, where price and R&D are both decision variables:

$$Q_D = Q(P, R) \tag{6.1}$$

$$C = C(Q, R) \tag{6.2}$$

where Q_D is the quantity demanded, P is price, R is current R&D expenditure, and C is costs. R is a fixed cost and the profit function can then be written:

$$\pi = PQ - C(Q) - R \tag{6.3}$$

where π is profit. Assuming profit maximisation, the following first order conditions are obtained:

$$\frac{\partial \pi}{\partial R} = \frac{P \partial Q}{\partial R} - \frac{dC}{dQ} \frac{\partial Q}{\partial R} - 1 = 0 \tag{6.4}$$

$$\frac{\partial \pi}{\partial P} = P \frac{\partial Q}{\partial P} + Q - \frac{dC}{dQ} \frac{\partial Q}{\partial P} = 0. \tag{6.5}$$

Multiplying (6.4) by R and Q/Q, and (6.5) by P and Q/Q gives:

$$\frac{\partial Q}{\partial R} \frac{R}{Q} \left(PQ - \frac{dC}{dQ} Q \right) = R \tag{6.4.1}$$

$$\frac{\partial Q}{\partial P} \frac{P}{Q} \left(PQ - \frac{dC}{dQ} Q \right) = -PQ \tag{6.5.1}$$

Dividing (6.4.1) by (6.5.1) gives the Dorfman–Steiner result:

$$\frac{R}{PQ} = \frac{(-\partial Q/\partial R)}{(\partial Q/\partial P)} \frac{R/Q}{P/Q} = \frac{-\eta_R}{\eta_P} \tag{6.6}$$

where η_R is the elasticity of demand with respect to R&D, η_P is the price elasticity of demand, and R/PQ is the ratio of R&D to sales. Hence, the more elastic demand is with respect to R&D, the higher will be R/PQ, *ceteris paribus*.

If there is more than one firm in the industry, and there is no collusion, the optimal R&D/sales ratio will depend on the firm's expectations of its rivals' R&D and price reactions, given its actions. Equation (6.6) may then be rewritten:

$$\frac{R_i}{P_i Q_i} = \frac{\left(\dfrac{\partial Q_i}{\partial R_i} + \dfrac{\partial Q_i}{\partial R_r} \dfrac{dR_r}{dR_i} \right) \dfrac{R_i}{Q_i}}{\left(\dfrac{\partial Q_i}{\partial P_i} + \dfrac{\partial Q_i}{\partial P_r} \dfrac{dP_r}{dP_i} \right) \dfrac{P_i}{Q_i}} \qquad (i = 1, 2 \ldots n) \tag{6.7}$$

where $\dfrac{dR_r}{dR_i}$ and $\dfrac{dP_r}{dP_i}$ represent firm i's conjectures about its rivals R&D and price responses to any change in its price and R&D. If there were no price responses the optimal R&D ratio would be reduced by interaction given that $\partial Q_i/\partial R_r < 0$ and $dR_r/dR_i > 0$ (Cowling 1972; Cowling *et al.* 1975). If Cournot behaviour is assumed, the equation reverts to the Dorfman–Steiner conditions of equation (6.6). Needham derives an expression similar to equation (6.7) to consider the effects of interdependence among firms (Needham 1975). If $\partial Q_i/\partial R_i$ is greater under oligopoly than under monopoly, expectations of imitative R&D behaviour by other firms will lead to the monopoly R&D level, while R&D will be larger than the monopoly level if less than imitative R&D reactions are expected. Equation (6.7) does make clear the important point that R&D decisions may depend on expectations of rivals' price and R&D decisions – although without considering time lags.

One of the main differences between R&D and advertising is that R&D may directly affect variable costs. Whereas advertising changes the image of a product, R&D is expected to result in changes in, or additions to, the physical characteristics of a product. These changes could increase or decrease the costs of production as well as shifting demand. R&D may also lead to process innovation only, which would be expected to reduce variable costs. Thus, R&D may have an effect both as a fixed cost and as a variable cost.

In the above equations, the price of R&D has been effectively normalised and set equal to unity. However, the effective cost of R&D may vary by industry and firm. For example, given the uncertainty attached to R&D, borrowing funds to finance R&D may be more expensive, and firms with a higher flow of funds be better placed to buy R&D inputs. The existence of other inputs complementary to R&D, such as other skilled staff and capital equipment, may also affect its effective cost. Expectations of potential duplication of R&D output may be less in a more concentrated industry which will affect the industry elasticity, η_R, but may also decrease uncertainty which can be seen as reducing the cost of R.

The preceding analysis can be extended to include the effects of R&D on variable costs (as done for the dynamic case by Leech and Stoneman (1976)) and without setting the price of R&D equal to one. The profit function may then be rewritten as:

$$\pi = PQ - C(Q, R) - \alpha R \tag{6.8}$$

where α is the price of R&D, and the first order condition for R written as:

$$\frac{\partial \pi}{\partial R} = \frac{P \partial Q}{\partial R} - \frac{\partial C}{\partial Q} \frac{\partial Q}{\partial R} - \frac{\partial C}{\partial R} - \alpha = 0 \tag{6.9}$$

where $\partial C/\partial R \gtrless 0$. This may be rewritten as:

$$\frac{\partial Q}{\partial R}\frac{R}{Q}\left(PQ - \frac{\partial C}{\partial Q}\frac{Q}{C}C\right) - \frac{\partial C}{\partial R}\frac{R}{C}C = \alpha R$$

$$= \eta_R(PQ - \eta_C C) - \eta_{RC}C = \alpha R$$

(6.10)

The first order condition for price, equation (6.5), can be re-expressed as:

$$\left(P - \frac{dC}{dQ}\frac{Q}{C}\frac{C}{Q}\right)\frac{\partial Q}{\partial P} + Q = 0 \tag{6.11}$$

multiplying by P:

$$PQ\frac{P}{Q}\frac{\partial Q}{\partial P} - \eta_C C\frac{P}{Q}\frac{\partial Q}{\partial P} + PQ = 0 \tag{6.12}$$

$$C = PQ\frac{(1 + \eta_P)}{\eta_P \eta_C} \tag{6.13}$$

Substituting (6.13) into (6.10) gives:

$$\alpha R = \eta_R PQ - \frac{PQ(1 + \eta_P)}{\eta_P \eta_C}(\eta_R \eta_C + \eta_{RC}) \tag{6.14}$$

hence:

$$\frac{\alpha R}{PQ} = \frac{-\eta_R}{\eta_P} - \frac{\eta_{RC}(1 + \eta_P)}{\eta_P \eta_C} \tag{6.15}$$

If $\eta_C = 1$ — i.e. constant returns to scale (Leech and Stoneman 1976) — (6.15) simplifies to:

$$\frac{\alpha R}{PQ} = \frac{-\eta_R - \eta_{RC}(1 + \eta_P)}{\eta_P} \tag{6.16}$$

The greater is α, the lower will R/PQ be. The sign of η_{RC} will indicate whether R&D is having a positive or negative effect on variable costs. If η_{RC} is negative (i.e. decreasing variable costs) this will increase the optimal R/PQ ratio. If η_{RC} is positive this reduces the effect of η_R. Since R/PQ cannot be negative, $|\eta_R|$ must then be greater than, or equal to, $|\eta_{RC}(1 + \eta_P)|$ when η_{RC} is positive. If R&D only reduces variable costs and does not affect demand, (6.16) becomes:

$$\frac{\alpha R}{PQ} = \eta_{RC}\frac{(1 + \eta_P)}{\eta_P} \tag{6.17}$$

If equation (6.16) correctly specifies the determinants of R&D expenditure relative to sales, then, to explain variation in R&D spending across industries, it is necessary to consider the determinants of η_R, η_{RC}, η_P and α and whether they are likely to vary across industries. However, while this may provide a means for categorising or defining some of the expected determinants of R&D expenditure, the application to R&D of an analysis derived in relation to advertising may be only approximate, or not applicable to all R&D expenditures. It is important to be aware of the limitations of this analysis.

Limitations of the model

Two differences between advertising and R&D have been introduced into the analysis: the effect of R&D on variable costs, and the possible variation in the effective price of R&D by industry. The risks and uncertainties associated with R&D and advertising are also likely to be different. For example, the risk of not doing the same level of R&D as a competitor may be greater than for advertising, since R&D may result in fundamental breakthroughs or changes in products and processes. However, in the short run the effect on demand of doing less or no R&D may be less than it would be for advertising. It is relatively easy to predict the effect of a certain amount of advertising expenditure, whereas not only is the output of R&D likely to be more uncertain, it is also new. Since R&D may change the characteristics of the product, not just its image, it may tend to shift industry demand to a greater extent, but less predictably. Also, since the same level of R&D in two firms may lead to different developments, R&D expenditures may be less cancelling in their effect on firms' demand than advertising. One further difference is that advertising can be directly linked to a firm's name or trademark, whereas R&D output has to be protected if a return is to be made on it — whether through monopoly, collusion, patents or secrecy.

There may, therefore, be more uncertainty attached to R&D expenditure than to advertising, and R&D may lead to changes in products and processes that cause jumps in supply and demand. This latter point is particularly important. The above analysis of R&D assumes that the effects of R&D on both output and costs are continuous. This is at best an approximation. Marginal changes in product characteristics and processes may have an effect that is virtually continuous, though very marginal changes may be due to design not to R&D inputs. The greater a change that results from R&D, and the more unevenly such changes occur, the more likely is the effect to be discrete and not continuous. It is then very difficult to provide a rigorous or general model of such changes, which would depend on the particular assumptions made about the structure of the market, consumers' tastes, producers' reactions and so on. Once non-marginal changes in products are considered, the price elasticity with respect to the new or developed product might also be very different.

It is precisely the non-marginal effects of innovation that Schumpeter stresses: 'competition which commands a decisive cost or quality advantage and which strikes not at the margins of the profits and the outputs of the existing firms but at their foundations and their very lives' (Schumpeter 1976, p. 84). He postulates a dynamic, disequilibrium competitive process which differs markedly from the profit-maximising equilibrium process underlying the Dorfman–Steiner approach. The application of the advertising analysis to R&D may therefore provide a useful approximation where innovations are relatively minor; where they are major or discontinuous in effect it may only throw some initial light on the problem. The likelihood of R&D having more discontinuous effects than those of advertising may also explain the finding that advertising tends to be associated with stability in market shares, and product development with instability (Caves and Porter 1978).

In considering the factors that determine or proxy the variables in equation (6.16) (η_R, η_{RC}, η_P and α), it is important to recognise that the underlying theory may be only an approximate explanation of some and not all of the determinants of R&D. The factors or proxies considered may, together with other influences, also affect the probability of R&D resulting in major changes. Hence, the optimal or the observed R&D level may be determined through various channels, not solely through those indicated in equation (6.16).

6.2 Specification of an estimating equation for R&D expenditure

In the light of the potential theoretical determinants of R&D discussed above and in Chapter 5, this section considers what factors may be expected directly to affect R&D and/or act as proxies for the variables that determine R&D in equation (6.16).

The following equation specifies the expected determinants of R&D that will be considered:

$$R = f(X, T, C, I, G, P, F) \tag{6.18}$$

where:
R = R&D
X = exports
T = technological opportunity
C = concentration
I = investment
G = expected profit
P = cash flow
F = foreign participation in production.

Exports

As discussed above, there have been several suggestions in the literature that exports may affect R&D. Exports will have a positive effect on R&D if there are differences in the nature of demand between export and domestic markets. In particular, if the elasticity of export demand with respect to R&D (η_{XR}) is greater than the elasticity of domestic demand (η_{DR}), then the larger the export share, the larger will be the overall elasticity (η_R).[1]

There are several reasons why η_{XR} may exceed η_{DR}. Firstly, as export markets of one industry will vary, in terms of consumers' preferences, entry barriers and elasticities, there may be a greater probability of R&D increasing demand in some of these markets than domestically. Thus, export markets will represent a higher return to R&D or, in terms of the current model, they will have a higher η_{XR}. Secondly, the R&D elasticity may also be higher in export markets if a Linder-type hypothesis is adopted (Linder 1961). If a minority of consumers in each country like variety, or differentiated goods, then, if R&D leads to variety and there are scale economies, this demand will be satisfied by exports. The responsiveness of this export demand to variety changes due to R&D will then be greater than the responsiveness of domestic demand, implying that η_{XR} is greater than η_{DR}. Furthermore, if certain goods are more susceptible to product differentiation, exports will be higher in these goods, and demand in these markets may be more responsive to variety changes – thus, again, there will be a positive relation between exports and η_R.

Finally, if competition is more intense in export markets – due to failure to recognise oligopolistic interdependence and/or due to the home market being protected – then, again, it may be expected that demand will be more responsive to R&D in those markets. Thus all these hypotheses imply that η_{XR} is greater than η_{DR} and, therefore, that exports will have a positive effect on R&D. However, this also requires that the higher η_{XR} is not outweighed by an equally higher η_P in export markets or a difference in η_{RC} between domestic and export markets. There does not seem to be any reason to expect the effect of R&D on variable costs to be less in export markets. A process innovation may be expected to have very similar effects on domestic and export production. If production costs change due to a product innovation this may vary between domestic and export markets, but in which direction cannot be predicted. The price elasticity may vary between export and domestic markets but the direction cannot be predicted, though it may be expected that the export elasticity will be greater, reflecting more competitive conditions in world markets. If consumers in export markets are more responsive to non-price aspects such as R&D, it is possible they may be less responsive to price than are domestic consumers, thus reinforcing the positive effect of exports on R&D. Even if the price elasticities differ initially, the price elasticities with respect to a new product will not be known with certainty, but could change. The price elasticity could therefore alter the effect of exports on R&D, but whether positively or negatively cannot be predicted.

Technological opportunity

The positive effect of technological opportunity on R&D may operate through various channels. The technological opportunity level reflects both the range and level of scientific knowledge that an industry may develop or use in its production processes and products. A higher technological opportunity level may be viewed as providing more opportunities for product and process development per input of a unit of R&D or, alternatively, it reduces the unit price of R&D. It may reduce the uncertainty associated with a given input of R&D, thereby reducing its expected cost. Technological opportunity may therefore reduce the price of R&D (α) and increase the expected (negative) change in costs for a change in R&D, or decrease the expected increase in costs (η_{RC}). It may increase η_R, since it will increase the output of new products for a given input of R&D, which will have a larger effect on demand.

In a Schumpeterian approach, technological opportunity would also be expected to have a positive relationship with R&D, since the extent of underlying scientific opportunities may be expected to stimulate competition based on innovation.

Concentration

The degree of concentration may have a positive effect on R&D for the Schumpeterian reasons discussed above, but may also be related to the preceding theoretical discussion. Cable (1972) has demonstrated that there may be a broadly quadratic relationship between concentration and advertising. This analysis may also be applied to R&D. In addition the possibility of exact duplication of R&D output by competitors may be less in a more concentrated industry. This will increase η_R relatively and, if it decreases uncertainty, reduce the price of R&D (α). However, Cable also shows that recognition of interdependence increases with concentration, which may exaggerate or suppress any R&D concentration relationship according to whether the effect of interaction is stronger for R&D or for price.

The final potential positive effect of concentration is that of appropriability. A higher degree of monopoly in an industry is likely to facilitate control of innovations. This does not fit directly into the R&D/advertising

framework, since appropriability is not a problem in advertising. It could be viewed as reducing the cost of R&D (α) or alternatively as ensuring that the effect of R&D on output (η_R) will not be transitory.

Investment

If the flow of investment, relative to capital stock or output, is high, this may reduce the cost of incorporating R&D output into the production process. The level of investment relative to the capital stock may reflect the general dynamism of the industry, which will positively affect the industry's attitude towards the riskiness and uncertainty of R&D. A higher relative level of investment may, therefore, reduce η_{RC} when it is positive and may also reduce α. However, if investment in capital equipment reflects allocation of funds among alternative uses, then a high level of investment would reflect a relatively low expected marginal product of R&D. Investment and R&D may then exhibit a negative relationship.

Expected profit

Given the theory that demand is a particularly, or the most, important determinant of R&D (Schmookler 1962, 1966), firms' expectations of future demand and future profitability of sales may have a strong influence on their R&D decisions (Bosworth 1981). The higher future demand and profits are expected to be, the more R&D the firm will undertake, since it will expect a relatively higher return to R&D. Expected profit will have a positive effect on R&D as it will increase the expected value of η_R.

Price elasticity

The price elasticity is inversely related to optimal R&D. Unlike the analysis of advertising, the relevant price elasticity — with respect to product innovations — is the future not the current elasticity. Use of the current elasticity is at best an approximation, since it refers to current goods and not to new products. Since the price–cost margin is inversely related to the price elasticity and positively to the degree of concentration (Cowling and Waterson 1976), the price–cost margin may be expected to have a positive relation to R&D and may substitute for a direct measure of the price elasticity. There is some similarity in the roles of the expected profit variable and the price–cost margin. However, they are not mutually exclusive since the former refers, in particular, to expected trends in demand while the latter is concerned with the nature of demand at a point in time. Nevertheless, given their similarity it may be difficult empirically to identify both effects.

Foreign participation in production

R&D may be carried out by subsidiaries of multinational enterprises (MNEs) both because technology transfer is not costless, and as subsidiaries' R&D may concentrate on specific aspects of the market being served (Mansfield and Romeo 1980; Hirschey and Caves 1981). If R&D is relatively cheaper in the host country for the MNEs, their subsidiaries may do more R&D than do indigenous firms. The extent of foreign participation will then be associated with relatively higher R&D/sales ratios. If subsidiaries tend to use parent company R&D, there will be a negative effect. These potential effects operate at the industry not the firm level. They do not relate directly to the R&D equation, equation (6.16).

Government

The effects of government expenditure on, and regulation of, R&D have not been included in the estimating equation specified. Government regulations may affect R&D spending in different industries but proper consideration of their effect would require a more detailed analysis, probably based on case study. The effects of the level and direction of government spending, particularly towards defence, would also require a more detailed analysis, including looking at effects on sectors over time; it may however be possible to consider whether industries with high defence R&D, such as aerospace, have different R&D behaviour.

6.3 Conclusions

This chapter has analysed a model of optimal R&D intensity developed as an extension of the Dorfman–Steiner advertising model. The uses and limitations of this approach were discussed. This model, together with the theories considered in Chapter 5, was then used in deriving an equation specifying the expected determinants of R&D spending. It was argued that, while the different theories are not entirely compatible, they may be complementary to the extent that they explain different aspects of R&D expenditure, according to whether R&D results in major or minor changes. Since the output of R&D cannot be distinguished in this study, a general R&D equation was specified drawing on the various theories analysed.

CHAPTER 7

Estimation of the composition of
U.K. manufactured exports, 1978

The potential determinants of export composition were analysed in Chapter 5. It was argued, in particular, that exports and R&D are simultaneously determined. Previous empirical studies of the technology and skill theories of trade have not, however, considered this potential simultaneity. This chapter first sets out the specification of the simultaneous system of export and R&D equations, and then the results of estimating the export equation for the U.K.[1] The R&D data used is more disaggregated than that employed in previous U.K. studies, which allows more precise estimation of the effect of technology on U.K. exports. In order to give a more comprehensive picture of U.K. trade composition, the final section of the chapter presents estimates of import penetration and the net trade balance.

7.1 Specification of the simultaneous system

The theoretical analysis of the determinants of export levels and R&D has demonstrated that the estimating equations for exports and R&D form a simultaneous system. Exports and R&D are, therefore, jointly endogenous. Ordinary least squares (OLS) estimation will result in biased and inconsistent parameter estimates.

The system is specified by the following two structural equations:

$$X_8 = a_0 + a_1 R_5 + a_2 FR_5 + a_3 HS + a_4 TP + a_5 C_5 + a_6 IK + a_7 SM + a_8 K \tag{7.1}$$

$$R_5 = b_0 + b_1 X_8 + b_2 FR + b_3 C_5 + b_4 IK + b_5 GL + b_6 PL + b_7 FL \tag{7.2}$$

where:

X_8 = [exports/gross output] 1978 in constant prices (1975 = 100)
R_5 = [R&D/value-added] 1975

FR_5 = $[\Sigma_i \text{ R\&D}_i/\Sigma_i \text{ value-added}_i]$ 1975; i = U.S., France, Germany, Japan

HS = [skilled manual labour/total labour employed] 1971

TP = [(professional and technical staff) — (scientists and engineers in R&D)] /total labour employed 1971

C_5 = five-firm sales concentration ratio 1975

IK = Σ_i (investment/capital stock)$_i/2$; i = 1974, 1975

SM = (scale elasticity 1963) × (minimum efficient scale 1975)

K = [capital stock/total labour employed] 1975

FR = $\Sigma_i [(\Sigma_j \text{ R\&D}_j)/(\Sigma_j \text{ value-added}_j)]_i/2$; i = 1973, 1975; j = U.S., Japan, France, Germany

GL = growth of gross output 1968–74 in constant prices (1975 = 100)

PL = $\Sigma_i [(\text{value-added} - (\text{wages and salaries}))/\text{value-added}]_i/3$; i = 1972, 1973, 1974

FL = [sales by foreign-owned firms/total sales] 1968

The equations are estimated in multiplicative form, the variables all being in logarithms,[2] except for *SM*.

The specification of the two equations indicates that both are over-identified. The export equation excludes *GL, PL, FL* and *FR*. The R&D equation excludes *HS, TP, SM, K* and *FR*$_5$. Given the similarities of the two variables *FR* and *FR*$_5$ they are not expected to provide clear identification, which would be problematic only if identification rested on these variables alone. The procedure used to estimate this system is that of instrumental variables, using as instruments all the exogenous variables in the system. Initially, this is identical to using two-stage least squares. However, if variables are excluded from the system, the reduced form estimates of X_8 and R_5 will differ according to whether they are two-stage or instrumental estimates. The advantage of the instrumental variable approach is that, when different specifications of the equation are compared, the reduced form estimates of X_8 and R_5 used will be the same in all cases, aiding direct comparison. Since additional instrumental variables cannot result in less precise or biased instrumental estimates of X_8 and R_5, the instrumental variables estimates are likely to be better than the two-stage least squares estimates.

Measurement of variables[3]

Exports

Exports in 1978 are measured relative to gross output to give a clear measure of the relative importance of exports across industrial sectors of different sizes. Though in policy terms it may be important to know which sectors have absolutely large exports, in relation to the current analysis it is important to assess what factors other than size are influencing exports in different industries. Exports are measured in 1978 in both equations, since it is argued that the simultaneous relation between exports and R&D will hold over time, even though there may be some lagged effects, and it is in the spirit of full information methods of estimating to ensure that both exports and R&D are the same in both equations.

R&D

R&D is measured relative to value-added both for size reasons, similar to those given for exports above, and because R&D relative to value-added may give a better indication of R&D intensity than sales (Walker 1979).

There may be lags in the effects of R&D, though these will vary considerably by industry (Mansfield 1968). Due to lack of detailed information, the analysis here assumes that lags are the same across industries, and that rates of depreciation of R&D across industries and countries are the same. It is also assumed that different stocks of R&D knowledge are reflected in current R&D expenditures. Various studies have commented on the tendency for R&D in the 1970s to be directed to short-run projects with returns expected in a few years (OECD 1980; Schott 1981). Measuring R&D in 1975 relative to exports in 1978 may make some small allowance for this.

The R&D data covers intra-mural R&D expenditure for forty-eight industries covering all U.K. manufacturing. Given that R&D is being used as the best available measure of technological intensity, and that this study is particularly concerned with assessing the effects of technology on trade, the empirical analysis was carried out at this level of aggregation, rather than disaggregate the R&D data further on some necessarily *ad hoc* basis, as done in other U.K. studies (Cable and Rebelo 1980; Smith *et al.* 1982; Lyons 1983). This measure of technology is considerably more disaggregated than that used in many studies, where two or three groups may be defined as high, medium and low technology-intensive groups, and more disaggregated than that used in any previous U.K. study. As analysed above, the relation between exports and R&D is expected to be positive in both equations.

Foreign R&D

Foreign R&D is measured as the sum of R&D relative to the sum of value-added for the four other largest R&D spending OECD countries, i.e. the U.S., Germany, Japan and France.[4]

In the export equation, foreign R&D (FR_5) is measured for 1975 since it is used to analyse the technology gap between the U.K. and foreign R&D in 1975. FR_5 is expected to be negative.

In the R&D equation, foreign R&D is used to proxy technological opportunity as it provides a more precise and less subjective measure than the technological opportunity dummies used in many other studies (for example,

Scherer 1965; Globerman 1973). A similar approach was adopted by Caves *et al.* (1980), who used U.S. R&D as a technological opportunity proxy. The advantage of taking an average across countries, and across two years, is that deviations in individual countries' R&D expenditure relative to the technological opportunity level of an industry are more likely to cancel out. *FR* is expected to be positive in the R&D equation.

Skilled labour

The skilled labour variables are introduced to test the human skills theory of trade. Two skill variables are used, since the relative importance of the two different types of labour represented — skilled manual and professional and technical staff — will vary across industries. The U.K. may have an advantage in one type of labour, not both, and the strength of the effect of each on exports may differ. The data was taken from another U.K. study (Smith *et al.* 1982) which constructed the series from the 1971 Census of Population. The professional and technical staff series was adapted for this study, by subtracting employment of scientists and engineers in R&D, to try to distinguish the effects of this skilled labour variable from the R&D variable, since the two are quite highly correlated. Thus, the hypotheses to be tested are that *HS* and *TP* are both positive.

Concentration

The five-firm sales concentration ratio for 1975 is used in the export equation to measure the effects of monopoly power on exports. As discussed above, this may have positive or negative effects on exports, and is also expected to be correlated with firm size which may have positive effects on exports. In the R&D equation the concentration ratio is used to test the hypothesis that the protection of monopoly power and the working of oligopolistic competition will increase R&D.

Investment

Investment expenditure is measured relative to the capital stock and averaged over two years, because of the lumpy nature of investment expenditures. *IK* is expected to have a positive effect on exports, as a higher level of investment indicates more modern equipment and processes may be in use, with consequently higher productivity or quality. Measuring investment relative to the capital stock also gives some indication of the rate of turnover of the capital stock and so, in part, of the general dynamism of the industry. There is expected to be some lag in new investment affecting exports; hence it is measured for 1974 and 1975.

In the R&D equation, investment is expected to be complementary to R&D since higher investment allows R&D results to be incorporated more easily and efficiently. However, since R&D may be considered in part as an investment expenditure itself (though not included in the measure *IK*), it may represent an alternative to other forms of investment expenditure and be competing rather than complementary.

Scale economies

Scale economies may have a positive or negative effect on exports, which will depend on whether U.K. industry is able to achieve available scale economies relative to its competitors. The measure of scale economies uses Hufbauer's measure (Hufbauer 1970).[5] A large scale elasticity will only be important if the plant size at which scale economies are achieved is also large relative to the market. A measure of minimum efficient scale was, therefore, constructed, defined as the average size of plants in the top 50 per cent of net output relative to total net output. This is similar to measures used in other studies (for example, Caves 1981). The product of this measure and the scale elasticity is then used as the measure of scale economies.

Some of the scale elasticities are negative, so the variable cannot be expressed in logarithms. However, the scale elasticity is measuring how productivity changes proportionately for a proportionate change in size weighted, in effect, by the measure of minimum efficient scale and so is already unit-free.

Capital intensity

Capital intensity is measured as capital stock relative to total employment in 1975. As argued above, it is not expected to have a significant effect. However, Baldwin (1979) finds negative effects of capital intensity even when human capital variables are included, but the effects are insignificant once natural resource industries are excluded.

Expected profit and profit margin

Growth of gross output (*GL*) is measured from 1968 to 1974 (at constant 1975 prices) and is used as a proxy for expected profit which is expected to have a positive effect on R&D. *PL* represents a measure of the profit margin (as an approximation to the price–cost margin). Since the price–cost margin is inversely related to the price elasticity and positively to the degree of concentration, *PL* may act as a proxy for the (inverse of the) price elasticity. *PL* could also be interpreted as a measure of available cash flow which will also have a positive effect on R&D (Bosworth 1981). There may be some overlap in the effects captured by *PL* and *GL*.

Foreign participation

Sales by foreign-owned firms are measured relative to total sales for 1968, the most recent year for which data is available. It is expected that the

Table 7.1. *Predicted effects of independent variables*

Dependent variable	R_s	FR_s	HS	TP	C_s	IK	SM	K	X_8	FR	GL	PL	FL
X_8	+	−	+	+	?	+	?	?					
R_s					+	+				+	+	+	?

extent of foreign participation in an industry may have a positive effect on U.K. R&D since, at least up to and including the mid-1970s, it was relatively cheaper to undertake R&D in the U.K. (OECD 1979). However, multinationals may do most of their R&D in the parent company and transfer results to subsidiaries, in which case there may be a negative correlation. Even in this case, though, introduction of new products and processes in foreign firms could stimulate R&D in domestic firms (Mansfield and Romeo 1980).

Having discussed the construction and expected effects of the variables in the simultaneous system of equations, their predicted effects are summarised in table 7.1.

Sample size

The sample size is based on the availability of data for R&D, which is at a level of disaggregation of forty-eight industries. As mentioned in the discussion of foreign R&D (Appendix 2), there is insufficient data on the ships and marine engines category, so this observation is dropped. The observation on other manufacturing is also dropped as this represents a number of different and distinct industries which would not be expected to behave in similar ways. Thus, the sample is restricted to forty-six manufacturing industries.

Instrumental variables estimate of R&D 1975

Prior to discussing the results, the instrumental variables estimate of R&D 1975 (R_5) used in estimating the export equation, is presented. It is obtained from the OLS estimation of R_5, using all the independent variables in the model as the instrumental variables to estimate R_5:

$$\text{OLS } R_5 = \underset{(-2.179)}{-4.743^*} \underset{(-1.394)}{- 2.265FR} + \underset{(1.697)}{2.719FR_5} \underset{(-0.070)}{- 0.053PL} +$$

$$\underset{(0.316)}{0.166GL} + \underset{(2.144)}{0.168^*FL} \underset{(-1.419)}{- 0.543IK} + \underset{(1.890)}{0.630C_5} +$$

$$\underset{(2.270)}{34.136^*SM} \underset{(-2.020)}{- 0.932HS} + \underset{(2.447)}{0.703^*TP} \underset{(-1.145)}{- 0.277K}$$

$$R^2 = 0.816 \qquad F_{11,34} = 13.688^* \qquad (7.3)$$

Figures in brackets are t-statistics; * denotes significance at 5 per cent level (here and throughout).

The overall explanatory power of the equation is quite high, as shown by the R^2. A very poor estimate might make it difficult to estimate the effect of R_5 in the export equation. However, no direct inference can be drawn from this equation on the role of the independent variables. Nevertheless, some of the significant and nearly significant variables have signs that are in line with the theoretical discussion. *SM, TP* and *FL* are significant, *HS* and C_5 close to significance. Positive relationships between scale and concentration and R&D may be expected, given the theoretical discussion. A positive relationship of R&D with technical and professional staff is expected, given some degree of complementarity in their functions. The negative relation with *HS* may then indicate that industries either have a high R&D and *TP* input or a high *HS* input, but the two are not complementary. This is also shown in the correlation matrix (table 7.2). The positive sign on *FL* probably reflects the greater prevalence of multinational companies in high technology industries.

The simple correlations between the variables in the export equation give some indication of any potential multicollinearity problems.[6] The strength of the correlations varies considerably, but there are no very high correlations indicating serious problems of multicollinearity. The highest correlation is 0.709 between R_5 and FR_5, which should still enable separate influences to be distinguished. Exports are quite strongly correlated with only three variables: R_5, FR_5 and *TP*. R_5 is fairly strongly correlated with five other variables – X_8, FR_5, *TP*, C_5 and *HS* – which could mean it will be more susceptible to effects of multicollinearity than any other variable.

7.2 Estimation of the export equation

In the initial estimation of the export equation as specified in equation (7.1), there were clear indications of the presence of heteroscedasticity. The results of this estimation, the tests for homoscedasticity and the adjustment made for the heteroscedasticity (by weighting the data) are described in Annexe 7.1.

Table 7.3 reports the results of estimating the export equation by instrumental variables having weighted the data to eliminate the heteroscedasticity. Equation (1), table 7.3, gives the results of estimating the full specification of the export equation. Equation (1a) gives the results of estimating the equation by OLS. The instrumental variables estimates of equation (1) give some support to the neo-technology theories – R_5 is positive and significant, FR_5 is negative and significant. However, if separate coefficients are calculated for the technology level and the technology gap, only the

Table 7.2. Correlation matrix of variables in the export equation

	X_8	R_s	FR_s	HS	TP	C_s	IK	SM	K	FL
X_8	1.0	0.492	0.409	-0.046	0.475	0.143	-0.066	0.097	-0.050	0.319
R_s		1.000	0.709	-0.528	0.690	0.519	-0.062	0.240	0.186	0.276
FR_s			1.000	-0.229	0.663	0.254	-0.010	-0.109	-0.029	0.089
HS				1.000	-0.410	-0.405	-0.047	-0.170	-0.464	-0.205
TP					1.000	0.270	-0.068	-0.007	0.316	0.069
C_s						1.000	-0.019	0.451	0.438	0.155
IK							1.000	-0.037	-0.386	0.192
SM								1.000	0.168	-0.179
K									1.000	-0.074
FL										1.000

gap is significant:

$$0.435R_5 + 0.306*(R_5 - FR_5)$$
$$(1.480) \qquad (1.875)$$

This result implies there is no effect of the technology level on exports, and that it is only relative technological positions that affect exports.

The effects of the two human skills variables are positive, as predicted by the human skills theory, but only skilled manual labour is significant. This supports the hypothesis that the U.K. may have a relative advantage only in skilled manual, not non-manual, labour. There may also be multicollinearity problems between R_5 and TP, but the results indicate that R_5 is having the dominant effect.

The investment variable is positive as hypothesised, but insignificant. Concentration and scale are both negative in their effect but neither is significant. This contrasts with another similar U.K. study (Smith *et al.* 1982), which found concentration and plant size to be positive – the former always insignificant, but the latter sometimes significant, though the sign on *SM* may support the results of a study of the U.K. relative to the U.S. (Katrak 1973). Capital intensity, as predicted, is very weak and insignificant, failing to support any role for the traditional factor endowment variable. Excluding the capital intensity variable from the equation results in some changes – concentration, in particular, is more significant (equation (2), table 7.3). This may be due to its positive correlation with K, which may have increased its standard error.

The OLS results contrast with the instrumental variables estimates. The coefficient on R_5 is larger in equation (1) than in (1a), the OLS estimation. This indicates that the OLS estimation results in a negative bias on R_5, though the discussion of the direction of the bias suggests it might tend to be positive (Appendix 4). The significance and coefficients of FR_5, HS, C_5 and SM are higher in equation (1) relative to (1a), while the opposite is true for TP, IK and K. The existence of some degree of collinearity means the simultaneity bias may have affected all variables. The consequences are seen to be serious.

Simultaneity

Before considering different specifications of the export equation, it is appropriate to test whether the simultaneous specification of the model is supported by the data. This can be assessed using a Hausman test (Hausman 1978, see Annexe 7.2). This tests the significance of the instrumental estimate of the simultaneous variable in an equation which also contains the actual variable. Thus, where $\hat{R}_5$ represents the instrumental estimate of R_5,

Table 7.3. *Results of the estimation of X_8 (weighted) by instrumental variables*
Mean of the dependent variable, $X_8 = -1.3115$

	Constant	R_s	FR_s	HS	TP	C_s	IK	SM	K	Standard error of the regression
(1)	2.922 (1.459)	0.741* (2.615)	−0.306* (−1.875)	0.835* (2.045)	0.057 (0.207)	−0.381 (−1.151)	−0.056 (−0.097)	−12.882 (−0.995)	−0.060 (−0.334)	0.5425
(2)	3.340* (2.075)	0.793* (3.278)	−0.306* (−1.919)	0.920* (2.808)	0.002 (0.002)	−0.448 (−1.658)	0.006 (0.025)	−13.696 (−1.047)		0.5583
(3)	3.341* (2.111)	0.795* (3.999)	−0.316* (−1.964)	0.920* (2.871)		−0.448 (−1.723)	0.006 (0.026)	−13.734 (−1.115)		0.5511
(4)	3.319* (2.519)	0.794* (4.096)	−0.316* (−2.000)	0.919* (2.982)		−0.449 (−1.752)		−13.719 (−1.131)		0.5436
(5)	3.271* (2.630)	0.691* (4.274)	−0.222* (−1.750)	0.819* (2.936)		−0.496* (−2.076)				0.5134
OLS										$\bar{R}^2$
(1a)	0.696 (0.552)	0.357* (3.335)	−0.156 (−1.482)	0.353 (1.417)	0.330* (1.807)	−0.102 (−0.438)	−0.307 (−1.303)	−4.538 (−0.465)	−0.276 (−1.711)	0.412
(5a)	1.761 (1.910)	0.427* (4.536)	−0.060 (−0.658)	0.499* (2.255)		−0.304 (−1.533)				0.398

Figures in brackets are t-statistics.[a]
* Denotes significance at the 5% level.

[a] As Maddala (1977, p. 241) points out, the finite-sample variance of two-stage least squares estimates may be infinite, which means the tails of the distribution are much thicker than is assumed in the asymptotic distribution. This is one justification for using t-tables though 'adjusting for degrees of freedom and using t-tables will usually be more conservative' (Maddala, 1977, p. 239).

the following equation is estimated:

$$\text{OLS } X_8 = \underset{(1.606)}{2.683} + \underset{(2.221)}{0.261*R_5} + \underset{(1.752)}{0.466\hat{R}_5} - \underset{(-2.298)}{0.312*FR_5} +$$

$$\underset{(2.267)}{0.772*HS} + \underset{(0.319)}{0.073TP} - \underset{(-1.368)}{0.376C_5} - \underset{(-1.368)}{0.116IK} -$$

$$\underset{(-1.248)}{13.445SM} - \underset{(-0.569)}{0.086K} \tag{7.4}$$

$\hat{R}_5$ is not quite significant, so the hypothesis of no simultaneity is not rejected. However, the power of the test is weak, due to the inevitable multicollinearity of R_5 and $\hat{R}_5$, and the t-statistic on $\hat{R}_5$ quite large, suggesting there may still be some presumption of simultaneity. Incorrect use of instrumental variables will give inefficient estimates. Incorrect use of OLS will result in biased estimates. The simultaneous estimation method is, therefore, retained. This approach is supported when the export equation is estimated without K. A Hausman test then rejects the hypothesis of no simultaneity, the t-statistic on $\hat{R}_5$ being 2.439. The capital intensity variable was included to test a more traditional trade hypothesis which was not expected to be supported. Given its clear insignificance, it seems appropriate to estimate the equation without K. The result of the subsequent Hausman test is important. It implies that estimation of the export equation by OLS will result in biased estimates of the coefficient on R_5 and elsewhere, due to the multicollinearity of R_5 with some of the other variables. This has serious implications for other empirical tests of the technology theory, none of which have used simultaneous methods.

The hypothesis of homoscedasticity is supported for equation (1), given the weighted adjustment to the data as explained in Annexe 7.1. The hypothesis is tested by regressing the squared residuals against any set of independent variables (Harvey 1981). NR^2 is then distributed as $\chi^2_{(r-1)}$ where N is the number of observations and r is the number of regressors.[7]

Specification of TP and IK

It may be argued that a comprehensive test of the neo-factor endowment theory should include all skilled professional and technical staff in the variable TP, and not exclude those in R&D. Estimating the export equation, with R&D staff included in TP, failed to improve the performance of this variable. Thus, even when a measure of R&D is included in the skilled labour variable, the R&D measure on its own continues to dominate the skilled labour variable.

The performance of the investment variable could also be affected by its measurement, given the uneven nature of investment expenditures. Re-calculating *IK* for an average of four years (1972–5) and re-estimating the export equation, *IK* was more significant than previously but remained negative, contrary to the hypothesis of a positive effect of investment. However, after *TP*, it remained the least significant variable in the equation (after the exclusion of *K*).

The poor performance of *TP* and *IK* is not shown to be attributable to details of their measurement. However, one factor that may affect the investment variable is the growing practice of leasing of capital goods during the 1970s. Thus, *IK* might not be giving a true picture of relative investment in capital goods across industries.

Re-specification of the equation

Equation (1), table 7.3, gives support to some, but not most, of the hypotheses advanced with respect to the different variables. There are various procedures that could be adopted at this point. If the export equation as specified represents the true model, then further estimation of different specifications is not required and is incorrect. However, as Winters (1981) points out, the literature on estimation assumes that the true model is known, while the literature on hypothesis testing does not provide a procedure to adopt once a particular hypothesis is rejected. It may therefore be argued that hypothesis testing can be used in the process of choosing a model, and may allow the removal of insignificant variables (Maddala 1977; Winters 1981). The procedure adopted here is therefore to eliminate the least significant variables in the equation one by one, to find the appropriate model to estimate U.K. export composition. This procedure may not work well if multicollinearity is a serious problem (Maddala 1977). However, as previously discussed, though there is likely to be some multicollinearity in the system, there is no evidence that it is very serious.

As referred to above, the capital intensity variable was not expected to have an effect and was included to test a more traditional theoretical approach. Given its insignificance it is excluded first from the equation. The hypotheses relating to the other variables are assessed from the variables' significance levels and the elimination procedure just described is adopted. The least significant variable is *TP*, which is omitted, and the equation re-estimated. This procedure is repeated resulting in the exclusion of *IK*. The results of this elimination procedure are set out in table 7.3. Equation (4) thus gives the results of the estimation having eliminated *K*, *TP* and *IK*. If the coefficients for the technology level and technology gap variables are calculated for equation (4) they are:

$$0.478*R_5 + 0.316*(R_5 - FR_5)$$
$$(5.204) \qquad (2.000)$$

The hypotheses of a positive effect of the technology gap and the technology level are now both supported. The significance of R_5 is now much higher than in the full specification of the equation. This may be due to the elimination of TP; the removal of this source of multicollinearity would be expected to reduce the standard error of the estimate of R_5. The hypothesis of a positive effect of skilled manual labour is supported. Concentration is negative and close to significance (on a two-tail test). The scale variable is negative, though insignificant. This may give some support to the conclusions of a U.S./U.K. study (Katrak 1973) which found that U.K. exports relative to those of the U.S. were relatively lower when scale economies were more important.

In its re-specified form, the export equation may no longer be simultaneous. A Hausman test rejects the hypothesis of no simultaneity for equation (4).[8] The presence of homoscedasticity is also again indicated.[9]

Final specification of the export equation

Omitting SM from the export equation, as the least significant variable, the estimated equation is then given by equation (5), table 7.3, with the OLS estimation given in equation (5a). Calculation of the technology level and gap coefficients for equation (5) gives:

$$0.469 * R_5 + 0.222 * (R_5 - FR_5)$$
$$(5.072) \qquad (1.750)$$

As before, the results give support to the technology theory of trade and some support to the human skills theory. The hypotheses of homoscedasticity and simultaneity are again both supported.[10] The model is, however, failing to explain a considerable part of the variation in export composition.

The results suggest that there are at least two distinct sources of competitive advantage for U.K. exports — technology and skilled manual labour — and that there are two aspects of the effects of technology. Both the intensity of R&D and the gap between U.K. and foreign R&D have a positive effect on exports. The result of a positive effect of R&D on U.K. exports is similar to that of many other studies which have found support for the technology theories of trade (for example Gruber, Mehta and Vernon 1967; Hufbauer 1970; Horn 1977; Stern and Maskus 1981). However, previous U.K. studies have varied in their results. All used OLS estimation methods. Two found a positive effect of technology level (Cable and Rebelo 1980; Lyons 1983) while one rejected this effect (Smith *et al.* 1982). Katrak failed to find a significant effect of the technology gap (Katrak 1973). Other studies have not found, or looked for, positive effects of both the level of technology and the technology gap together. The results presented here show that not only will differences in technology across countries, as proxied by R&D, have a positive effect on export levels, but that the level of technology itself will have a positive effect on exports, through channels such as the combination of product differentiation and scale economies, and by allowing entry into new markets. The additional effect of the level may thus reflect a general U.K. advantage in R&D-intensive products; alternatively, it could reflect the higher tradeability of more technologically advanced goods.

The results of equation (5) support the hypothesis of a negative effect of concentration. This could be a result of firms with monopoly power choosing not to export if they can then no longer discriminate between home and export markets, or it may reflect lower competitiveness, lack of dynamism and greater inefficiencies of these sectors and firms. It shows that industry structure can have an important influence on trade. It offers no support for the idea that oligopolists may use spare capacity – created to inhibit entry – to supply export markets. It also suggests caution in advocating large firm size as potentially beneficial to export intensity, if increased firm size results also in greater concentration. Results of other studies including a concentration variable have been varied. Concentration has not always or often been significant but seems more frequently to have been found to be positive (Baldwin 1971; Goodman and Ceyhun 1976; Pagoulatos and Sorensen 1976; Smith *et al.* 1982; Utton and Morgan 1983). Although significant only in equation (5), the concentration variable is consistently negative in the equations estimated in this study.

The positive effect of the human skills variable, *HS*, lends partial but not complete support to the human capital theory. Other studies have often used either one general skill variable, or just one variable similar to the technical and professional staff variable employed here. Smith *et al.* (1982), using the same data though including R&D employment in *TP*, found a positive and significant effect of *TP*, but an insignificant though positive effect of *HS*. The results of that study and the current study, though conflicting, confirm the hypothesis that it is relevant to define more than one category of skilled labour. The importance of this is particularly underlined by the current results since here it is the less commonly used measure, *HS*, that is significant.

The differences in results between the current study and that of Smith *et al.* (1982) are important to understand, since these studies represent detailed analyses of the neo-technology and neo-factor endowment theories for the U.K. – using similar skilled labour and R&D data – but obtain different results.

One major difference lies in the level of disaggregation and the disaggregation procedures used. Although the study of Smith *et al.* is more disaggregated than is the current study, they use R&D data from a more aggregated level than used here and then allocate it — by guesswork — from thirty-two sectors to their ninety-seven sectors. In contrast, their skilled labour data is calculated separately for each of the ninety-seven sectors — and their *TP* variable includes R&D staff. The current study takes their skilled labour data (removing R&D staff from the *TP* variable) and aggregates it up to the same level at which the R&D data is obtainable — forty-six industries. Thus, the R&D data is not disaggregated by guesswork, making a clearer comparison possible between the effects of skill and R&D. In addition to this major difference, the two studies use in general somewhat different specifications, variables and estimation methods. This underlines the importance of a clear theoretical underpinning in determining such factors, but also must raise doubts about the robustness of the results not only of these but of other similar studies. In particular, the effect of simultaneous estimation has been shown to be important here, but the Smith *et al.* study — in common with many others — uses single equation estimation. They also present no tests for homoscedasticity.

Tests of homoscedasticity are infrequently presented in empirical studies. It is important, therefore, to consider whether failure to ensure homoscedasticity is likely seriously to affect results. This will depend on the particular sample, the model and the form of the heteroscedasticity. In the current model, if the adjustment for heteroscedasticity described in Annexe 7.1 is not made, both FR_5 and C_5 are insignificant. If the adjustment had not been made, the hypotheses of no effect of the technology gap and of no effect of industry structure would have been accepted. The final equation would then have been:

$$\text{IV } X_8 = 0.673 + 0.364*R_5 + 0.616*HS$$
$$\phantom{\text{IV } X_8 = } (1.286) \quad (4.524) \quad\quad (2.354) \quad\quad\quad\quad \sigma = 0.5430 \quad\quad (7.5)$$

The full set of results for the unadjusted estimation are set out in table 7.6 (Annexe 7.1). In the current analysis, failure to adjust for heteroscedasticity seriously alters the conclusions that can be drawn from the results.

Outliers and industry groups in the export equation

The residuals of equation (5) have been shown to be homoscedastic. It may still be the case that there are systematic patterns in the residuals by industry group — such as chemicals, electrical engineering, etc. — or that certain outlying observations are dominating the results. Inspection of the pattern of residuals does not indicate any systematic patterns by industry group. Food, drink, telecommunications and wheeled tractors remain among the larger residuals. Food is over-estimated, which may be due to it being directed to the domestic market and being a perishable good. Drink is under-estimated, possibly due to the particularly differentiated nature of some U.K.-produced drinks, which will not be captured by the independent variables. Telephone and telegraph apparatus is over-estimated, which may be due to its role as a nationalised industry which, though advanced in R&D, has aimed to provide a service for the U.K. when changes in design, or increased variety, may be necessary to export. Wheeled tractors is under-estimated. This is a product with, relatively, very low R&D and a very high export/sales ratio. By its nature, this product may be expected to lead to large exports, if it is required by less developed, more highly agriculture-based countries without the means or competitiveness to produce themselves. Of the remaining residuals greater than one standard error of the regression, specific characteristics, particularly weight, may explain three: fertilisers, timber and bricks, cement etc. Organic chemicals may also face relative transport difficulties, while printing is likely to be particularly directed to the domestic market. There seems to be no clear explanation for the other larger residuals: synthetic resins, metal goods, textile machinery, construction equipment, and other textiles.

Technology and skilled labour

The results of equation (5) show that technological intensity and the proportion of skilled manual labour represent two positive determinants of the U.K.'s export composition. These two factors are not directly linked; the highest technology industries will not necessarily be those with the highest skilled manual labour — the two variables are, in fact, negatively correlated. However, the combination of skilled manual labour with R&D within an industry may be crucial in ensuring a successful follow-up to R&D activities. Thus, the ability to translate R&D results into full production may depend precisely on the level and nature of skilled labour. This proposition is, however, not directly tested by the above model, nor does it explain why technical and professional staff should not be of similar importance. One possible explanation could be that the U.K. is becoming relatively weak in terms of its quantity, quality or use of technical and professional staff, and so it is failing to maintain exports where these staff are particularly important.

These results do not offer any direct support for the hypothesis of a 'low technology syndrome' in the U.K., which suggests the U.K. has fallen behind its main competitors through failing to increase R&D fast enough, and through misdirecting R&D, particularly to defence, with consequent negative effects on technology-intensive exports (Freeman 1978; Katrak 1982). Nor do they clearly reject it either, however, since this would require an analysis of the U.K.'s exports both relative to other countries and over time. They do show that R&D has some positive effect, though it could be less effective than competitors' R&D. The results indicate channels through which the low technology syndrome could operate – through both the level of R&D intensity and U.K. R&D relative to its competitors. Thus, to the extent that U.K. R&D is falling increasingly behind that of the U.S., Japan and Germany, and given that the U.K. allocates relatively more R&D spending to defence than do Japan and Germany, this must be expected to affect U.K. exports.

7.3 Alternative specification, estimation methods and hypotheses

This section considers the results of (i) a different method of simultaneous estimation, (ii) estimating the equation for 1972, (iii) a different specification of the export equation, and (iv) the inclusion of a foreign participation variable. Various hypotheses are then tested with respect to different industries – namely aerospace, and food, drink and tobacco – and to different categories of industries – grouped by technology class, and by type of industry – capital goods and chemicals, basic goods and consumer goods.

Full information maximum likelihood

Given the simultaneous specification of the system, as corroborated by the Hausman test, the question arises of whether it is preferable to use a full information method of estimation. The model, as initially specified (equations (7.1) and (7.2)), was estimated by full information maximum likelihood (FIML). However, the estimation was very sensitive to the specification of the system and to initial starting values of the coefficients, frequently failing to converge or converging to a point that was clearly not maximising the likelihood. Given these problems, estimation with FIML was not pursued. One set of converged results are given for information, though little weight may be attached to them:

$$X_8 = \begin{array}{c} 1.395 \\ (0.754) \end{array} + \begin{array}{c} 0.324^*R_5 \\ (8.223) \end{array} - \begin{array}{c} 0.027FR_5 \\ (-0.288) \end{array} - \begin{array}{c} 0.052HS \\ (-0.411) \end{array} + \begin{array}{c} 0.134^*TP \\ (2.038) \end{array}$$

$$- \begin{array}{c} 0.382C_5 \\ (-1.365) \end{array} - \begin{array}{c} 0.086IK \\ (-0.251) \end{array} + \begin{array}{c} 7.627^*SM \\ (2.108) \end{array} - \begin{array}{c} 0.065K \\ (-1.076) \end{array} \quad \begin{array}{l} \text{Residual sum of} \\ \text{squares} \\ \text{(RSS)} = 13.400 \end{array}$$

$$(7.6)$$

$$R_5 = \begin{array}{c} -4.016 \\ (-1.131) \end{array} + \begin{array}{c} 1.906^*X_8 \\ (14.987) \end{array} + \begin{array}{c} 0.243FR \\ (1.375) \end{array} + \begin{array}{c} 0.969^*C_5 \\ (1.841) \end{array} - \begin{array}{c} 0.095IK \\ (-0.136) \end{array}$$

$$+ \begin{array}{c} 0.115GL \\ (0.392) \end{array} + \begin{array}{c} 0.134PL \\ (0.302) \end{array} + \begin{array}{c} 0.087^*FL \\ (2.024) \end{array} \quad \text{RSS} = 58.987$$

$$(7.7)$$

Log of likelihood function $= -77.884$.

The export results still confirm the positive and significant effect of R_5, and a negative effect of C_5. HS and FR_5 are now very insignificant. By contrast, TP is positive and significant, suggesting it may be possible to identify separately the influences of R&D and of technical and professional staff. SM is now positive and significant, reinforcing those studies that have found positive effects of plant size (Smith *et al.* 1982; Wolter 1977; Lyons 1983). The results do not completely contradict the results of the instrumental variables estimation but do lend support to some different hypotheses. Given the lack of robustness of these results, little emphasis can be placed on them. However, they do suggest caution in accepting or rejecting different hypotheses and imply that results may be sensitive to specification and estimation methods.

Exports 1972

It is of interest to consider whether estimation of exports for an earlier year will reinforce the conclusions of the previous section. Exports for 1972 (X_2) were estimated using R&D, skilled manual labour, foreign R&D, and concentration. R&D was still measured in 1975 since R&D in 1972 and 1975 are highly correlated and since the simultaneous nature of the system implies temporal deviations are not crucial. The instrumental estimate of R&D 1975 also produced a better fit, so this was preferred. HS is measured for 1971 already. Foreign R&D (FR_3) was measured for 1973. Concentration (C_5) was not changed. The following result was obtained:

$$IV\ X_2 = \underset{(1.929)}{2.872} + \underset{(4.121)}{0.779{*}R_5} - \underset{(-1.830)}{0.269{*}FR_3} + \underset{(2.593)}{0.875{*}HS} - \underset{(-1.507)}{0.437C_5}$$

$$\sigma = 0.6396 \qquad (7.8)$$

These results are very similar to those of equation (5), table 7.3. The coefficients on the independent variables are similar to those obtained previously. The main difference is the insignificance of the concentration variable, though C_5 still has a negative effect and is quite close to significance — and is measured for a later year. A Hausman test rejects the hypothesis of no simultaneity, the t-statistic on $\hat{R}_5$ being 2.411. The results of estimating exports in 1972 therefore provide some confirmation both of the results for exports in 1978 and of the adoption of a simultaneous estimation method.

Technology and factor endowments

A more traditional specification of the export equation would exclude industry structure variables. SM and IK were not significant in the previous analysis but C_5 was, so omission of these variables will alter the results.

It is interesting to compare the results of a more traditional specification with the results given above. Estimating the export equation, including only technology, human capital and capital intensity, gives the following result:

$$\text{IV } X_8 = \underset{(2.562)}{1.453} + \underset{(3.189)}{0.428^*R_5} - \underset{(-1.502)}{0.165FR_5} + \underset{(2.287)}{0.618^*HS} + \underset{(1.410)}{0.264TP}$$

$$\underset{(-1.537)}{-0.159K} \qquad\qquad \sigma = 0.4690 \qquad (7.9)$$

As previously, the hypotheses of a positive effect of R_5 and HS on exports are supported. The technology gap is not quite significant. The technical and professional staff variable is now much closer to significance, as is the capital intensity variable, which is negative (as in other U.K. studies (Smith *et al.* 1982)). Thus, having omitted industry structure variables, TP and K are more likely to be seen as affecting exports. Hence, studies that omit industry structure variables could bias their results in favour of these more traditional variables.

If TP is omitted from the equation, the significance level of K falls and it becomes the least significant variable. This may be due to the positive correlation of TP and K. The significance of FR_5 also falls, R_5 and HS remaining the only significant variables. This more traditional specification of the equation would therefore lead to a failure to reject the hypothesis of no effect of the technology gap. This suggests that the results of equation (5) depend on the relation between FR_5 and C_5. Also, in this more traditional specification the coefficient on R_5 is lower than in equation (5). This may be due to the elimination of C_5 which is positively correlated with R_5. FR_5 is strongly positively correlated with R_5 also, as well as with X_8 but weakly correlated with C_5. These correlations could therefore result in the reduction of the coefficient on R_5 and the reduction of the (negative) coefficient of FR_5.

An F-test could show whether C_5 and FR_5 are jointly significant. This could not be done. Once the sum of squared residuals from the second stage regressions – of X_8 on R_5 and HS, and of X_8 on R_5, HS, FR_5 and C_5 – were adjusted (Maddala 1977, p. 239), the sum of squares of the former equation were greater than the latter. As an approximate test, an F-test was done using the unadjusted sums of squares. This gave a value of 2.8215, where $F_{2,40} = 3.23$, supporting the hypothesis that C_5 and FR_5 are jointly insignificant. The economic interpretation of this result is unclear. It implies that, together, FR_5 and C_5 are not making a significant contribution to the explanation of the variation in exports, though they are separately significant. However, since the variables separately are only just significant, and together just insignificant, the results may simply reflect the borderline nature of the significance of these coefficients. This may be due in part to the correlations discussed above.

Foreign multinational enterprises

The main reason for considering the effect of foreign MNEs in the export equation is that, in estimating changes in exports over time (Chapter 9) one hypothesis to be tested is that foreign MNEs have a negative effect (Panić and Joyce 1980). It is therefore helpful to assess their effect in the exports levels equation. It is frequently suggested that the presence of foreign multinationals may have a positive effect on exports. Although there may be expected to be a positive correlation between exports and multinationals, this does not necessarily indicate causation. Multinationals would be expected to be positively related to tradeability and to technology level. If MNEs are to have a separate effect on exports there must exist a third identifiable influence. It has been suggested that foreign MNEs export relatively more than do domestic firms in the same industry (Dunning 1979). One study matched firms by various characteristics and found that this no longer held (Solomon and Ingham 1977). Foreign MNEs may have some specific factor – such as management, way of organising production or use of R&D results from the parent company – that could affect exports more than domestic sales, in particular if they are using the U.K. as a base to export from, or using U.K. labour or other resources. Foreign MNEs might have superior knowledge of, or links with, foreign markets.

It may be difficult to observe if foreign MNEs do have a separate effect. This depends on identifying an effect other than tradeability and technology. Foreign MNEs' participation is measured by the proportion of foreign sales in output, FL. If this is correlated with tradeability, proxied by exports (X), and technology, proxied by R&D (R), then the foreign sales variable may be expressed as:

$$FL = \alpha_1 X + \alpha_2 R + \alpha_3 Z \tag{7.10}$$

where Z is any separate effect FL may have on exports. This equation is not intended to imply any direct causation from X and R to FL. If the export equation is written as follows:

$$X = \beta_0 + \beta_1 R + \beta_2 FL + \beta_3 Y \tag{7.11}$$

where Y represents all other independent variables, this may be re-expressed (substituting (7.10) into (7.11)):

$$X = \frac{1}{1 - \beta_2 \alpha_1} (\beta_0 + (\beta_1 + \beta_2 \alpha_2)R + \beta_2 \alpha_3 Z + \beta_3 Y) \tag{7.12}$$

FL only has a separate effect through *Z*. However, (7.11) not (7.12) is estimated, so *FL* is likely to capture some of the R&D effect and some export effect, causing simultaneity problems. Since $\beta_2\alpha_1$ and $\beta_2\alpha_2$ are expected to be positive, insignificant *FL* would be quite a strong rejection of the hypothesis of a positive effect of *Z*, i.e. that $\beta_2\alpha_3$ is greater than zero.

If *FL* is included in the initial specification of the export equation, it is positive but not significant. Eliminating insignificant variables, the following result is obtained:

$$\text{IV } X_8 = \begin{array}{ccccc} 3.113^* & +\,0.613^*R_5 & -\,0.167FR_5 & +\,0.798^*HS & -\,0.437C_5 \\ (2.686) & (3.804) & (-1.336) & (3.083) & (-1.932) \end{array}$$

$$\begin{array}{ll} +\,0.069FL & \sigma = 0.4900 \qquad (7.13) \\ (1.302) & \end{array}$$

The effect of *FL* is weak and insignificant, failing to reject the hypothesis of no effect of foreign sales. This contrasts with the results of the Department of Industry study (Smith *et al.* 1982), which found some positive and significant results for the same foreign sales variable when included. However, they too were doubtful about the justification for including this variable. The inclusion of *FL* results in FR_5 not being significant while C_5 is close to significance. *FL* is the least significant variable, so, following the procedure adopted previously and omitting *FL*, the equation will then be the same as equation (5), table 7.3. Foreign participation does not, therefore, alter the results of the estimation based on the model adopted in this study.

Aerospace

One particular industry that might be expected to be different from the other observations is aerospace. Many studies also work with manufacturing industry excluding food, drink and tobacco.

Although included in the sample, it may be thought that the aerospace observation may have a particularly dominating influence on the results. It is the U.K.'s most research-intensive industry and its research is heavily directed towards defence which may affect the R&D/export relationship (*Business Monitor* MO14 1979). A dummy variable, *DA*, was added to the estimating equation (taking the value 1 for aerospace, 0 for all other industries) with the following result:

$$\text{IV } X_8 = \begin{array}{ccccc} 3.288^* & +\,0.692^*R_5 & -\,0.219FR_5 & +\,0.827^*HS & -\,0.493^*C_5 \\ (2.600) & (4.227) & (-1.667) & (2.860) & (-2.036) \end{array}$$

$$\begin{array}{ll} -\,0.072DA & \sigma = 0.5192 \qquad (7.14) \\ (-0.128) & \end{array}$$

This result fails to reject the hypothesis that aerospace is similar in its behaviour to the other observations.[11]

Effects of industry groups

Although examination of the residuals showed no obvious patterns by industry groups, there might be effects of different classifications such as by type of product, or by technology class. These effects can be considered by using dummy variables for the categories drawn up. This is not a rigorous procedure since it may not always be precisely clear in which category an industry should be, and also because the significance or otherwise of a dummy variable may be due to other factors, or influences, that are correlated with some or most of the industries in a particular group. The interpretation of dummy variables may therefore not always be clear.

The effects of technology on exports may vary by technology class – high technology industries may have a closer association with tradeability which would be reflected in their intercept, or their R&D may have a relatively stronger effect, changing the slope of R_5. The industries in the sample were informally categorised into high, medium and low technology industries and intercept and slope dummies were constructed (Appendix 1). Slope dummies were put on R_5 and FR_5, and on R_5 only. None of the dummies were significant. An F-test failed to reject the hypothesis that the dummies were jointly insignificant. Similar results held for the intercept dummies.

A separate hypothesis has been proposed (Freeman 1978) that the effect of technology on exports may vary according to industry group – capital and chemicals, consumer goods, and basic goods. The strongest relation is predicted in capital and chemicals, since here 'comparative advantage in human capital and R&D intensity is most firmly established' (Freeman 1978, p. 61) while price competition may be more crucial in basic goods, and technical change in consumer goods may not be picked up by conventional measures. This may be tested by constructing slope dummies (Appendix 1) for the technology variables, R_5 and FR_5. Including slope dummies on both R_5 and FR_5, for capital and chemicals and for basics, none is significant. An F-test fails to reject the hypothesis that they are jointly insignificant. However, if slope dummies on R_5 alone are included the capital and chemicals dummy is significant. Excluding the basic goods dummy which is insignificant, the following result is obtained:

$$\text{IV} \quad X_8 = \quad 1.995 \quad + 0.617 * R_5 - 0.118 * DCKR - 0.273 * FR_5 + 0.733 * HS$$
$$(1.562) \quad (4.096) \quad (-2.122) \quad (-2.323) \quad (2.865)$$

$$- 0.362 C_5 \qquad\qquad\qquad \sigma = 0.4650 \qquad (7.15)$$
$$(-1.608)$$

where $DCK = 1$ for capital and chemicals, 0 otherwise; $DCKR = DCK \times R_5$.

If the equation is estimated with an intercept dummy the following result is obtained:

$$\text{IV } X_8 = \begin{array}{l} 1.629 + 0.553^*R_5 + 0.480^*DCK - 0.271^*FR_5 + 0.745^*HS \\ (1.202) \quad (3.447) \quad\quad (2.224) \quad\quad\quad (-2.295) \quad\quad (2.897) \end{array}$$

$$\begin{array}{ll} - 0.343C_5 & \sigma = 0.4691 \quad\quad (7.16) \\ (-1.501) & \end{array}$$

Contrary to Freeman's hypothesis, $DCKR$ in (7.15) is negative. This suggests that these industries require a relatively higher R&D input to have the same effect on exports. $DCKR$ may be picking up a more general effect of relatively poor performance in these industries, possibly connected to non-price factors (such as poor delivery, poor after-sales servicing or reliability) that may be particularly important in these industries. However, this should affect the intercept, not the slope. The intercept dummy DCK in equation (7.16) is positive. Contrary to the hypothesis proposed, this suggests either that the U.K. has some advantage in capital goods and chemicals or that they have higher tradeability. This effect could explain why the sign of $DCKR$ was negative, if it was picking up a positive intercept effect, and suggests Freeman's hypothesis needs to be re-expressed in terms of these industries' tradeability or other factors, not R&D. If DCK and $DCKR$ are entered in the same equation, neither is significant, though $DCKR$ is very insignificant. The DCK dummy may be split into two dummies, one for capital goods and one for chemicals. A t-test fails to reject the hypothesis that their coefficients are the same.

The inclusion of the DCK dummy results in the constant no longer being significant, and in C_5 being insignificant. This suggests that C_5 captures industry structure effects which are partly dominated by the structure effects represented by DCK. However, as discussed above, caution needs to be exercised in the use and interpretation of dummy variables. Here, the interpretation of DCK is not completely clear. It does not test the Freeman hypothesis as initially formulated, and for which purpose the industry categories were drawn up. For these reasons, the final equation including C_5 is preferred – though the results here suggest that the industry structure results captured by C_5 may be complex.

7.4 Import penetration and the net trade balance

A broader picture of the U.K.'s international trade position may be obtained by considering the level of import penetration and the net trade balance. The main disadvantage of these measures is that determinants of exports and imports will vary. In particular, imports are likely to be affected by tariff and non-tariff barriers, and may reflect preferential trading arrangements and other peculiarities in sources of supply of particular goods. This will affect the results of the net trade balance and import equations.

The import equation is specified with the same independent variables as the equation to estimate the export/output ratio:

$$M_8 = \beta_0 + \beta_1 R_5 + \beta_2 FR_5 + \beta_3 HS + \beta_4 TP + \beta_5 C_5 + \beta_6 IK + \beta_7 SM + \beta_8 K$$

$$(7.17)$$

where $M_8 = [(\text{imports})/\text{gross output} - \text{exports} + \text{imports})]$ 1978 (1975 = 100) and the other variables are as defined previously.

It may be expected that imports will have a negative relationship with the technology gap between U.K. and foreign R&D, so FR_5 would be predicted to have a positive sign. Having adjusted for the technology gap, imports may then be positively related to technology level if this reflects more opportunity for product differentiation, higher demand and higher levels of tradeability. If the U.K. is relatively more competitive in the production of high technology goods, the sign will be negative. Overall, the expected sign is therefore indeterminate.

There is no clear expectation of the signs of the two skilled labour variables. Given the positive effect of HS on exports, if this reflects relative U.K. advantage in skilled labour, it may be expected that it will have a negative effect on imports.

It is usually expected that concentration will have a positive relation with imports, due to the effect of monopoly power on profit rates and on prices of differentiated goods (White, L.J. 1974). However, if high concentration reflects barriers to entry that also affect imports, C_5 may be negative. IK is predicted to have a negative sign; the expected sign of SM is not clear. As with the export equation, capital intensity is not expected to have a strong effect.

Table 7.4 presents the results of estimating the import equation by OLS.

Equations (1) to (6) are not significant. U.K. R&D is positive and significant, while FR_5 is negative. A technology gap variable would therefore have an implausible sign. The results support the hypothesis of a positive effect of technology level on imports. Skilled manual labour is positive, suggesting that this variable may be reflecting some aspect of tradeability not comparative advantage, since it is also positive in the export equation. The signs of C_5 and IK are also contrary to those predicted, but insignificant. There is no sign of heteroscedasticity.

The question arises as to whether there is any reason to expect a simultaneous relationship between imports and R&D. This would require imports to have some effect on R&D. It may be possible that imports would affect R&D, though this could operate through various channels. A higher level of

Table 7.4. *Results of the estimation of M_8 by OLS*

	Constant	R_s	FR_s	HS	TP	C_s	IK	SM	K	$\bar{R}^2$	F
(1)	1.529 (0.803)	0.330* (2.128)	−0.091 (−0.597)	0.745 (1.989)	−0.022 (−0.080)	−0.317 (−0.948)	0.107 (0.313)	−5.666 (−0.388)	0.084 (0.421)	0.006	1.033
(2)	1.178 (0.696)	0.311* (2.118)	−0.107 (−0.728)	0.676* (2.030)	0.028 (0.112)	−0.251 (−0.859)	0.032 (0.110)	−6.008 (−0.417)		0.027	1.181
(3)	1.066 (0.798)	0.310* (2.144)	−0.106 (−0.730)	0.672* (2.057)	0.026 (0.105)	−0.251 (−0.870)		−6.020 (−0.423)		0.052	1.412
(4)	1.034 (0.804)	0.315* (2.323)	−0.101 (−0.742)	0.665* (2.097)		−0.253 (−0.891)		−6.144 (−0.439)		0.075	1.735
(5)	1.180 (0.959)	0.297* (2.318)	−0.078 (−0.628)	0.650* (2.082)		−0.298 (−1.139)				0.094	2.163
(6)	1.091 (0.899)	0.240* (2.674)		0.608 (2.008)		−0.273 (−1.063)				0.107	2.793
(7)	−0.053 (−0.094)	0.203* (2.450)		0.666* (2.233)						0.104	3.613*

Figures in brackets are *t*-statistics.
*Denotes significance at the 5% level.

imports might reduce the expected return to R&D, or it might provoke a competitive reaction of increased R&D. However, a Hausman test on equation (1), including the instrumental estimate of R_5 used in the export equation, clearly fails to reject the hypothesis of no simultaneity. If M_8 is included in the R&D equation it is negative but not quite significant on a one-tail test. Given its lack of significance, the result of the Hausman test, and the clearer theoretical justification for R&D as an independent variable in the import equation, the estimation is continued using OLS.

Equation (7) is significant; however the overall explanatory power of the equation is low. The hypothesis of a positive effect of technology level is supported, as is the hypothesis of a positive effect of skilled manual labour. There is no effect of the technology gap on imports. The positive sign of *HS* is surprising given its sign in the export equation. This may reflect different specialisations within industries — and so a high level of intra-industry trade in industries with high *HS*. The hypothesis of homoscedasticity is supported. The poor performance of the equation may be due in part to omitted variables, in particular, variables containing information on trade barriers.

The effect of foreign participation on M_8 is tested. It will be positive if there is high intra-firm trade by MNEs and if MNEs have tended to disinvest and are supplying the U.K. market by imports. It will be negative if MNEs are based in industries where the U.K. has a comparative advantage not fully reflected in other variables. As with the export equation, it could have a spurious positive sign due to its correlation with tradeability and technology. Including foreign participation in the equation, it is positive but not significant, suggesting there is no strong effect of foreign participation.

Estimation of the net trade balance

The net trade balance equation is specified with the same independent variables as the import equation. The net trade balance is measured as:

XM_8 = (exports/imports) 1978 at constant 1975 prices

Since a simultaneous relation is expected between exports and R&D, there is a presumption of simultaneity between the net trade balance and R&D. The equation is therefore estimated by instrumental variables (IV), the instrumental estimate of R&D being the same as that used in the export equation. Results of the estimation are given in table 7.5.

As with imports, the explanatory power of the equations is very low. None of the independent variables are close to significance, suggesting none can contribute to an explanation of the net trade balance. The hypothesis

Table 7.5. *Results of the estimation of XM_8 by instrumental variables*

Mean of dependent variable, $XM_8 = 0.287$

	Constant	R_s	FR_s	HS	TP	C_s	IK	SM	K	Standard error of the regression
(1)	1.495 (0.586)	0.222 (0.611)	−0.109 (−0.504)	0.142 (0.274)	0.278 (0.765)	0.084 (0.201)	0.009 (0.025)	5.413 (0.317)	−0.085 (−0.364)	0.697
(2)	2.069 (1.011)	0.297 (0.975)	−0.125 (−0.579)	0.259 (0.629)	0.198 (0.672)	−0.011 (−0.032)	0.096 (0.312)	4.116 (0.241)		0.711
(3)	2.021 (1.485)	0.293 (1.089)	−0.123 (−0.599)	0.258 (0.637)	0.200 (0.710)		0.095 (0.316)	4.052 (0.243)		0.700
(4)	2.090 (1.559)	0.335 (1.636)	−0.153 (−0.906)	0.290 (0.749)	0.178 (0.662)		0.100 (0.330)			0.705
(5)	1.730* (2.260)	0.325 (1.630)	−0.145 (−0.882)	0.270 (0.717)	0.175 (0.661)					0.694
(6)	1.521* (2.144)	0.380* (2.053)	−0.129 (−0.781)	0.269 (0.702)						0.707
(7)	1.084* (3.332)	0.293* (2.230)	−0.076 (−0.540)							0.676
(8)	1.139* (3.803)	0.237* (3.007)								0.656

Figures in brackets are *t*-statistics.
* Denotes significance at the 5% level.

of homoscedasticity is supported. A Hausman test fails to reject the hypothesis of no simultaneity: the t-statistic on the instrumental estimate of R_5 is 1.235. This increases to 1.693 if the test is repeated when the equation is estimated without K. Thus, although not significant, given the weak power of the test and the simultaneous relationship found between exports and R&D, the estimation is continued using instrumental variables.

Omitting insignificant variables, R_5 becomes significant in equation (6), supporting the hypothesis of a positive effect of the technology level on the net trade balance. This suggests the U.K. does have a comparative advantage in R&D-intensive goods. The insignificance of HS further supports the suggestion that this variable may be capturing tradeability but not comparative advantage effects. This contrasts with another U.K. study in which R&D was negative and insignificant, and the only significant variable was manual labour, which was negative (Cable and Rebelo 1980). The positive sign of R&D is comparable to Katrak's result for the U.K. that the R&D intensity of exports relative to imports is greater than unity, though no tests of significance were done (Katrak 1982).

The hypothesis of homoscedasticity is supported. A Hausman test rejects the hypothesis of no simultaneity:

$$XM_8 = \quad 1.139^* - 0.235R_5 + 0.472^*\hat{R}_5$$
$$\quad (4.163) \quad (-1.553) \quad (2.815)$$

where $\hat{R}_5$ is the instrumental estimate of R_5.

Foreign participation in production

The hypothesis of a positive effect of foreign participation in production on exports or on imports was rejected in both the import and the export equations. In both equations foreign participation (FL) had a positive sign; hence it may not be expected that there will be a clear effect of FL on the net trade balance. The advantage of testing the effect of FL on the net trade balance is that this should remove to a large extent the correlation of FL with tradeability. Estimating the full specification of the equation, including FL, gives the following result:

$$\text{IV } XM_8 = \quad -2.002 \quad -0.783R_5 + 0.396FR_5 - 0.669HS + 0.944TP$$
$$\quad (-0.601) \quad (-1.110) \quad (1.060) \quad (-0.935) \quad (1.739)$$

$$+ 0.526C_5 - 0.543IK + 46.515SM - 0.323K + 0.255FL$$
$$\quad (1.053) \quad (-1.066) \quad (1.545) \quad (-1.159) \quad (1.670)$$
$$\sigma = 0.7072 \qquad (7.19)$$

FL has a positive effect, though not quite significant. SM and TP now both have more clearly positive effects. The signs on R_5 and FR_5 are opposite to those predicted. These results suggest that the effect of FL on XM_8 is positive, which may be for comparative advantage reasons or due to superior performance of foreign MNEs. The signs on R_5 and FR_5 are surprising. Although the correlation of R_5 with TP and FL, in particular, may lower the significance of R_5 it would not be expected to change its sign.

If the final form of the equation, as in equation (8), table 7.5, is estimated with FL, it is then insignificant while R_5 is significant:

$$\text{IV} \quad XM_8 = \begin{array}{ccc} 1.212 & +0.218*R_5 & +0.052FL \\ (3.856) & (2.640) & (0.748) \end{array} \qquad \sigma = 0.6545 \qquad (7.20)$$

This result suggests it is the interacting effect of some of the other independent variables which resulted in the near-significance of FL and the negative sign on R_5. If least significant variables are omitted from equation (7.19), the following result is obtained:

$$\text{IV} \quad XM_8 = \begin{array}{ccccc} 1.663* & -0.103R_5 & +0.111FR_5 & +25.284SM & +0.423TP \\ (3.622) & (-0.417) & (0.625) & (1.447) & (1.560) \end{array}$$

$$\begin{array}{l} +0.141FL \\ (1.607) \end{array} \qquad \sigma = 0.5988 \qquad (7.21)$$

Again, the opposite signs to those predicted on R_5 and FR_5 are observed. SM, TP and FL remain positive but none are significant. These results for the net trade balance equation have two alternative interpretations. Either the hypothesis of a positive effect of R&D on XM_8 is rejected and the full equation must be re-specified without either U.K. or foreign R&D, or FL is proxying comparative advantage effects not well captured by other variables in the equation and so dominating R_5. In the latter case, it may be argued that there is not a strong theoretical justification for including FL in the equation and, since it is not significant in the initial or final forms of the equation, it should be omitted, the hypothesis of a role for FL being rejected. The insignificance of FL in equation (7.20) tends to support the omission of FL, and suggests that its near-significance in the full equation may be due to correlations and collinearity between the independent variables, and not to a separate, identifiable effect of FL.

7.5 Conclusions

This chapter analysed the results of estimating an export equation for U.K. manufacturing industry. It also presented results for imports and the net trade balance. The main aim of this analysis was to explain the U.K.'s export composition in 1978; in particular, to consider the explanatory power of the neo-technology and neo-factor endowment theories of trade, and to test the hypothesis that the relationship between technology and trade is simultaneous. The export results supported the predictions of the neo-technology theory and also gave partial support to the human skills theory. Two results were derived with respect to the neo-technology theory: first, that the technological intensity level of an industry had a positive effect on exports, and, second, that the gap between the U.K.'s and competitors' R&D levels had a positive effect on exports. The analysis rejected the hypothesis of a positive effect of professional and technical staff on exports, but found that skilled manual labour — a less frequent measure in tests of the human skills theory — did have a positive relationship with U.K. exports. The more traditional factor endowment variable, capital intensity, was not found to play any role. Nor did a more traditional specification of the equation — excluding industry structure variables — result in significance of the capital intensity or the technical and professional staff variables. It did, however, weaken the effect of the technology gap. Industry structure was found to be important. The scale and investment variables were not significant, but concentration had a negative effect on exports. The effect of concentration was slightly weakened by the inclusion of a dummy for the capital goods and chemicals industries, though the interpretation of this dummy was unclear. No justification was found for treating other industries or industry groups separately, nor was foreign participation significant. Re-estimating the final export equation for 1972 supported the results for 1978, though the concentration effect was weaker.

Hausman tests supported the hypothesis that there was a simultaneous relationship between exports and R&D, and therefore that OLS estimation would lead to biased results. The importance of testing for the existence of homoscedasticity was also shown, and the potentially serious effect on results if heteroscedasticity is not adjusted for.

The results therefore indicate that there are at least three separate determinants of U.K. export composition — technology, skill and industry structure — which affect the U.K.'s competitive position. However, the results fail to explain a large part of the variation in U.K. exports. This might be due, in part, to lack of information on various factors, such as: the geographical breakdown of U.K. exports; historical, and other, trading ties with other countries; the extent and duration of foreign direct investment; and other non-price influences such as design. The current analysis is also limited in that it focuses on one year and is for the U.K. only.

To gain a broader picture, the chapter also briefly considered the determinants of import penetration and the net trade balance. Results of estimating these equations were relatively weak. The net trade balance was found to depend positively on R&D intensity. Imports were positively related both to R&D intensity and to skilled manual labour, suggesting tradeability factors may explain part of these variables' significance in the import and the export equation.

A general analysis of the role of technology, skill and industry structure, and of other variables, in export performance should also consider changes in exports over time, and the determinants of exports relative to another country or countries – this is done in Chapters 9 and 10.

Annexe 7.1 Adjustment for heteroscedasticity

If the export equation is estimated by instrumental variables without any adjustments to the data, the hypothesis of homoscedasticity is not supported. Results of this estimation are given in table 7.6.

If a Hausman test is carried out on equation (1), table 7.6, the t-statistic on $\hat{R}_5$ is 1.816. This is not significant but, given the weak power of the test and as the t-statistic is quite large, there may be some presumption in favour of simultaneity. Once the capital intensity variable is omitted – being very insignificant – a Hausman test then rejects the hypothesis of no simultaneity, the t-statistic on $\hat{R}_5$ being 2.023.

The hypothesis of homoscedasticity is clearly rejected. Regressing the squared residuals from equation (1) against estimated X_8 does not reject the hypothesis of homoscedasticity, which suggests that the logarithmic transformation is acceptable. However, regressing the squared residuals against the independent variables in the export equation, including the instrumental estimate of R_5, rejects the hypothesis of homoscedasticity: NR^2 is 17.443 where χ_8^2 is 15.507 at the 5 per cent level. Regressing the squared residuals against all the independent variables in the system also rejects the hypothesis: NR^2 is 24.172 where χ_{11}^2 is 19.675. The existence of ,heteroscedasticity means the parameter estimates are still unbiased but are no longer efficient. The estimate of the variance is biased.

Inspection of the equations estimating the squared residuals suggests the problem of heteroscedasticity may lie, in part, with the investment variable. One adjustment to try to eliminate heteroscedasticity could be to divide through all the variables in the export equation by the square root of the investment coefficient, in the residuals equation, multiplied by IK. However, since IK is in logarithms it is negative and its square root cannot be taken. As an alternative to this, the variables could be divided through by the square root of the predicted values of the squared residuals, regressed on IK and a constant. However, whether regressed only on IK or on all the variables in the export equation, some of the predicted values are negative and so, again, the square root cannot be taken.

Given the problems of adjusting for heteroscedasticity in these ways,

Table 7.6. Results of the estimation of X_8 (unweighted) by instrumental variables

Mean of dependent variable, $X_8 = -1.328$

	Constant	R_s	FR_s	HS	TP	C_s	IK	SM	K	Standard error of the regression
(1)	3.141 (1.335)	0.668* (1.996)	−0.271 (−1.360)	0.898* (1.884)	0.085 (0.256)	−0.371 (−0.964)	0.106 (0.301)	−7.475 (−0.474)	0.036 (0.163)	0.6425
(2)	2.904 (1.618)	0.637* (2.385)	−0.264 (−1.397)	0.850* (2.350)	0.119 (0.460)	−0.332 (−1.138)	0.070 (0.262)	−6.938 (−0.464)		0.6231
(3)	2.627 (1.843)	0.625* (2.419)	−0.256 (−1.398)	0.833* (2.384)	0.119 (0.468)	−0.328 (−1.146)		−6.711 (−0.458)		0.6117
(4)	2.612 (1.914)	0.563* (2.676)	−0.212 (−1.424)	0.784* (2.461)	0.151 (0.647)	−0.344 (−1.264)				0.5885
(5)	2.668 (1.905)	0.629* (3.330)	−0.209 (−1.369)	0.789* (2.408)		−0.394 (−1.468)				0.6024
(6)	1.794 (1.575)	0.410* (4.482)		0.585* (2.195)		−0.251 (−1.114)				0.5501
(7)	0.673 (1.286)	0.364* (4.524)		0.616* (2.354)						0.5430

Figures in brackets are t-statistics.
* Denotes significance at the 5% level.

a simpler approach was adopted. Inspection of the squared residuals indicated there were four observations that were acting as outliers: food, drink, telephone and telegraph apparatus and equipment, and wheeled tractors. The ratio of the mean square errors of the remaining forty-two observations relative to the mean square errors of these four observations in the export equation was calculated, giving a value of 0.1318. The square root of this ratio was then used as a weight for those four observations while the remaining observations had weights of 1. These weights were applied after the instrumental estimate of R_5 was calculated, since there was no evidence of heteroscedasticity there. Comparing the results in tables 7.2 and 7.6 demonstrates that failure to adjust for heteroscedasticity does affect the results obtained.

Annexe 7.2 The Hausman test

Hausman (1978) illustrates his test for simultaneity in the following very simple regression framework:

$$y = X\beta + \epsilon \tag{i}$$

with the standard stochastic specifications:

(a) $E(\epsilon|X) = 0$ or in large samples plim $\dfrac{1}{T} X'\epsilon = 0$

(b) $V(\epsilon|X) = \sigma^2 I$

If (a) is true, then estimation by OLS or two-stage least squares will result in consistent estimation of β; but OLS will be the more efficient method.

Rewriting (i) and decomposing X into $(\hat{X} + u)$ where u is the estimated residual:

$$y = \beta\hat{X} + \beta u + \epsilon \tag{ia}$$

If there is no simultaneity the two estimates of β will be the same, but under the alternative hypothesis the coefficient on u will vary because u is related to y via the simultaneous relationship. Hence:

$$y = \beta\hat{X} + \gamma u + \epsilon \tag{ib}$$

Adding and subtracting βu allows the test of equality of β and γ to be formulated as:

$$y = \beta(\hat{X} + u) + (\gamma - \beta)u + \epsilon$$
$$= \beta X + \alpha u + \epsilon \tag{ii}$$

Thus, $H_o: \alpha = 0$ tests the difference between β and γ. Alternatively, (ii) may be reformulated:

$$y = \beta X + (\gamma - \beta)(X - \hat{X}) + \epsilon$$
$$= \gamma X - (\gamma - \beta)\hat{X} + \epsilon$$
$$= \gamma X + \alpha \hat{X} + \epsilon \tag{iia}$$

where again $\alpha = 0$ tests $\beta = \gamma$, i.e. whether or not there is simultaneity.

CHAPTER 8

Estimation of the R&D intensity of
U.K. manufacturing industry, 1975

This chapter reports the results of estimating the determinants of R&D intensity from the simultaneous system specified in Chapter 7. The results of the previous chapter demonstrated that R&D has significant and positive effects on exports. This suggests that an understanding of the determinants of R&D expenditure are important in an analysis of U.K. export composition and of changes in that composition. There is, however, little evidence for the U.K. on the determinants of R&D, and there have been no tests of the role of exports in U.K. R&D. The results presented here are, therefore, of interest, not only in the context of export performance but more generally in gaining a fuller understanding of the various factors determining R&D intensity in the U.K.

8.1 Specification of the R&D equation

The precise specification of the R&D equation and the expected signs of the independent variables are discussed in Chapter 7. For convenience, the R&D equation (7.2) is repeated here:

$$R_5 = b_0 + b_1 X_8 + b_2 FR + b_3 C_5 + b_4 IK + b_5 GL + b_6 PL + b_7 FL \qquad (8.1)$$

where:

R_5 = [R&D/value-added] 1975
X_8 = [Exports/gross output] 1978
FR = $\Sigma_i(\Sigma_j \text{R\&D}_j/\Sigma_j \text{value-added}_j)/2$; i = 1973, 1975; j = U.S., Japan, France, Germany
C_5 = five-firm sales concentration ratio 1975
IK = $\Sigma_i(\text{investment/capital stock})_i/2$; i = 1974, 1975

GL = growth of gross output 1968–74 in constant prices (1975 = 100)
$PL = \Sigma_i[(\text{value-added} - (\text{wages and salaries}))/\text{value-added}]_i/3$; $i = 1972$, 1973, 1974
FL = [sales by foreign-owned firms/total sales] 1968

It is predicted that X_8 will have a positive effect on R&D. As discussed above, exports are measured in 1978 to ensure consistency with the export equation. It is expected that the simultaneous relation will hold over time and this allows full information methods of estimating also to be used. Technological opportunity, proxied by FR, is predicted to have a positive effect as is concentration. GL represents expected profit and is expected to be positive. However, it may be difficult to identify the effects of both PL and GL since, even if theoretically distinct, the measurement of the variables are not completely separate in the effects they are proxying. PL could represent an expected profit proxy. For this reason, the equation is also estimated with only PL, not GL, and vice versa. IK is predicted to have a positive effect on R&D since it allows the incorporation of R&D output. It may also reflect a demand effect. Finally, the foreign participation variable may have a positive effect, if foreign MNEs take advantage of relatively cheap R&D output from the parent company.

Instrumental variables estimate of X_8

As in the instrumental variables estimate of R_5, all the exogenous variables in the system are used to obtain an instrumental variables estimate of X_8:

$$\text{OLS } X_8 = 0.807 - 0.110FR - 0.067C_5 + 0.040PL + 0.004GL$$
$$(0.465)(-0.085) \quad (-0.254) \quad (0.065) \quad (0.009)$$
$$- 0.269IK + 0.166^*FL + 0.177FR_5 + 19.755SM$$
$$(-0.880) \quad (2.660) \quad (0.138) \quad (1.610)$$
$$+ 0.368HS + 0.526^*TP - 0.132K$$
$$(1.001) \quad (2.295) \quad (-0.685)$$
$$R^2 = 0.443 \qquad F_{11,34} = 2.458^*$$

$$(8.2)$$

The overall explanatory power of the equation is quite low, which means that the estimate of X_8 may be a poor proxy for actual X_8. FL and TP are significant and positive, which may be expected given their positive correlation with R_5. The two foreign R&D variables are very weak. This may be a result of their high collinearity and of the combined effects of the expected

Table 8.1. *Correlation matrix of variables in the R&D equation*

	X_8	R_s	FR	C_s	IK	GL	PL	FL
X_8	1.0	0.492	0.407	0.143	-0.066	0.185	-0.104	0.319
R_s		1.0	0.710	0.519	-0.062	0.369	0.139	0.276
FR			1.0	0.267	-0.007	0.238	-0.147	0.088
C_s				1.0	-0.019	0.109	0.257	0.155
IK					1.0	0.355	0.059	0.192
GL						1.0	0.378	0.256
PL							1.0	0.069
FL								1.0

negative sign of foreign R&D relative to exports and the expected positive sign of U.K. R&D, with which they are quite highly correlated.

Table 8.1 presents a correlation matrix for the variables in the R&D equation. The highest correlation is between FR and R_5, and then that between R_5 and C_5. X_8 is quite highly correlated with R_5 and FR. The remaining correlations are quite weak. Though there may be potential multicollinearity problems due to the interaction of variables, the matrix here indicates no serious cause for concern.

8.2 Estimation of the R&D equation

Table 8.2 presents the results of estimating the R&D equation by instrumental variables.

Equation (1), table 8.2, gives the results for the full specification. The export variable is significant and positive, despite its poor instrumental estimate, supporting the hypothesis that the more open a sector, in terms of the proportion of its output exported, the more R&D will be carried out by that sector *ceteris paribus*. This suggests that there could be a virtuous circle, such that export success encourages R&D expenditures which may further reinforce export performance.[1]

The results support the hypothesis of a positive effect of technological opportunity (FR) on R&D − the underlying level of scientific potential of an industry positively affects the amount of R&D undertaken. There is, however, a problem of avoiding tautologous definitions of technological opportunity. The variable used here may be preferable to the use of crude dummies, but if R&D was estimated at the level of the world economy clearly a variable such as FR could not be used. The idea of some industries being related to a wider scientific base than others is not, in itself, controversial, though these relations may change over time. What is problematic is a satisfactory measure of the scientific base − the results here must be interpreted with this in mind.[2]

Table 8.2. Results of the estimation of R_5 by instrumental variables
Mean of dependent variable, $R_s = -3.5986$

Constant		X_s	FR	C_s	PL	GL	IK	FL	Standard error of the regression
(1)	−4.245 (−1.708)	1.108* (2.132)	0.497* (3.106)	0.872* (2.623)	0.643 (1.178)	0.593 (0.893)	−0.272 (−0.622)	0.008 (0.066)	0.8965
(2)	−4.231 (−1.721)	1.127* (2.638)	0.494* (3.289)	0.874* (2.658)	0.646 (1.198)	0.594 (0.900)	−0.264 (−0.632)		0.8903
(3)	−3.205 (−1.715)	1.189* (2.824)	0.493* (3.289)	0.868* (2.610)	0.701 (1.302)	0.418 (0.691)			0.9007
(4)	−2.711 (−1.545)	1.260* (3.038)	0.509* (3.341)	0.839* (2.503)	0.874* (1.805)				0.9151
OLS									R^{-2}
(1a)	−5.496* (−2.645)	0.382* (1.740)	0.625* (5.113)	0.898* (3.069)	0.454 (0.967)	0.829 (1.452)	−0.477 (−1.297)	0.098 (1.106)	0.669
(4a)	−3.474* (−1.545)	0.525* (2.522)	0.663* (5.605)	0.897* (3.067)	0.779* (1.846)				0.660

Figures in brackets are t-statistics.
*Denotes significance at the 5% level.

The results also give support to the hypothesis of a positive effect of monopoly power on R&D. The concentration variable has a clear positive and significant effect in addition to the effects of the technological opportunity variable, contradicting the hypothesis that the main cause of an observed positive influence of concentration is due to its correlation with technological opportunity. If concentration has a separate effect this may be due to the advantages of monopoly power in appropriating returns to R&D, or it may, in part, reflect the stimulating effects of oligopolistic competition. However, the concentration ratio is, inevitably, a very poor measure of this latter concept.

Neither the profit margin nor the expected profit variable is significant, though both are positive as predicted. As discussed above, this may in part be due to the fact that they are not capturing completely separate effects.[3] By contrast, the investment variable is negative and insignificant, rejecting the hypothesis of a positive effect of investment expenditure on R&D. This supports Pavitt's finding (1981) of an apparent tendency for there to be a positive correlation between other countries' R&D and investment trends but not for the U.K. This could also indicate a relative inefficiency of U.K. R&D if its output is not so easily or quickly incorporated into production.[4]

The coefficient of FL is weak and very insignificant which fails to reject the hypothesis that foreign participation has no effect on U.K. R&D. Given that both positive and negative effects of foreign sales were hypothesised, these may cancel out resulting in a coefficient not significantly different from zero. Thus, for example, multinational enterprises may be more research-intensive, but the subsidiary may use R&D output from the parent company in place of some of its own R&D activity. In addition, it is not possible — due to lack of data — to take account of any effects of U.K. firms that are multinationals, though their behaviour may differ from that of U.K. firms that produce only in the U.K.

OLS results are given in equation (1a), table 8.2. The OLS coefficient is lower than that of the instrumental variables estimate. The OLS and IV results are otherwise quite similar, though the significance levels of most variables are higher in OLS. The ranking of variables by significance level will vary between the OLS and IV estimations. The estimation method is therefore important, both due to biased coefficients in OLS and if the estimation procedure is adopted of omitting the least significant variable from the equation as outlined above.

It is appropriate, therefore, to test whether the simultaneous specification of the R&D equation is supported by the data. As for the export equation, this is assessed using a Hausman test, entering both the actual and instrumental values of X_8 into the equation where $\hat{X}_8$ is the instrumental estimate.

This gives the following result:

$$\text{OLS } R_5 = -4.245 + 0.165X_8 + 0.943\hat{X}_8 + 0.497^*FR + 0.872^*C_5$$
$$(-2.000)\ (0.681)\quad (1.864)\quad (3.637)\qquad (3.071)$$
$$+ 0.643PL + 0.593^*GL - 0.272IK + 0.008FL$$
$$(1.380)\quad (3.071)\quad (-0.728)\quad (0.078)\qquad\qquad (8.3)$$

$\hat{X}_8$ is not quite significant but, given the weak power of the test, this may be interpreted as indicative of the presence of simultaneity. In addition, since the Hausman tests on the export equation tended to reject the hypothesis of no simultaneity, there must be a presumption in favour of estimating both equations in the model by simultaneous methods.

The R&D equation, like the export equation, is also estimated under the hypothesis of homoscedasticity. This is supported.[5]

Re-specification of the equation

As in the estimation of X_8, the procedure is adopted of eliminating the least significant variables one by one. The results of this estimation procedure are set out in table 8.2. The variables *PL* and *GL* fail to achieve significance when both are entered in the R&D equation, which suggests they may be capturing or representing similar effects. When *GL* is omitted, *PL* becomes significant. If the equation is estimated without *PL*, and *FL* is omitted as the least significant variable, the following result is obtained:

$$\text{IV } R_5 = -5.921^* + 1.006^*X_8 + 0.461^*FR + 1.007^*C_5 + 0.977^*GL$$
$$(-3.030)\quad (2.496)\qquad (3.219)\qquad (3.353)\qquad (1.744)$$
$$-0.344IK$$
$$(-0.861)\qquad\qquad\qquad\qquad\qquad\qquad \sigma = 0.8642\ (8.4)$$

The results of this estimation are similar to the previous results, but now also give support to the hypothesis of a positive effect of expected profit on R&D. Thus, with the omission of *PL*, *GL* is significant and has a strong effect on R_5. Investment is negative as before. However, if *IK* is omitted from the equation *GL* is insignificant, which may be due to the positive correlation of these two variables. Finally, therefore, the results fail to reject the hypothesis of no effect of expected profit, as proxied by *GL*.

If the R&D equation is estimated in its full form without *GL*, both *FL* and *IK* are insignificant as before. The final specification of the equation, equation (4), is then the same as is arrived at with the inclusion of *GL*, since *GL* is the least significant variable in equation (3). In equation (4), table 8.2,

PL is positive and significant. This supports the hypothesis of a positive effect of the profit margin on R&D. If the profit margin proxies the price elasticity, this indicates a negative relationship with the price elasticity. *PL* could also be interpreted as a (somewhat crude) proxy for the flow of funds. The positive sign then reinforces the results of other studies that have found positive effects of cash flow variables but not of expected profit (Smyth, Samuels and Tzoannos 1972; Grabowski 1968) and contrasts with those finding no role for these variables (Scherer 1965), though these studies have tended to be at firm, not industry level. However, since one further interpretation of *PL* could be as an expected profit proxy (as *GL* is), and since *PL* and *GL* seem, in part at least, to be capturing similar effects, the significance of *PL* cannot be taken as complete confirmation of the effect either of the price elasticity or of cash flow.

The results for the other independent variables in equation (4) are similar to those for the full specification of the equation. The hypothesis of a positive effect of exports on R&D is supported – this effect being stronger when estimated by instrumental variables. This adds to the results of a U.S. study (Mansfield, Romeo and Wagner 1979) which found that export levels were important in decisions on R&D expenditure in a firm level analysis, though it was not clear if this was due to a simple extension of market size or to other factors. The results contrast with those of a Canadian study (Caves *et al.* 1980) which found a negative, though not usually significant, effect of exports and also of imports. However, the Canadian results may be specific to that economy and its particular relationship with the U.S. economy.

The hypothesis of a positive effect of concentration is supported, even in the presence of a positive and significant technological opportunity variable. This contrasts with many of the results in the literature which have not found a clear role for concentration (Kamien and Schwartz 1975) and with a U.K. study, at a higher level of aggregation and using a different concentration measure – the Herfindahl index, which found no significant effect (Leech and Stoneman 1976).

The positive and significant effect of technological opportunity is a similar result to those of many other studies, using various different measures of technological opportunity (for example, Scherer 1965; Scherer 1982; Stoneman 1979; Wilson 1977) and to that of Caves *et al.* (1980) who used U.S. R&D expenditures – a similar measure to the one used here. The results, therefore, do not support Schmookler's hypothesis (1962, 1966) that demand alone is the main determinant of R&D expenditure rather than the inherent characteristics of the industry itself. Rather, they suggest that a combination of inherent characteristics – as represented by *FR* – and structural, performance and demand factors all have a positive influence on R&D. The results also highlight the importance of taking account of the openness of an economy, and not just analysing domestic variables.

In its restricted version, equation (4), it is appropriate to test the hypothesis of simultaneity for the R&D equation. A Hausman test gives the following result:

$$\text{OLS } R_5 = -2.711 + 0.165X_8 + 1.095^*\hat{X}_8 + 0.509^*FR + 0.839^*C_5$$
$$(-1.890)\ (0.697)\quad (2.645)\quad (4.085)\quad (3.061)$$
$$+ 0.874^*PL$$
$$(2.208) \tag{8.5}$$

This clearly rejects the hypothesis of no simultaneity. It is a stronger result than that for the fuller specification – equation (8.3). The result, therefore, supports the use of a simultaneous method of estimation, rather than OLS, which reinforces the use of simultaneous methods in the estimation of the export equation. The hypothesis of homoscedasticity is again supported.

The effects of using OLS estimation, not instrumental variables, are less serious here than for the export equation. Equation (4a), table 8.2, shows the OLS estimation of equation (4) – the main difference is in the size of the coefficients but these differences are quite large.

8.3 Alternative estimation methods and hypotheses

This section looks at the results of a different method of simultaneous estimation and of estimating the R&D equation for 1972. The hypothesis of a non-linear effect of concentration is tested using a dummy variable. Various hypotheses are then tested, with respect to specific industries and to different industry groups classified by technological opportunity level.

Full information maximum likelihood

As explained in Chapter 7, the simultaneous model as initially specified was estimated by full information maximum likelihood (FIML). For the reasons set out in that chapter, no great weight may be attached to these results. The R&D results (7.7) are repeated here to enable comparison with the instrumental variables estimates of the R&D equation:

$$R_5 = -4.016 + 1.906^*X_8 + 0.243FR + 0.969^*C_5 - 0.095IK$$
$$(-1.131)\ (14.987)\quad (1.375)\quad (1.841)\quad (-0.136)$$
$$+ 0.115GL + 0.134PL + 0.087^*FL \qquad \text{RSS} = 58.987$$
$$(0.392)\quad (0.302)\quad (2.024)$$

Log of likelihood function $= -77.884$.

The results for the R&D equation confirm the role of exports and concentration but reject the hypotheses of positive effects of *FR*, *GL* or *PL*. Also in contrast to the IV results, foreign participation has a positive and significant effect suggesting the presence of multinationals increases research intensity. While these results are not very robust, they suggest that some caution must be exercised in the interpretation of the IV results, and that certain variables may be sensitive to specification and estimation methods.

R&D 1972

As in the case of the export equation, it is of interest to consider whether estimation of R&D for an earlier year will reinforce the conclusions of the previous section. As mentioned above, if exports 1972 are entered in the R&D 1975 equation, the hypothesis of no effect of exports on R&D is rejected. If equation (4) is re-estimated with exports and R&D measured in 1972, the following result is obtained:

$$\text{IV } R_2 = -2.239 + 0.442X_2 + 0.684^*FR + 0.594C_5 + 0.838PL$$
$$(-1.083) \quad (1.392) \quad (4.249) \quad (1.506) \quad (1.496)$$

$$\sigma = 1.0641$$

$$(8.7)$$

where $R_2 = (\text{R\&D/value-added})$ 1972;
$X_2 = (\text{exports/gross output})$ 1972

Only the technological opportunity variable *FR* retains significance, although the other variables are fairly close to significance. However, if the equation is estimated with a growth of output variable 1968–71 (GL_8), *PL* drops out, GL_8 is clearly significant and C_5 is again significant, though X_2 remains insignificant. The superior performance of GL_8 to the profit margin variable (*PL*) may be due in part to the fact that *PL* was retained from the 1975 analysis, due to data availability, and so is not measured for the appropriate years. The significance of GL_8 reinforces the conclusion above that it may be more appropriate to interpret the *PL* variable in the 1975 analysis as an expected profits variable. Alternatively, it could be the case that in 1975 cash flow was a more serious restriction than it was in 1972.

The export variable is positive but not significant. Although this weakens the earlier results, the specification of the equation is not so good, since all the variables are not measured for the appropriate time period. The result might also indicate that when future profit expectations are important, exports have a weaker influence – as firms get more optimistic about domestic demand responses. Alternatively, the results might be related to the relatively high level of the exchange rate in 1972, which made exports less profitable than in earlier years and also affected expectations. Apart from the weaker export result, the results tend to reinforce the results for 1975, though again highlighting the similarity between the two variables *PL* and *GL*.

Concentration

It has been found here that concentration has a positive and significant effect on R&D. Some other studies that have also found a positive relationship have suggested that there is a cut-off point between concentration ratios of about 50–60 per cent where concentration has a weaker effect or becomes negative (Scherer 1967; Comanor 1967; Kamien and Schwartz 1975), though one study found suggestions of a non-linear concentration effect that was positive (Caves *et al.* 1980). To test this hypothesis in the current model, a dummy variable (*DC*) was constructed, with values of 1 where concentration ratios were less than or equal to 55 per cent, and 0 otherwise (Appendix 1). The results of estimating the R&D equation were then:

$$\text{IV } R_5 = -2.596 + 1.263^*X_8 + 0.509^*FR + 0.815^*C_5 + 0.873^*PL$$

$$(-1.083) \ (2.990) \qquad (3.296) \qquad (1.683) \qquad (1.777)$$

$$-0.008DCL \qquad\qquad\qquad\qquad \sigma = 0.9275$$

$$(-0.071) \tag{8.8}$$

where $DCL = DC \times C_5$.

This fails to reject the hypothesis that there are no significant differences in the relationship between concentration and R&D dependent on the actual level of concentration. While concentration does have a positive effect even in the presence of technological opportunity, it does not appear to be a non-linear effect.

Aerospace

For similar reasons to those discussed in the export section, the aerospace observation may not be similar in behaviour to the other observations, in particular due to the high defence component of its R&D and since it has the highest proportion of government-funded R&D (*Business Monitor* MO14 1979). Equation (4) is re-estimated with the addition of a dummy for aerospace, with the following result:

$$\text{IV } R_5 = -2.679 + 1.310^*X_8 + 0.466^*FR + 0.818^*C_5 + 0.933^*PL$$

$$(-1.473) \ (3.014) \qquad (2.774) \qquad (2.348) \qquad (1.838)$$

$$+0.810DA \qquad\qquad\qquad\qquad \sigma = 0.9483$$

$$(0.773) \tag{8.9}$$

where $DA = 1$ for aerospace, 0 otherwise.

This result fails to reject the hypothesis that aerospace is similar in behaviour to the other observations, as was also found for the export equation. Thus, the particular characteristics of aerospace are not observed to be significantly altering its behaviour in the context of this model.

This does not represent a direct test of the argument that the U.K. has misdirected its R&D to aerospace (Freeman 1978), in particular as Freeman's argument relates to the exploitation of R&D output through scale economies in production, at which the U.S. may have an advantage. In addition, since *FR* for aerospace is measured by U.S. R&D alone (see Appendix 2), the test may not be very strong. However, when using cruder dummies for technological opportunity, aerospace is still not found to be significantly different from the other observations.

Technological opportunity

It has been argued that *FR* is a measure of technological opportunity which is preferable to that used in many other studies, since it is more detailed and does not involve arbitrary or subjective categorisation. It is then of interest to see whether a cruder categorisation of technological opportunity — similar to that used in other studies — significantly affects the results obtained. It could also be argued that technological opportunity does not vary as much as the use of *FR* implies and that there are only three or four main categories of technological opportunity. In this case, the results may falsely lend support to the positive effects of technological opportunity and obscure the effects of other variables, given the high correlation between R_5 and *FR*. To see whether this would alter which hypotheses were accepted or rejected, three groups were constructed representing high, medium and low technological opportunity, using the foreign R&D data as a guide (Appendix 1). The dividing lines between the groups are necessarily arbitrary. Inclusion of dummies for high and medium technology industries in the final specification of the R&D equation gives the following result:

$$\text{IV } R_5 = -4.847^* + 1.341^*X_8 + 1.655^*DH + 0.785^*DM + 0.860^*C_5$$
$$(-2.673) \quad (3.331) \quad\quad (3.827) \quad\quad (2.187) \quad\quad (2.496)$$
$$+ 1.242^*PL \quad\quad\quad\quad\quad\quad\quad \sigma = 0.9162$$
$$(2.409) \quad\quad\quad\quad\quad\quad\quad\quad\quad\quad (8.10)$$

where *DH* = 1 for high technology industries, 0 otherwise;
       DM = 1 for medium technology industries, 0 otherwise.

These results do not alter the main conclusions drawn above. X_8, C_5 and *PL* are positive and significant as previously. *PL* has a larger coefficient and smaller standard error — this stronger effect may be observed due to *PL*'s correlation with *FR*. If the dummies are used in the initial specification of the equation, the results still fail to reject the hypotheses of no effect of investment, foreign participation and expected profit.

The use of technology dummies raises the possibility that the effect of technological opportunity, as measured by *FR*, may be non-linear. It may vary by technological opportunity group, which could affect the intercept or slope. If differences in technological opportunity levels between industries had different effects at higher or lower levels of *FR*, this would affect *FR*'s slope across groups. Higher technological opportunity industries might require larger initial lump sums of R&D to be able to produce R&D output, affecting the intercept, or a certain initial amount of R&D may be more productive for higher technological opportunity industries. Introducing two slope dummies, applying *DH* and *DM* to *FR*, both were negative and insignificant.

If intercept dummies are introduced in the final equation with *FR*, *FR* is insignificant. This suggests the effect of technological opportunity does not vary within the technology groups. However, collinearity between the dummies and *FR* is inevitable, making an interpretation of this result difficult. It suggests, though, that the information in *FR* may be too detailed relative to the actual effects of technological opportunity. However, *FR* has advantages over these dummy measures. It is not subjective and arbitrary, as they inevitably are, and it is less likely to be capturing other influences resulting from the industry groups used. It does contain more precise and comprehensive information. For these reasons the use of *FR* is preferred. Nevertheless, while caution is needed in using dummies, the results presented here − equation (8.10) − suggest that use of crude technological opportunity groups (where better data is not available) may not seriously affect results.

8.4 Conclusions

This chapter has presented the results of estimating an R&D equation for U.K. manufacturing industry. The aim of the analysis was to identify the determinants of R&D and to test and examine the simultaneous relationship between exports and R&D. The results gave support to most, but not all, of the hypotheses advanced with respect to R&D. R&D was found to depend on a group of variables reflecting inherent characteristics of the industry, and structural, performance and demand characteristics. Thus, technological opportunity, concentration, the profit margin and exports were found to have positive, significant effects on R&D. The investment, expected profit and foreign participation variables were not found to have significant effects. Hausman tests indicated that the relationship between R&D and exports was simultaneous. Use of dummies raised the possibility that the measure of technological opportunity was too detailed, though without seriously affecting the results. Use of a concentration dummy rejected the hypothesis of a break in the concentration/R&D relationship at levels of concentration of 55 per cent. The profit margin/cash flow variable performed better than the expected profit variable, but it appeared possible that a separate effect was not being captured; both variables could reflect an expected profit effect.

These results, therefore, show that a number of factors affect R&D and that any theoretical explanation that focuses exclusively on one variable — whether demand, technological opportunity, concentration or other variables — will be misleading. The significant variables in the current analysis suggest that R&D will be affected both by the underlying characteristics of an industry, and by competitive and demand factors. Explanations presented only in terms of demand or focusing solely on oligopolistic competition and industry structure, in the Schumpeterian tradition, may therefore fail to recognise the importance of a group of different but inter-related factors affecting R&D. Since some of the factors affecting R&D are industry-specific, notably technological opportunity, further insights into the determinants of R&D may be gained by a cross-country study, so industry characteristics are matched and need not be proxied. This is done in Chapter 10.

CHAPTER 9

U.K. trade performance 1972–8

Many studies have emphasised the relatively poor trade performance of the U.K. economy (for example, Blackaby 1978). In the 1970s this performance deteriorated further. This was largely due to the rate of increase of import penetration in U.K. manufacturing industry; by 1979 the import penetration ratio exceeded the export/sales ratio. This chapter analyses U.K. trade performance in the period 1972 to 1978, in an attempt to throw further light on the determinants of the rate of change of U.K. exports, imports and the net trade balance.

9.1 The change in the export/sales ratio

The equation to estimate the change in the export/sales ratio is specified as:

$$XC = \alpha_0 + \alpha_1 RD + \alpha_2 RDC + \alpha_3 FR + \alpha_4 FRC + \alpha_5 IK + \alpha_6 IKC + \alpha_7 HS$$
$$+ \alpha_8 TP + \alpha_9 GWC + \alpha_{10} XPC \qquad (9.1)$$

where:

XC = (percentage change in exports/gross output) 1972–8 measured in constant prices (1975 = 100)

RD = $\Sigma_i[(\text{R\&D/value-added})_i]/2; i = 1972, 1975$

RDC = percentage change in (R&D/value-added) 1972–5

FR = $\Sigma_i[(\Sigma_j \text{ R\&D}_j)/(\Sigma_j \text{ value-added}_j)_i]/2; \; i = 1973, 1975; \; j = \text{U.S.,}$ France, Germany, Japan

FRC = percentage change in (Σ_j R&D/Σ_j value-added) 1973–5; $j = $ U.S., France, Germany, Japan

IK = $\Sigma_i(\text{investment/capital stock})_i/2; i = 1974, 1975$

IKC = percentage change in (investment/capital stock) 1972–6

HS = skilled manual labour/total labour employed 1971

123

TP = [(professional and technical staff) – (scientists and engineers in R&D)] /total labour employed 1971
GWC = Percentage growth in world demand 1972–8 (1975 = 100)
XPC = Percentage change in export unit values relative to percentage change in import unit values 1972–8 (1975 = 100)

The variables are measured in logarithms, the percentage changes being changes in logarithms. Exports are estimated from 1972 to 1978, both because those years are at similar points in the trade cycle and also because they are years in the 1970s that were not directly affected by any sharp external or internal shocks.

The R&D variables

The level of U.K. R&D may have a positive effect on the change in exports. Unlike the traditional factor endowment variables, a continuing level of R&D creates new innovative output. This will not necessarily completely supplant old output and may create, or provide entry into, new markets. Thus, over time, the cumulative effects of R&D may lead to a higher level of exports. In addition, any gap between U.K. and foreign R&D will be expected to reinforce this positive effect. The coefficient on foreign R&D would therefore measure the effect of the technology gap. The level of R&D may have additional effects. It has been suggested that the U.K. R&D effort has been misdirected, in particular, to prestige, high technology and defence projects, and that, consequently, higher R&D expenditures have not had proportionately higher effects on exports. It has also been argued that the U.K. has relatively low technology levels, the 'low technology syndrome', which may affect its competitiveness more in the more R&D-intensive industries where competition among the advanced countries is particularly intense (Freeman 1978; M. Kaldor 1980; Katrak 1982). If the U.K. is less competitive in the more R&D-intensive industries, this may not be fully captured by the measure of the technology gap, and a negative relation may then be observed between U.K. R&D and the change in exports. The technology gap may not fully reflect U.K. relative competitiveness if there are associated aspects of competitiveness, not captured by the independent variables, which are correlated with the R&D-intensive industries. Relatively poor U.K. performance in the R&D-intensive industries may be due not only to its relative R&D input, but to the use it makes of the output and complementary factors such as design and marketing. The innovation process requires more than just R&D expenditure, and if the U.K. spends less on subsequent stages of the innovation process (ACARD 1978), this will affect its competitiveness. It may spend relatively less in the more R&D-intensive industries, or this may be more important in these industries.

Any changes in the nature of R&D and its implementation may affect he change in exports. For example, the greater emphasis on relatively short-un, less risky R&D in the 1970s (Schott 1981) may have a greater, negative ffect on the R&D/export relation of the more R&D-intensive industries. f less R&D-intensive industries tend to focus on less risky projects anyway, r alternatively feel less need to reduce the risk related to a small expendi-ure, then the slope of the R&D/export relation would change. Over time, R&D would then have a negative relation with the change in exports. In he estimates of export composition in Chapter 7, the coefficient on R&D n the export equation for 1972 was greater than that for 1978. In estimating quation (9.1) it is expected that there will be a positive effect of the change n U.K. R&D on XC and a negative effect of both the level and the change in oreign R&D. These effects may be difficult to identify, given the various redicted effects of the levels of U.K. R&D. Since there is no *a priori* nformation on lag structures and since more disaggregated data is available or U.K. R&D 1972, the change in R&D (RDC) was measured from 1972 o 1975, and the change in foreign R&D (FRC) from 1973 to 1975, the losest available year to 1972. Given these measures, it may be difficult to lentify separately all four R&D variables.

nvestment

: is possible that the level of investment will have a positive effect on the hange in exports. If IK represents relative dynamism and modernity across ndustries, then differences in IK by industry may lead to an increasing gap etween industries' exports. The hypothesis of a positive effect of IK on the vel of exports was rejected, but it may still have a positive effect on the nange in exports. In addition, the change in investment may have a positive ffect on the change in exports, though given the failure to observe a signifi-nt effect on export composition this may be unlikely. The change in vestment is initially measured from 1972 to 1976, and the effect of an ternative measure, averaging the end years over 1971 and 1972, and 1975 nd 1976, is also tested. As with the R&D variables, the inclusion of the vel and the change of the investment variable may make it difficult to entify both effects.

:illed labour

lthough endowments are not expected to change, except very slowly, it possible that the U.K.'s relative comparative advantage or competitiveness shifting in either type of skilled labour (Katrak 1982). Positive or negative fects of the coefficients of either of the skilled labour variables may then dicate the direction of change of countries' relative endowments or whether their relative utilisation of those endowments is changing, though a precise interpretation of the coefficients is not possible without more information on countries' endowments. The expected signs of the two skilled labour variables cannot be predicted, although increasing competition from developing countries might lead to negative effects.

The capital/labour ratio is added into the estimating equation, below, to test whether its insignificant effect found for export levels carries over into the change in exports equation. This also enables a comparison with other studies that have looked at the changing pattern of comparative advantage in terms of technology and endowment variables (Heller 1976; Cable and Rebelo 1980; Katrak 1982; Lyons 1983).

Growth of demand and price changes

As world income grows, it is to be expected that export demand will grow. Holding other influences constant, varying income elasticities of demand will mean that growth of demand is not constant across products. World demand growth would, therefore, be expected to have a positive effect on the change in exports. The effect of different income elasticities could not be directly assessed in the export level equation.

Similarly, while there was no role for relative price in the export level equation, there may be in the change in exports equation. If it is assumed that those differences in domestic and foreign prices due to factors such as different product specifications remain constant over time, then changes in domestic relative to foreign prices should reflect changing competitiveness and have a negative effect on the change in exports. If differences due to product specification and the extent of product heterogeneity do not remain constant over time, this may obscure any observed effects of changes in relative prices.

Growth of world demand (GWC), is proxied by the growth of industrial production from 1972 to 1978 in Canada, Italy, Japan, Sweden, West Germany, the U.K. and the U.S., constructed as a weighted average, using each country's gross output shares in each industry, 1975, as weights (Appendix 2).

Exports and imports in 1972 and 1978 are measured in current relative to constant prices, and the change in export relative to import values (XPC) is then measured. Since this is in fact a measure of change in unit values, increases in unit value partly reflected increases in quality not captured elsewhere, this would have some positive effect on exports (Saunders 1978) which may reduce the coefficient on XPC or even reverse the sign. Import prices proxy the prices of those goods with which U.K. exports are competing; how good a proxy they are cannot be ascertained. They are used as a proxy since they are available for the same classification and base year as the export data.

Concentration and scale

The industry structure variables, concentration and scale, are expected to change only very slowly. Hence, changes in these variables are not expected to affect the change in exports over a relatively small number of years. Their expected effects in the export level equation do not suggest that there may be further effects of their levels on the change in exports. Scale effects, whether via relative country size, size of firm or in relation to variety and intra-industry trade, are not expected to increase over time. Similarly, the effects of concentration may work through factors such as firm size, and the ability to discriminate between markets. Again, it is not clear that these factors should affect export changes over a relatively short time period.

Simultaneity

The levels of R&D and exports were estimated as a simultaneous system. This implies there may be a simultaneous relationship between changes in R&D and changes in exports. It was argued in the estimation of the levels of R&D and exports that lags in their relationships did not remove the simultaneity, as the relationship between the two was essentially long-run. However, the same argument does not necessarily apply to the changes in these variables. The simultaneity of the levels, for different years, arises due to those parts of exports (1978 and 1972, for example) that are similar. The variation across years in exports may then not be simultaneous with the variation in R&D across years. Time lags may be important in determining the effects of R&D changes on changes in exports.

An instrumental estimate of the change in R&D ($R\hat{D}C$) was calculated, and a Hausman test carried out on the XC equation as specified in equation 9.1) including the instrumental estimate of RDC. This test clearly failed to reject the hypothesis of no simultaneity (Annexe 9.1). The estimation of the equation was, therefore, done by OLS.

Table 9.1 presents the simple correlations between the variables in the changes in exports equation. The proportion of output produced by foreign firms (FL) is included, as this variable is added to the estimating equation, below, to test the Panić/Joyce hypothesis (1980).

Most of the correlations are relatively weak. As in the export levels equation, RD, FR and TP are quite strongly positively correlated. These three variables, in particular TP and FR, are also positively correlated with GWC, suggesting that demand growth may be higher in the more technology-intensive

Table 9.1. *Correlation matrix of variables in the XC equation*

	XC	RD	RDC	FR	FRC	IK	IKC	HS	TP	GWC	XPC	FL
XC	1.0	− 0.22	− 0.16	− 0.08	0.18	0.04	− 0.16	0.10	− 0.29	− 0.03	− 0.23	− 0.46
RD		1.0	− 0.08	0.71	− 0.07	− 0.09	0.16	− 0.51	0.71	0.42	0.07	0.26
RDC			1.0	0.05	− 0.02	0.16	0.31	− 0.08	− 0.09	− 0.05	0.03	0.23
FR				1.0	− 0.09	− 0.008	0.38	− 0.24	0.67	0.63	− 0.01	0.09
FRC					1.0	− 0.04	− 0.10	0.26	− 0.19	− 0.22	− 0.002	− 0.002
IK						1.0	0.14	− 0.05	− 0.07	0.14	− 0.40	0.19
IKC							1.0	− 0.10	0.33	0.24	− 0.31	− 0.06
HS								1.0	− 0.41	− 0.26	− 0.25	− 0.21
TP									1.0	0.51	0.17	0.07
GWC										1.0	− 0.20	0.20
XPC											1.0	0.19
FL												1.0

and skill-intensive industries. *FR* has the highest correlation with *GWC*. This suggests foreign R&D may be more closely related to 'world' growth of demand than is U.K. R&D. All the R&D variables, except *FRC*, have a negative correlation with *XC*, the highest being with *RD* (which is similar to that of *TP*). *IKC* and *GWC* both have weak negative correlations with *XC*, contrary to their predicted sign. *XPC* and *FL* are both negatively correlated with *XC*, *FL* having the strongest correlation with *XC* of all the independent variables.

Estimating the full specification of the *XC* equation gives the following result:

$$XC = -0.249 - 0.076RD - 0.080RDC + 0.090FR + 0.299FRC$$
$$(-0.477)(-1.526) \quad (-1.089) \qquad (1.546) \qquad (1.163)$$

$$-0.057IK - 0.076IKC - 0.158HS - 0.098TP - 0.100GWC$$
$$(-0.488) \quad (-0.683) \quad (-1.186) \quad (-0.936) \quad (-0.170)$$

$$-0.157XPC$$
$$(-1.534) \qquad\qquad \bar{R}^2 = 0.045 \qquad F_{10,\,35} = 1.210 \qquad (9.2)$$

The results of the estimation are poor; the equation as a whole is not significant. *RD* is negative while *FR* is positive, so a technology gap variable would be implausible. The signs of *RDC* and *FRC* are opposite to those predicted, as are the signs of *IK, IKC* and *GWC*. The hypothesis of homoscedasticity was supported.

Given the signs on *RDC* and *FRC*, and the expected difficulty of identifying all the R&D variables, *RDC* and *FRC* were omitted from the equation. An *F*-test failed to reject the hypothesis that they were jointly insignificant. Re-estimating the equation without *RDC* and *FRC*, the equation remained insignificant. Including the capital/labour ratio in the equation to test the hypothesis of no effect of this variable, the hypothesis was supported, the variable being very insignificant and negative. Cable and Rebelo (1980) also found capital intensity to be insignificant in estimating the change in exports over the years 1970 to 1978. However, it became close to significance when exporting areas were broken down, suggesting this could be a fruitful extension of the analysis.

Omitting the least significant variable from the equation, and re-estimating the equation, results in the following order of elimination of variables: *GWC, IK, HS* and *TP*. The following estimate is then obtained:

$$XC = 0.323^* - 0.063RD + 0.059FR - 0.170IKC - 0.160^*XPC$$
$$(2.701)(-1.697) \quad (1.274) \quad (-1.876) \quad (-2.018)$$

$$\bar{R}^2 = 0.095 \qquad F_{4,41} = 2.176 \qquad (9.3)$$

The equation remains insignificant. The hypothesis of a negative effect of prices is supported. *IKC* is negative. If the equation is re-estimated with *IKC* measured with the end years averaged over 1971 and 1972, and 1975 and 1976, it remains negative, but its significance level falls. *RD* is negative, but not significant, giving some support to the hypothesis that the U.K.'s performance is worse in the more R&D-intensive industries. *XPC* is negative and significant, supporting the hypothesis of a negative effect of price changes.

If *FR*, then *RD*, then *IKC* are omitted from the equation, *XPC* also becomes insignificant, and the equation remains insignificant. These poor results compare with those of other U.K. studies of the change in exports (Cable and Rebelo 1980; Lyons 1983). These also failed to estimate significant equations. Both studies used the independent variables from their levels equations to estimate the change in exports.

It is unclear why the results of estimating the change in exports in the 1970s are so poor. The reason may, in part, be a failure to measure correctly certain variables, such as the price variable. It may also be the case that the various external and internal shocks experienced by the U.K. in the 1970s affected industries differently, which is not taken account of by the cross-section analysis. The specification of time lags could be important, and measurement and omission of variables will create noise in the equation.

However, better results were achieved when testing the effect of foreign participation on the change in exports (Panić and Joyce 1980). Panić and Joyce found that there was a positive correlation between the extent of foreign participation and both the exports/sales ratio and the net trade balance. They also found that, in a regression of the change in the net trade balance, in the 1970s, on foreign participation, there was a negative relation. They suggested this may reflect disinvestment by foreign MNEs in the U.K., and increased investment abroad.

The inclusion of the level of foreign-owned production is in fact not a direct test of this hypothesis, unless it is argued that sectors with higher foreign participation are expected to disinvest more. A more direct test would look at the change in foreign-owned production, but data is not available for the level of disaggregation of the current study. The variable used to test the Panić/Joyce hypothesis is foreign-owned sales/total sales in 1968 (*FL*).

Table 9.2 presents the results of estimating the change in exports equation including *FL*. The variables *RDC* and *FRC* again have the wrong signs. An *F*-test fails to reject the hypothesis that they are jointly insignificant.

Equation (2), table 9.2, gives the estimates of the restricted equation, omitting *RDC* and *FRC*. The equation is significant and there is no evidence of heteroscedasticity. The hypothesis of a negative effect of foreign-owned

Table 9.2. Results of the estimation of the change in the export/sales ratio 1972–8, including FL, OLS

	Constant	RD	FR	IK	IKC	HS	TP	GWC	XPC	FL	RDC	FRC	$\bar{R}^2$	F
(1)	−0.281 (−0.558)	−0.008 (−0.155)	0.041 (0.752)	0.056 (0.500)	−0.831 (−0.826)	−0.092 (−0.752)	−0.166 (−1.704)	0.529 (0.929)	−0.038 (−0.378)	−0.085* (−3.005)	−0.023 (−0.334)	0.299 (1.286)	0.223	2.174*
(2)	−0.145 (−0.296)	0.005 (0.094)	0.039 (0.735)	0.060 (0.542)	−0.107 (−1.177)	−0.042 (−0.376)	−0.173 (−1.818)	0.476 (0.855)	−0.036 (−0.364)	−0.087* (−3.222)			0.229	2.481*
(3)	−0.149 (−0.308)		0.042 (0.985)	0.057 (0.546)	−0.109 (−1.245)	−0.047 (−0.471)	−0.169* (−2.063)	0.458 (0.889)	−0.040 (−0.446)	−0.086* (−3.562)			0.249	2.867*
(4)	−0.139 (−0.291)		0.041 (0.979)	0.076 (0.793)	−0.098 (1.178)	−0.041 (−0.416)	−0.178* (−2.289)	0.535 (1.115)		−0.090* (−3.940)			0.265	3.318*
(5)	−0.048 (−0.113)		0.041 (0.982)	0.080 (0.849)	−0.108 (−1.386)		−0.166* (−2.332)	0.545 (1.150)		−0.088* (−3.963)			0.281	3.926*
(6)	−0.338 (−1.392)		0.038 (0.920)		−0.095 (−1.247)		−0.174* (−2.484)	0.616 (1.324)		−0.085 (−3.886)			0.286	4.599*
(7)	−0.423 (−1.890)				−0.081 (−1.087)		−0.143* (−2.336)	0.802* (1.922)		−0.085* (−3.904)			0.288	5.558*
(8)	−0.445 (−1.994)						−0.160* (−2.693)	0.757* (1.819)		−0.082* (−3.799)			0.285	6.987*

Figures in brackets are t-statistics.
*Denotes significance at the 5% level.

production on XC is supported. The professional and technical staff variable has a negative sign, suggesting that any U.K. comparative advantage is shifting away from this type of skilled labour. The U.K. R&D variable is now positive but very insignificant. Since RD and TP are quite highly correlated, and RD is more strongly correlated with FL than TP is, this may suggest that the negative sign on RD in the previous estimation is now captured by FL and TP. The negative effect of these two variables may be reflecting generally poor U.K. export performance in industries with higher tradeability levels. Relative to equation (9.3) the price variable is very insignificant. Though not highly correlated, this may also be due in part to the joint effect of TP and FL.

Equation (8), table 9.2, presents the final XC equation having omitted the least significant variables. The hypothesis of a positive effect of the growth of world demand is supported. This variable becomes significant when FR is omitted, reflecting some degree of collinearity between these two variables. TP is negative and significant. Since TP was not significant in the export levels equation, this result suggests the U.K. may be developing a comparative disadvantage in this type of skilled labour but that this is not, or not yet, sufficiently strong to be apparent in estimating the determinants of the level of exports. TP does not appear to be capturing the same effect as the RD variable, since if equation (8) is estimated with RD not TP, RD is negative but not close to significance, and GWC is then insignificant. The hypothesis of a negative effect of foreign-owned production on the change in exports is supported, complementing at a more disaggregated level the results of Panić and Joyce (1980). If Panić and Joyce are correct that the negative relation is due to disinvestment by foreign MNEs, the specification here in fact implies that disinvestment is higher, the higher the initial level of participation. If U.K. competitiveness is worse in the higher trade industries, correlated with FL, then there may be both higher disinvestment in these industries by MNEs, and also a relative decline in exports due to lack of competitiveness. If there has been more than proportionate disinvestment in industries with higher foreign participation, then this might imply that MNEs in these industries will supply the U.K. market from other bases, and so a positive correlation with the change in imports would be expected. However, these hypotheses with respect to MNEs cannot be clearly tested without data on the change in multinational participation.

9.2 The change in import penetration

The equation to estimate the change in import penetration (MC) is specified with the same independent variables as in the change in the export/sales ratio equation (equation (9.1)) with two exceptions. First, there is no growth in

Table 9.3. *Correlation matrix of weighted variables in the MC equation*

	MC	RD	FR	IK	IKC	HS	TP	MPC	FL
MC	1.0	0.118	0.154	−0.469	−0.313	−0.048	0.002	0.752	0.138
RD		1.0	0.710	−0.089	0.161	−0.513	0.712	0.029	0.256
FR			1.0	−0.008	0.375	−0.243	0.672	−0.056	0.088
IK				1.0	0.142	−0.047	−0.068	−0.347	−0.192
IKC					1.0	−0.100	0.333	−0.313	−0.064
HS						1.0	−0.410	−0.082	−0.205
TP							1.0	0.113	0.069
MPC								1.0	0.143
FL									1.0

where MC = percentage change in [(imports)/(gross output + imports − exports)] 1972–8, in constant 1975 prices.

world demand variable. The appropriate growth variable, for the import equation, is the growth in domestic demand (GDC). This is the change in the denominator of the dependent variable, and is therefore constrained to have a coefficient of 1. This constraint is tested. Secondly, the price variable for the import equation (MPC) is the change in domestic prices relative to the change in import prices, and is expected to have a positive sign.

As in the change in exports equation, RDC and FRC have the opposite signs to those predicted. RDC is significant. The significance of RDC may be due to the problems of multicollinearity among the four R&D variables. The interpretation of RDC and FRC, given their signs, is unclear. Since their signs are theoretically inconsistent and since the XC equation was estimated without these variables, they are excluded from the equation.

The hypothesis of homoscedasticity is supported for the initial specification of the equation. Once RDC and FRC are omitted from the equation, the hypothesis is not supported. The same procedure is therefore followed as in the export levels equation (Chapter 7) − the largest outliers are adjusted by weights.[1] Re-estimating the weighted full equation, RDC is no longer significant.

Table 9.3 presents the correlations of the weighted variables in the import equation.

Most of the correlations presented are similar to those discussed for the XC equation. RD and FR are both positively correlated with MC, though the gap effect of RD may be predicted to have a negative sign. IK and IKC both have negative signs, as predicted by the model. The two skill variables have very weak correlations. The import price variable is quite strongly positively correlated with MC while FL is positively but weakly correlated with MC.

Table 9.4 presents the results of estimating the determinants of the change in import penetration 1972–8. Both investment and technical and professional staff have a significant negative effect on the change in imports. The change in relative prices has the expected positive effect.

Given the signs on *RD* and *FR*, a measure of the technology gap can be constructed for equation (2), table 9.4, as follows:

$$0.151^*RD - 0.136^* \, (RD - FR)$$
$$(3.082) \quad (-3.391) \tag{9.4}$$

This supports the hypothesis of a positive effect of technology level and a negative effect of the technology gap. The positive effect of *RD* may indicate a continuation, in the change in imports equation, of the positive influence of technology observed for the level of imports. Alternatively, the positive sign on *RD* may support the hypothesis that the U.K. is becoming relatively less competitive in the more R&D-intensive industries.

Since the negative effect of the technical and professional staff variable was also observed in the *XC* equation it cannot here be interpreted as indicating an increasing U.K. comparative advantage in this type of skilled labour. Its negative sign in both equations suggests there has been a relative shift in both world and domestic demand from products of high *TP* industries. This is not directly explicable in the current model. Changes in technique and advances in knowledge may have resulted in substitutes for these goods being produced in other industries. This seems implausible. Alternatively, the higher *TP* industries may have been more affected by relatively slower income growth in the 1970s. In contrast, Cable and Rebelo (1980) found a positive effect of non-manual labour. The other skilled labour variable (*HS*) is also negative, though insignificant, as it was in the *XC* equation. Thus, in both the import and export levels equations *HS* has a positive effect while, in looking at changes over time, it is insignificant, possibly suggesting that the levels relationships are roughly equilibrium ones. The superior performance of *IK* in the change in imports equation may similarly suggest it is proxying dynamic, disequilibrium effects not captured in the levels equation.

If the capital intensity variable is included in the *MC* equation it is negative and insignificant, failing to reject the hypothesis of no effect of capital intensity. In contrast, Cable and Rebelo (1980) and Lyons (1983) found it to be negative and significant. The foreign participation variable is positive, as hypothesised, but not significant, and remains insignificant if other, less significant variables are omitted. This suggests that while MNEs may have disinvested in the U.K., to produce in other countries and not supply them with exports from a U.K. base, MNEs are still producing in the U.K. to supply the domestic market, rather than supplying it by imports.

The restriction that the denominator of *MC*, domestic demand growth *GDC*, is equal to one is supported. For the test statistic, one minus the

Table 9.4. Results of the estimation of the change in import penetration (weighted), 1972–8, OLS

	Constant	RD	RD after adjusting for techno-logy gap	FR	IK	IKC	HS	TP	MPC	RDC	FRC	$\bar{R}^2$	F
(1)	−0.336 (−0.837)	0.023 (0.571)	0.153* (3.950)	0.130* (3.118)	−0.228* (−2.496)	−0.113 (−1.267)	0.027 (0.257)	−0.218* (−2.627)	0.665* (7.405)	0.050 (0.747)	−0.101 (−0.488)	0.688	12.038*
(2)	−0.388 (−0.995)	0.010 (0.390)	0.152* (4.582)	0.136* (3.391)	−0.219* (−2.463)	−0.084 (−1.044)	−0.006 (−0.064)	−0.229* (−2.948)	0.658* (7.501)			0.698	15.873*
(3)	−0.373 (−1.208)	0.016 (0.459)	0.152* (4.216)	0.136* (3.472)	−0.218* (−2.529)	−0.085 (−1.123)		−0.228* (−3.033)	0.658* (7.599)			0.706	19.003*
(4)	−0.446 (−1.473)	0.026 (0.758)	0.150* (4.330)	0.124* (3.281)	−0.220* (−2.544)			−0.253* (−3.511)	0.690* (8.433)			0.704	22.402*

Figures in brackets are t-statistics.
*Denotes significance at the 5% level.

coefficient on *GDC*, for equation (2), the *t*-static is 0.895. The hypothesis of homoscedasticity is also supported.

If insignificant variables are omitted from the change in imports equation, *HS* and *IKC* are dropped. All other variables remain significant as above.

In contrast to the change in exports equation, the *MC* equation indicates a significant role for the technology variables and for prices, and also for investment. The price variable for the import equation is closer to the measure theory would imply than the export price measure. This may have affected the relative performance of the two equations. The superior performance of the *MC* equation to the results of Cable and Rebelo (1980) and Lyons (1983) may also be in part due to the inclusion of a price variable. The similar performance of *TP* in both the *XC* and *MC* equations suggests that the equations are capturing trends other than relative competitiveness or performance effects. These common trends may be more likely to cancel out in estimating the change in the net trade balance. That equation may, therefore, give a clearer indication of the determinants of changing trade performance.

9.3 The change in the net trade balance

The equation to estimate the change in the net trade balance is specified in the same way as the change in the export/output ratio with the addition of the domestic growth variable (*GDC*). The dependent variable (*XMC*) is measured as the percentage change in (exports/imports) from 1972 to 1978. The expected signs of the independent variables are the same as for the *XC* equation. The signs on *HS* and *TP* cannot be predicted in advance, nor do the results of the separate *XC* and *MC* equations indicate what effect, if any, of these variables may be expected. *GDC* is expected to be negative. For the same reasons as discussed above, the equation may not be expected to be simultaneous. A Hausman test clearly fails to reject the hypothesis of no simultaneity (Annexe 9.1). The equation is therefore estimated by OLS.

The correlation matrix for the variables in the change in the net trade balance equation is presented in table 9.5. As with the import equation, most of the correlations are the same as those presented for the *XC* equation with similar interpretation.

Like *XC*, *XMC* is negatively correlated with three of the R&D variables: *RD*, *RDC* and *FR*. It is positively correlated with *IK* and *IKC* and strongly negatively correlated with *XPC*, and with *FL*. *XMC* is very weakly correlated with both the demand growth variables, positively correlated with *HS* and negatively with *TP*.

Table 9.6 presents the results of estimating the change in the net trade balance, 1972–8. If the full equation is estimated, including the two R&D variables, *RDC* and *FRC*, then as before these variables have the opposite

Table 9.5. *Correlation matrix of variables in the XMC equation*

	XMC	RD	RDC	FR	FRC	IK	IKC	HS	TP	GWC	XPC	FL	GDC
XMC	1.0	−0.22	−0.22	−0.17	0.03	0.39	0.13	0.11	−0.23	0.09	−0.80	−0.43	0.05
RD		1.0	−0.08	0.71	−0.07	−0.09	0.16	−0.51	0.71	0.42	0.07	0.26	0.35
RDC			1.0	0.05	−0.01	0.16	0.31	−0.08	−0.09	−0.05	0.03	0.23	−0.05
FR				1.0	−0.09	−0.01	0.38	−0.24	0.67	0.63	−0.01	0.09	0.18
FRC					1.0	−0.54	−0.10	0.26	−0.19	−0.22	−0.002	−0.003	−0.22
IK						1.0	0.14	−0.05	−0.07	0.14	−0.40	0.19	0.28
IKC							1.0	−0.10	0.33	0.24	−0.31	−0.06	0.10
HS								1.0	−0.41	−0.26	−0.25	−0.21	0.11
TP									1.0	0.51	0.17	0.07	0.43
GWC										1.0	−0.20	0.20	0.40
XPC											1.0	0.19	−0.12
FL												1.0	0.29
GDC													1.0

Table 9.6. Results of the estimation of the change in the net trade balance, 1972–8, OLS

	Constant	RD	FR	IK	IKC	HS	TP	GWC	GDC	XPC	RDC	FRC	$\bar{R}^2$	F
(1)	−0.665 (−0.854)	−0.154* (−2.228)	−0.017 (−0.206)	0.124 (0.751)	0.073 (0.479)	−0.529* (−2.899)	0.068 (0.449)	−0.064 (−0.076)	−0.204 (−0.808)	−1.090* (−7.790)	−0.291* (−2.896)	0.358 (1.017)	0.714	11.198*
(2)	−0.401 (−0.478)	−0.124 (−1.662)	−0.050 (−0.550)	0.069 (0.382)	−0.124 (−0.826)	−0.359 (−1.916)	0.165 (1.040)	0.022 (0.025)	−0.226 (−0.820)	−1.167* (−7.780)			0.656	10.543*
(3)	−0.394 (−0.504)	−0.124 (−1.759)	−0.049 (−0.645)	0.069 (0.387)	−0.125 (−0.849)	−0.360 (−1.978)	0.166 (1.073)		−0.224 (−0.861)	−1.169* (−8.266)			0.665	12.191*
(4)	−0.651 (−1.589)	−0.130 (−1.899)	−0.045 (−0.608)		−0.122 (−0.838)	−0.374* (−2.120)	0.160 (1.054)		−0.196 (−0.793)	−1.187* (−9.006)			0.673	14.229*
(5)	−0.666 (−1.638)	−0.151 (−2.564)			−0.141 (−1.002)	−0.387* (−2.229)	0.132 (0.918)		−0.168 (−0.696)	−1.182* (−9.059)			0.678	16.811*
(6)	−0.726 (−1.845)	−0.148* (−2.543)			−0.131 (−0.946)	−0.359* (−2.140)	0.099 (0.735)			−1.156* (−9.304)			0.682	20.339*
(7)	−0.904* (−2.927)	−0.122 (−2.677)*			−0.089 (−0.708)	−0.374* (−2.254)				−1.129* (−9.549)			0.686	25.574
(8)	−0.954* (−3.197)	−0.130* (−2.976)				−0.395* (−2.439)				−1.106* (−9.804)			0.670	34.339*

Figures in brackets are *t*-statistics.
*Denotes significance at the 5% level.

Table 9.7. Results of the estimation of the change in the net trade balance, 1972–8, including FL, OLS

	Constant	RD	FR	IK	IKC	HS	TP	GWC	GDC	XPC	FL	RDC	FRC	R̄²	F
(1)	-0.800 (-1.144)	-0.064 (-0.933)	-0.070 (-0.906)	0.259 (1.674)	0.066 (0.484)	-0.429* (-2.570)	-0.054 (-0.380)	0.685 (0.867)	-0.064 (-0.278)	-0.917* (-6.658)	-0.119* (-3.057)	-0.213* (-2.284)	0.346 (1.099)	0.770	13.563*
(2)	-0.607 (-0.834)	-0.022 (-0.316)	-0.102 (-1.273)	0.250 (1.527)	-0.073 (-0.555)	-0.280 (-1.707)	-0.017 (-0.117)	0.864 (1.053)	-0.047 (-0.193)	-0.932* (-6.412)	-0.144* (-3.606)			0.742	13.954*
(2a)[a]	-0.560 (-0.846)	-0.015 (-0.239)	-0.108 (-1.474)	0.151 (0.984)	-0.151 (-1.232)	-0.215 (-1.424)	0.025 (0.186)	0.589 (0.781)	-0.060 (-0.271)	-1.048* (-7.537)	-0.095* (-2.348)			0.774	16.416*
(3)	-0.570 (-0.881)	-0.026 (-0.413)	-0.103 (-1.309)	0.249 (1.545)	-0.078 (-0.648)	-0.279 (-1.730)	-0.057 (-0.253)	0.841 (1.071)		-0.940* (-7.278)	-0.142* (-3.852)			0.749	15.940*
(4)	-0.586 (-0.921)	-0.030 (-0.505)	-0.098 (-1.305)	0.240 (1.547)	-0.081 (-0.684)	-0.275 (-1.735)		0.775 (1.059)		-0.940* (-7.332)	-0.143* (-3.944)			0.756	18.389*
(5)	-0.480 (-0.808)		0.123* (2.244)	0.262* (1.777)	-0.078 (-0.665)	-0.233 (-1.748)		0.856 (1.210)		-0.923* (-7.562)	-0.149* (-4.406)			0.760	21.400*
(6)	-0.565 (-0.979)		-0.137* (-2.706)	0.256* (1.748)		-0.247 (-1.898)		0.280 (1.254)		-0.905* (-7.664)	-0.148* (-4.422)			0.764	25.253*
(7)	-0.267 (-0.504)		-0.098* (-2.431)	0.256* (1.738)		-0.279* (-2.164)				-0.948* (-8.338)	-0.140* (-4.223)			0.760	29.567*
(8)[a]	-0.501 (-1.016)		-0.109* (-2.974)	0.148 (1.055)		-0.245* (-2.060)				-1.024* (-9.493)	-0.096* (-2.789)			0.787	34.185*
(9)[a]	-0.963* (-4.204)		-0.113* (-3.055)			-0.257* (-2.174)				-1.082* (-11.628)	-0.082* (-2.579)			0.786	42.337*

[a] Variables weighted to eliminate heteroscedasticity.
Figures in brackets are t-statistics.
*Denotes significance at the 5% level.

signs to those predicted. *RDC* is significant. Following the procedure adopted in the import equation, *RDC* and *FRC* are omitted from the equation and it is re-estimated. Omitting insignificant variables, the final results (equation (9), table 9.6) show negative effects of U.K. R&D, skilled manual labour and relative price changes on the change in the net trade balance. Similar results are obtained if foreign participation (*FL*) is included in the equation. Table 9.7 presents results of the estimation once *FL* is included. *FL* has a consistently negative and significant effect. Equation (7), table 9.7, shows that skilled manual labour and relative prices have negative effects as before, but foreign R&D, not U.K. R&D, now has a significant negative effect. In addition, the level of investment has a significant positive effect.

TP is negative but very insignificant, suggesting that its negative sign in the *XC* and *MC* equations is not related to changing U.K. competitiveness in that type of labour. If capital intensity is included in equation (2), table 9.7, it is positive but very insignificant. The positive sign accords with Katrak's results, which found an increase in the capital intensity of exports to imports from 1972 to 1978 (Katrak 1982). Katrak also finds a slight fall in the relative skill intensity of exports to imports from 1968 to 1972, his definition of skilled labour being close to the *TP* variable here, but including skilled labour in R&D. Thus the sign of *TP* is consistent with his results, though insignificant.

If the least significant variables are omitted, table 9.7 indicates the following order of exclusion: *TP, GDC, IKC, GWC, FR, IK*. *FR* would be omitted if the technology gap were calculated, since *RD* is then significant and negative while $(RD - FR)$ is not quite significant. However, if the measure of the gap is not calculated *RD* is omitted and *FR* remains (and *IK*), as shown in equation (7). This result suggests that *FR* and *RD* are capturing the same effect of declining U.K. competitiveness in R&D-intensive industries. This may then throw doubt on the calculation of the technology gap for the change in the import/sales equation, since without this adjustment *RD* would also have been excluded from that equation.

However, the hypothesis of homoscedasticity is rejected for equation (7), though not for the previous equations. When the *XMC* equation is estimated without *FL*, the final equation contains *RD, HS* and *XPC* and is homoscedastic. This suggests the heteroscedasticity may be related to *FL* and *IK*. Following the procedure adopted previously, clear outliers are given weights.[2]

Equations (8) and (9), table 9.7, show the effect of the adjustment for heteroscedasticity. *IK* is insignificant, suggesting that the existence of heteroscedasticity decreased its standard error.

The hypothesis of homoscedasticity is supported for equations (8) and (9). Re-estimating the full *XM* equation with weights, as in equation (2a), table 9.7, alters the results little, though the significance levels of some variables fall. The technology gap is still not quite significant, thus, the weighted results also imply the interchangeability of *RD* and *FR*.

The results of equation (9), table 9.7, support the hypothesis of negative effects of foreign participation in production and of relative price changes. The hypotheses of declining U.K. competitiveness in skilled manual labour and in high technology products are also supported. This implies that the U.K. is losing competitiveness over time in areas where it has some advantage, as indicated by the results of the export level equation. The results of the import level equation suggested that skilled manual labour and R&D might, in part, be associated with tradeability. Equation (9) may then be interpreted as reflecting relatively declining U.K. competitiveness in the more highly traded products. However, the results of estimating the level of the net trade balance did suggest that the U.K. had a comparative advantage in R&D. Over time, it would now appear to be losing this advantage.

9.4 Conclusions

A comparison may be drawn between the results obtained from estimating the change in exports, imports and net trade balance from 1972 to 1978. A comprehensive picture can be obtained by also considering these results in relation to the levels results for this sample of industries. These results are summarised in table 9.8.

The export and import changes equations – equations (5) and (6), table 9.8 – both indicate relatively declining trade in products of industries with high ratios of professional and technical staff, while the change in the net trade balance equation, equation (7), demonstrates that this is not related to changing U.K. competitiveness in this type of labour. The change in exports and the net trade balance equations both support the Panić/Joyce finding of a negative influence of foreign participation in production (Panić and Joyce 1980). The results do not give any more indication of why this negative influence exists, though the insignificance of *FL* in the change in imports equation must cast doubt on the hypothesis that MNEs are disinvesting in the U.K. to supply its market from abroad. The results may suggest MNEs are disinvesting to supply other foreign markets directly, not by exports, but continuing to supply the U.K. market from U.K. production bases. The import changes equation supports the hypothesis of a negative effect of investment, but this variable was not significant in the export or net trade equations, though positive in the latter. The change in imports and the net trade balance equations both have the expected sign for relative prices. The export changes equation also supported the hypothesis of a negative effect of relative price changes, but this was not significant once *FL* was included. The change in imports and net trade equations both give support to the

Table 9.8. Summary of results of estimating U.K. trade composition and performance

	Estimation method	Dependent variable	Constant	R_5	FR_5	HS	C_5			Standard error of the regression	$\bar{R}_2^2$	F
(1)	IV	X_8	3.271* (2.736)	0.691* (4.446)	−0.222* (−1.820)	0.819* (3.055)	−0.496* (−2.159)			0.4936		
			Constant	X_8	FR	C_5	PL					
(2)	IV	R_5	−2.711 (−1.545)	1.260* (3.038)	0.509* (3.341)	0.839* (2.503)	0.874* (1.805)			0.9151		
			Constant	R_5	HS							
(3)	OLS	M_8	−0.053 (−0.094)	0.203* (2.450)	0.666* (2.233)						0.104	3.613*
			Constant	R_5								
(4)	IV	XM_8	1.139* (3.803)	0.237* (3.007)						0.6560		
			Constant	TP	GWC	FL						
(5)	OLS	XC	−0.445 (−1.994)	−0.160* (−2.693)	0.757* (1.819)	−0.082 (−3.799)					0.285	6.987*
			Constant	RD	$RD-FR$	IK	TP	MPC				
(6)	OLS	MC	−0.446 (−1.473)	0.150* (5.300)	−0.124* (−3.281)	−0.220* (−2.544)	−0.253* (−3.511)	0.690* (8.433)			0.704	22.404*
			Constant	FR	HS	XPC	FL					
(7)	OLS	XMC	−0.963* (−4.204)	−0.113* (−3.055)	−0.257* (−2.174)	−1.082* (−11.628)	−0.831* (−2.579)				0.786	42.337*

Figures in brackets are t-statistics.

hypothesis of declining U.K. competitiveness in R&D-intensive industries, and the import equation indicates a role for the technology gap. The interpretation of the negative sign on the technology variable in the net trade equation, equation (7), table 9.8, does suggest that there is, in some sense, a gap between U.K. and foreign R&D. However, since this is not captured by the technology gap variable, it suggests there is more than proportionately poorer U.K. competitiveness in more R&D-intensive industries. Thus either there are other aspects of competitiveness which are relatively poor in these industries and are not measured here, or technology gaps in these industries may be having relatively stronger effects over time. If competition is more intense in these industries, it may be expected to affect all or most aspects of competitive performance. The change in the net trade balance equation also suggests the existence of declining U.K. competitiveness in skilled manual labour.

The change in imports and the net trade balance equations have much higher explanatory power than has the export equation, possibly because of the superior performance of the price variable in these equations and, for the latter equation, because the net trade balance may more clearly capture or reflect trends in U.K. competitiveness. The change in net trade balance equation does not appear to be performing better than the export equation, due to the inclusion of imports in the dependent variable and the superior performance of the import equation, since the significant explanatory variables in both equations are not all the same.

In conjunction with the levels equations — equations (1), (3) and (4), table 9.8 — the results of the equations estimating the change in trade performance give a complementary explanation of determinants of U.K. export and import composition and performance. The export equation (1) and the net trade equation (4) both show the U.K. to have some relative advantage in technology-intensive goods, and the former also shows a role for the technology gap. The positive sign of R_5 in the import equation suggests that tradeability factors may also be involved, and similarly with HS. In those industries where the U.K. has a relative advantage and/or high exports, exports or net trade are shown to be relatively declining over time. Given the simultaneity of the relationship between exports and R&D — found in the export, net trade and R&D equations, (1), (2) and (4) respectively — relatively declining exports in high technology industries are of particular concern, since this could have a cumulative effect. The changes equations also indicate the importance of various factors not captured in the levels equations — notably price competitiveness, investment and foreign participation — while the export level equation suggests a role for another aspect of industry structure, concentration.

The results summarised in table 9.8 show a variety of factors having a combined effect on U.K. exports and trade, at a point in time and over time. Some of these factors – notably R&D and skilled manual labour – appear, in part, to be capturing tradeability factors, while others – in particular *TP* – are reflecting trends with common effects on both exports and imports. The effects of tradeability and other industry-specific factors can be neutralised through a cross-country study. This is done in the following chapter. The results here, for this level of disaggregation, show that there are factors other than, or in addition to, tradeability and common trends determining U.K. trade composition and performance.

Annexe 9.1 Hausman tests on *XC* and *XM*

The following instrumental estimate of *RDC* was obtained:

OLS $RDC =$ $0.048 - 0.888^*GLC + 0.460IKC_2 - 0.574PLC - 0.118RD$
$\qquad\quad (0.411)(-2.071)\qquad (1.035)\qquad (-1.041)\qquad (-1.138)$

$\qquad\quad + 0.108FR - 0.039FRC - 0.018IK + 0.271IKC$
$\qquad\quad\;\;\, (0.813)\quad (-0.068)\quad (-0.070)\quad (0.750)$

$\qquad\quad - 1.367GWC - 0.255HS - 0.123XPC$
$\qquad\quad\;\;\, (-1.084)\quad (-0.855)\quad (-0.471)$ $\hfill (9.5)$

$\qquad\qquad\qquad\qquad\qquad R^2 = 0.354 \qquad F = 1.695$

where $GLC =$ (growth of gross output 1972–4) – (growth of gross output 1968–71)

$\qquad IKC_2 = \Sigma_i$ (investment/capital stock)$_i/2 - \Sigma_j$ (investment/capital stock)$_j/2; i = 1974, 1975; j = 1971, 1972$

$\qquad PLC =$ (value-added – wages and salaries)/(value-added) 1974 – (value-added – wages and salaries)/(value-added) 1972

GLC, IKC_2 and PLC are all measured in logarithms.

A Hausman test estimating *XC*, including *RDC* and the instrumental estimate $R\hat{D}C$, gave the following result:

OLS $XC = -0.304 - 0.054RD + 0.076FR + 0.185R\hat{D}C - 0.112RDC$
$\qquad\quad\;\; (-0.541)(-0.986)\qquad (1.267)\qquad (0.989)\qquad (-1.397)$

$\qquad\quad + 0.264FRC - 0.091IK - 0.155IKC - 0.094HS - 0.099TP$
$\qquad\quad\;\;\, (1.015)\quad (-0.748)\;(-1.130)\quad (-0.630)\quad (-0.943)$

$\qquad\quad + 0.065GWC - 0.181XPC$
$\qquad\quad\;\;\, (0.106)\quad (-1.720)$ $\hfill (9.6)$

$R\hat{D}C$ is not significant, failing to reject the hypothesis of no simultaneity.

A Hausman test, estimating XM, including RDC and $R\hat{D}C$, gave the following result:

$$\text{OLS } XM = -0.573 - 0.188^*RD + 0.003FR - 0.285R\hat{D}C - 0.240^*RDC$$
$$(-0.735)(-2.498) \qquad (0.034) \quad (-1.121) \quad (-2.193)$$

$$+ 0.413FRC + 0.179IK + 0.194IKC - 0.629^*HS + 0.071TP$$
$$(1.168) \qquad (1.043) \quad (1.041) \quad (-3.106) \qquad (0.474)$$

$$- 0.216GDC - 0.305GWC - 1.054XPC$$
$$(-0.861) \qquad (-0.354) \qquad (-7.364)$$

Again $R\hat{D}C$ is not significant, failing to reject the hypothesis of no simultaneity.

CHAPTER 10

Export performance and R&D effort of the U.K. and West Germany – a comparative study

This chapter analyses the relative export performance and relative R&D effort of the U.K. and West Germany. Such a comparative study has a number of benefits. A cross-country study removes industry-specific characteristics – such as tradeability or technological opportunity – that otherwise may be only imperfectly captured by the independent variables. Using data for two similar countries means that industries can be matched and industry-specific characteristics should cancel out. This may reduce any problems of heteroscedasticity or of industry-related patterns in the residuals. It reduces or removes the need to normalise due to size, and may reduce collinearity problems among the independent variables. Such a study shifts the emphasis from analysing performance or competitiveness between different industries to an analysis of causes of relative competitiveness between countries. An analysis of only two countries does not allow separate estimation for each industry but does mean that relative competitiveness between the two countries is emphasised. Thus there are theoretical and statistical advantages to be gained from estimating the model of exports and innovation across countries, as well as for one country.

This chapter estimates the export and R&D equations, specified in Chapter 7, both for the U.K. and Germany separately, and for the U.K. relative to Germany. The aggregation level adopted here is determined by the availability of German R&D data. As previously 'ships' and 'other manufacturing' are omitted. There are then sixteen industry categories covering manufacturing industry (Appendix 3). This relatively high level of aggregation means that the results may be only suggestive and that further analysis at a more disaggregated level would be desirable. The combination of the aggregation level with some data difficulties and differences in definitions or classifications for Germany relative to the U.K. (Appendix 3) may result in poorer or less robust results than those obtained for the more disaggregated study. Nevertheless, the different level of aggregation allows, for the U.K., a comparison of these results with the earlier results both to see whether they are supported or otherwise and to see the effect of the aggregation. The export and R&D equations are estimated separately for the U.K. and Germany before combining the two countries' data sets. This not only enables comparison with the earlier U.K. results, but also allows comparison of the separate U.K. and Germany results, and comparison with the estimation of U.K. relative to Germany.

Simultaneity

The theoretical discussion and previous estimation for the U.K. (Chapters 7 and 8) have supported the hypothesis that there is a simultaneous relationship between exports and R&D. At the current level of aggregation, Hausman tests clearly fail to reject the hypothesis of no simultaneity in both the export and the R&D equations. The cause of these results is not clear. It may be a consequence both of the level of aggregation which could have acted to reduce the bias, and of the poorer results of these equations relative to the more disaggregated study. More importantly, the small sample size might result in bias of the instrumental estimates as well as of the OLS estimates, since instrumental variables estimates are consistent only (Maddala 1977) and the Hausman test is then likely to be inappropriate. Given the results of the Hausman test, the equations were estimated by OLS and these results are reported. The equations were also estimated by instrumental variables but, as would be expected, this made little difference to the results. The rejection of the simultaneity hypothesis here does not seriously undermine the earlier results since they are for a level of aggregation much more appropriate to the attempt to define individual industries. The result does, though, suggest the crucial importance of the aggregation level.[1]

10.1 Estimation of the export equations

The export equations for the U.K. and Germany are specified in the same form as the more disaggregated U.K. equation:

$$X_8 = a_0 + a_1 R_{5i} + a_2 FR_5 + a_3 HS + a_4 TP + a_5 C_{5i} + a_6 IK_i$$
$$+ a_7 SM + a_8 K_i \tag{10.1}$$

where $i = $ u, g; u and g are subscripts for the U.K. and Germany respectively.

The variables are in logarithms and are measured as in the disaggregated U.K. export equation (see Appendix 3). FR_5 is measured as previously, except that German R&D/value-added is now excluded from the variable. The German concentration ratio is a six-firm concentration ratio for 1970. Due to data problems, *HS, TP* and *SM* are the same in both equations, using U.K. data.

This should not be a serious problem with respect to the scale variable to the extent that this reflects the technical characteristics of an industry. It may also be argued that skill rankings of industries are likely to be similar across the two countries. This is an assumption, however, and so the estimation does not represent an exact test of the effect of skilled labour on exports, nor does it provide independent information on the relative skill endowments of the two countries (Leamer 1980).

Results are presented first for the separate U.K. and German export equations and then for the estimation of the U.K. relative to Germany.

The U.K. export equation

Table 10.1 presents the results of estimating the export equation for the U.K. at the higher level of aggregation. If equation (10.1) is estimated it is not significant (equation (1), table 10.1). Capital intensity is negative but insignificant and is omitted. Omitting the least significant variables, first *TP* and then *HS* are excluded. Equation (4) is then significant.

The hypothesis of a positive effect of R&D on exports is supported. Foreign R&D has the predicted positive sign, as does investment. As in the more disaggregated study, concentration is negative but here it is not significant. Omitting the insignificant variables, IK_u, *SM* and then FR_5 are omitted. The significance of C_{5u} increases, but remains insignificant. Thus, no significant effect of any variable other than R&D is found. Though providing some support for the more disaggregated result, these results are very poor. The performance of skilled manual labour is particularly poor relative to its significance in the earlier study. The hypothesis of a positive effect of R&D is quite robust, but this is not so for the other hypotheses. If foreign participation is included in the equation, foreign participation is positive but not significant. The specification of equation (8), table 10.1, means that if the system were estimated by simultaneous methods, the R&D equation would not be identified. Thus, if it is accepted that there is a simultaneous relationship between exports and R&D, the R&D equation is not identified at this level of aggregation. It can be argued, however, that the results of the export equation are poorer than those of the more disaggregated study partly because of the aggregation level and so that theoretically, though not statistically, the R&D equation is identified.

Table 10.1. *Estimation of X_{8u} by OLS*

	Constant	R_{su}	FR_s	IK_u	C_{su}	SM	HS	TP	K_u	$\bar{R}^2$	F
(1)	0.182 (0.046)	0.490 (1.608)	−0.379 (−1.437)	−0.355 (−0.471)	0.041 (0.062)	−0.918 (−0.026)	−0.380 (−0.471)	0.416 (0.897)	−0.473 (−1.084)	0.382	2.159
(2)	3.170 (1.297)	0.685* (2.765)	−0.271 (−1.097)	0.249 (0.483)	−0.391 (−0.721)	−18.465 (−0.582)	0.234 (0.404)	−0.115 (−0.307)		0.368	2.250
(3)	2.984 (1.329)	0.704* (3.085)	−0.248 (−1.111)	0.248 (0.508)	−0.394 (−0.765)	−20.024 (−0.674)	0.213 (0.390)			0.432	2.910
(4)	2.974 (1.385)	0.700* (3.209)	−0.254 (−1.189)	0.214 (0.467)	−0.483 (−1.097)	−17.259 (−0.625)				0.480	3.770*
(5)	2.515 (1.366)	0.677* (3.304)	−0.242 (−1.186)		−0.563 (−1.440)	−11.158 (−0.476)				0.517	5.015*
(6)	2.775 (1.608)	0.676* (3.410)	−0.234 (−1.190)		−0.628 (−1.770)					0.548	7.066*
(7)	2.850 (1.640)	0.484* (4.146)			−0.640 (−1.776)					0.534	9.585*
(8)	−0.173 (−0.459)	0.343* (3.726)								0.462	13.881*

Figures in brackets are t-statistics.
*Denotes significance at the 5% level.

Table 10.2. *Estimation of X_{8g} by OLS*

	Constant	R_{5g}	FR_5	IK_g	C_{6g}	SM	HS	TP	K_g	$\bar{R}^2$	F
(1)	2.334 (0.807)	0.310* (2.042)	-0.065 (-0.426)	0.586 (1.621)	-0.350 (-1.153)	16.597 (1.014)	0.654 (1.260)	-0.141 (-0.505)	0.253 (0.863)	0.558	3.364
(2)	0.066 (0.055)	0.213* (2.128)	-0.081 (-0.545)	0.468 (1.423)	-0.133 (-0.794)	12.574 (0.815)	0.314 (0.944)	-0.012 (-0.053)		0.572	3.861*
(3)	0.100 (0.105)	0.211* (2.320)	-0.083 (-0.600)	0.469 (1.509)	-0.135 (-0.877)	12.746 (0.896)	0.318 (1.034)			0.619	5.065*
(4)	0.486 (0.720)	0.170* (2.955)		0.540* (1.948)	-0.161 (-1.118)	12.419 (0.903)	0.396 (1.472)			0.644	6.417*
(5)	0.424 (0.636)	0.165* (2.902)		0.556* (2.025)	-0.127 (-0.923)		0.404 (1.512)			0.650	7.950*
(6)	0.059 (0.111)	0.132* (2.986)		0.629* (2.410)			0.471* (1.844)			0.654	10.445*

Figures in brackets are t-statistics.
*Denotes significance at the 5% level.

The West German export equation

Table 10.2 presents the results of estimating the export equation for West Germany. As for the U.K., both foreign R&D and concentration have negative signs but are not significant. However, German R&D has a positive and significant effect. This supports the hypothesis of a positive effect of R&D separate from that arising due to technology gaps. This conclusion is not very strong, however, given the relatively approximate nature of the measure of the technology gap and the level of aggregation. In addition to R&D, both skilled manual labour and investment have positive effects on German exports. These results are interesting, since they suggest that the U.K. and Germany may derive export strength from similar characteristics; the insignificance of HS in the more aggregated U.K. study may indicate, though, a clearer German advantage in skilled manual labour. Investment has a positive effect on German exports while no effect is discernible on U.K. exports. This may suggest that German investment is better directed towards those areas where it has some trading advantage. The U.K. may not be investing sufficiently in those areas, or may be investing relatively too much in other areas, or else, for other reasons, the potential efficiency and dynamism effects of investment are not feeding through into U.K. exports.

The German results may be compared with other studies of German exports, which also found support for the R&D or technology factor. In a study of fifty-five single products, a strong relation was found between R&D effort and trade performance in research-intensive goods (Horn 1977). Wolter (1977) found both the neo-factor endowment and neo-technology theories could contribute to an explanation of German exports, though the two explanations competed rather than being complementary as in the results presented here. He also found a clear change in German comparative advantage towards the high skill/technology industries. Thus, the positive effect of R&D on German exports, confirmed by these studies, may have become stronger in the 1970s, compared to the early 1960s.

Estimation of U.K. exports relative to West German exports

As explained at the start of the chapter, a cross-country analysis may provide a different perspective on the determinants of export performance, in particular by normalising for industry-specific characteristics. Estimating a cross-country equation is of interest in order to see whether it gives emphasis to the same set of independent variables as the separate equations for each country. The equation to estimate the determinants of U.K. relative to German exports is specified as follows:

$$XKG = a_0 + a_1 RGK + a_2 CGK + a_3 IGK + a_4 HS + a_5 TP + a_6 SM + a_7 K_u$$

$$(10.2)$$

where the variables are measured in logarithms and:

XGK = U.K. exports 1978 $-$ German exports 1978
RGK = U.K. R&D 1975 $-$ German R&D 1975
CGK = $C_{5u} - C_{6g}$
IGK = $IK_u - IK_g$

The remaining variables are as defined previously. New variables have, therefore, been constructed for exports, R&D, concentration and investment. The scale, capital intensity and skill variables are treated as comparative advantage variables. It is assumed that it is not the differences between the countries in these variables that are important, but their relative endowments, or country characteristics, that will determine the relationship between their relative exports and these variables. Foreign R&D is no longer in the equation since the relationship of U.K. and German R&D to other countries' R&D should cancel out. The equation thus estimates the effect of the overall gap between U.K. and German R&D.

Exports and R&D are no longer normalised to adjust for size effects. This is an advantage, since differences across countries in the normalisation of variables might affect the estimation, and also since U.K. and German exports compete directly against each other. Their relative export levels directly reflect their relative competiveness, rather than their relative exports/sales ratios.

It is expected that RGK and IGK will be positive. The signs of the other variables cannot be predicted *a priori.* As suggested above, the results of the two separate country equations may indicate that Germany has a relative advantage in manual skilled labour.

Table 10.3 presents the simple correlations between the variables in the export equation, where FGK = foreign participation in production, U.K. $-$ Germany.

There are no very strong correlations. The correlation of XGK with RGK is positive as predicted but weak, while XGK is negatively correlated with IGK, and with HS. The strongest correlation of XGK is with TP, suggesting some possible U.K. advantage. TP itself is quite strongly negatively correlated with all the other variables that measure the U.K. relative to Germany, i.e. RGK, CGK and IGK.

Table 10.4 presents the results of estimating the comparative export equation. Estimating the full form of the equation, the equation as a whole is not significant. The hypothesis of a positive effect of relative R&D expenditures is supported. IGK has the opposite sign to that predicted but is very insignificant. HS is negative, as it was suggested it might be, but is not significant. TP is positive and quite close to significance, while capital intensity is negative suggesting some possible relative advantage of Germany in capital-intensive goods.

Table 10.3. *Correlation matrix of variables in the U.K./Germany export equation*

	XGK	RGK	CGK	IGK	HS	TP	SM	K_u	FGK
XGK	1.0	0.184	−0.168	−0.205	−0.252	0.459	−0.170	−0.074	0.011
RGK		1.0	0.394	0.345	0.034	−0.462	−0.040	0.008	−0.299
CGK			1.0	0.320	0.015	−0.525	−0.044	−0.290	0.465
IGK				1.0	0.406	−0.559	0.127	−0.435	−0.009
HS					1.0	−0.445	−0.070	−0.598	−0.229
TP						1.0	0.008	0.328	−0.038
SM							1.0	0.164	−0.247
K_u								1.0	−0.103
FGK									1.0

Contrary to the procedure adopted elsewhere in this analysis, the capital intensity variable is not omitted from the equation since it is quite close to significance and may, contrary to expectation, have some explanatory role to play.

Omitting the least significant variables the following order of exclusion is found: *SM, IGK, CGK* and *HS*. At this point, capital intensity is again negative, but remains insignificant. It was therefore omitted. Including relative foreign participation (*FGK*) in the equation, it was positive but never significant, suggesting that once common industry and tradeability characteristics are eliminated there is no other role for *FGK*.

Equation (6), table 10.4, therefore presents the final form of the equation. These results support the hypothesis of a positive effect of the gap in R&D expenditure between Germany and the U.K. on relative exports. The results also support the hypothesis that the U.K. has a comparative advantage relative to Germany in technical and professional staff. This is somewhat surprising since *TP* did not have a significant role in the results for either of the earlier U.K. estimations.

The results explain only a small part of the variation in relative exports. However, given the similarity in the two countries' export compositions – with a correlation in the current sample of 0.674 – it is encouraging that some of the variation can be systematically explained. In contrast, a study of the U.S. found significant results vanished when normalising U.S. exports by either U.K. or German exports, which was suggested to be due to the similarity of their export composition to that of the U.S. (Gruber, Mehta and Vernon 1967). The results contrast with those of a study of the U.K. relative to the U.S. (Katrak 1973). The study found little support for the human skills theory and strongest support for the effect of scale economies. This effect of scale may be expected to be more important in analysing the trade of countries of different sizes. In the current study, these findings are reversed. There is a clear and important role for the technology gap, some

Table 10.4. *Estimation of XGK by OLS*

	Constant	RGK	CGK	IGK	HS	TP	SM	K_u	$\bar{R}^2$	F
(1)	1.329 (0.841)	0.534* (2.148)	−0.288 (−0.632)	−0.164 (−0.368)	−0.610 (−0.810)	0.707 (1.765)	−9.126 (−0.312)	−0.431 (−1.633)	0.208	1.562
(2)	1.292 (0.864)	0.545* (2.324)	−0.289 (−0.668)	−0.199 (−0.485)	−0.608 (−0.852)	0.705 (1.856)		−0.449 (−1.832)	0.287	2.007
(3)	1.643 (1.306)	0.521* (2.365)	−0.283 (−0.682)		−0.629 (−0.919)	0.761 (2.189)		−0.418 (−1.839)	0.342	2.557
(4)	1.834 (1.533)	0.491* (2.333)			−0.433 (0.715)	0.874* (2.925)		−0.357 (−1.751)	0.347	3.238
(5)	2.763* (2.234)	0.511* (2.506)				0.948* (3.461)		−0.282 (−1.648)	0.399	4.323*
(6)	1.070 (1.420)	0.447* (2.098)				0.779* (2.883)			0.320	4.530*

Figures in brackets are *t*-statistics.
*Denotes significance at the 5% level.

role for one category of skilled labour and no role for scale. Some theories suggest scale may be important in leading to trade, even between countries of similar size (for example, Krugman 1981), but this is not supported here.

10.2 Estimation of the R&D equations

As with the estimation of the export equations, the determinants of R&D are first estimated separately for the U.K. and Germany, and then their relative R&D effort is considered.

The individual R&D equations for Germany and the U.K. are specified as the more disaggregated U.K. equation was, i.e.:

$$R_{5i} = a_0 + a_1 X_{8i} + a_2 FR + a_3 C_{5i} + a_4 IK_i + a_5 PL_i + a_6 GL_i + a_7 FL_i$$

$$(10.3)$$

where $i = $ u, g (subscripts for the U.K. and Germany respectively).

The variables are measured as defined for the earlier U.K. R&D estimation, except that FR no longer includes Germany. For the German estimation, concentration is measured by a six-firm concentration ratio for 1970 (C_{6g}) and FL is measured for 1978.

The U.K. R&D equation

Table 10.5 presents the results of estimating the R&D equation for the U.K. at the higher level of aggregation.

The hypotheses of a positive effect of exports and concentration on R&D are supported in equation (1). Investment and technological opportunity are positive but not significant. The cash flow and expected profit variables are both insignificant. Even when PL_u is omitted, GL_u increases in significance only slightly, so their insignificance is not attributable to collinearity. Foreign participation in production has a negative sign, which may reflect subsidiaries' use of parent company R&D output, but is not significant.

Omitting insignificant variables, table 10.5 shows that there is a consistent positive effect of exports, concentration and technological opportunity on R&D. These results confirm most of the results of the more disaggregated U.K. study, except for the insignificance of PL_u.

The West German R&D equation

Table 10.6 presents the results of estimating the R&D equation for West Germany. In the full estimation, equation (1), only technological opportunity has a positive effect on R&D. None of the other variables are significant,

Table 10.5. Estimation of R_{su} by OLS

	Constant	X_{su}	FR	C_{su}	IK_u	PL_u	GL_u	FL_u	$\bar{R}^2$	F
(1)	−6.124 (−1.458)	0.761* (2.306)	0.413 (1.561)	1.333* (2.315)	0.237 (0.462)	0.037 (0.043)	1.286 (0.659)	−0.136 (−1.093)	0.857	13.797*
(2)	−6.268* (−2.660)	0.758* (2.474)	0.407* (1.979)	1.345* (2.837)	0.229 (0.507)		1.344 (1.016)	−0.138 (−1.205)	0.872	18.104*
(3)	−6.534* (−2.966)	0.730* (2.517)	0.416* (2.112)	1.240* (3.023)			1.168 (0.951)	−0.116 (−1.137)	0.882	23.412*
(4)	−5.335* (−2.952)	0.590* (2.371)	0.537* (3.597)	1.068* (2.914)				−0.057 (−0.706)	0.883	29.291*
(5)	−4.627* (−3.143)	0.542* (2.313)	0.581* (4.374)	0.950* (2.974)					0.888	40.583*

Figures in brackets are t-statistics.
*Denotes significance at the 5% level.

	Constant	X_{8g}	FR	C_{6g}	IK_g	PL_g	GL_g	FL_g	$\bar{R}^2$	F
(1)	0.033 (0.012)	0.794 (1.185)	0.981* (3.245)	0.310 (0.550)	0.812 (0.969)	-0.378 (-0.487)	1.206 (0.944)	-0.466 (-0.788)	0.879	16.557*
(2)	-0.209 (-0.081)	0.885 (1.438)	0.916* (3.535)	0.446 (0.949)	0.971 (1.317)		1.342 (1.125)	-0.628 (-1.342)	0.889	21.063*
(3)	2.014 (1.838)	0.842 (1.379)	1.098* (6.343)		0.869 (1.197)		1.409 (1.190)	-0.370 (-0.976)	0.890	25.347*
(4)	2.470* (2.496)	1.083* (1.941)	1.043* (6.387)		0.679 (0.973)		1.652 (1.429)		0.891	31.581*
(5)	1.989* (2.326)	1.406* (3.143)	1.054* (6.481)				1.554 (1.353)		0.891	41.981*
(6)	2.424* (2.990)	1.339* (2.921)	1.109* (6.828)						0.884	58.333*

Figures in brackets are t-statistics.
*Denotes significance at the 5% level.

although the signs are as predicted except for that of PL_g. As in the U.K. estimation, FL is negative. Omitting least significant variables, exports become significant in equation (4). This adds confirmation to the role of exports and technological opportunity in the U.K. equations. Contrary to the U.K. results, concentration though positive is not significant. GL_g is also positive but not significant.

Estimation of U.K. R&D relative to German R&D

As in the relative export equation, exports, R&D and foreign participation need not be normalised in estimating the R&D equation. In addition, here the cash flow variable can also be measured without normalisation. The equation is specified as:

$$RGK = b_0 + b_1 XGK + b_2 CGK + b_3 IGK + b_4 PGK + b_5 GGK + b_6 FGK$$

$$(10.4)$$

where:

$$PGK = \Sigma_i[(\text{value-added})_i - (\text{wages} + \text{salaries})_i] \quad \text{U.K.} - \text{Germany}; i =$$
$$1972, 1973, 1974$$
$$GGK = GL_u - GL_g$$

and the other variables are as defined previously.[2] FR, being the same in both equations, drops out. It is predicted that the effect of all the variables will be positive, except for that of FGK which may be positive or negative. The negative sign of FL in both the U.K. and the German equations suggests that its sign may be negative. The simple correlations of the variables in the relative R&D equation are presented in table 10.7.

The correlations are not strong. The correlations with the dependent variable have the signs predicted by the model. FGK has a negative correlation with RGK. The weakest correlations with RGK are those of XGK and PGK. PGK has quite a strong correlation with XGK, suggesting that both could be reflecting relative efficiency.

Table 10.7. *Correlation matrix of variables in the U.K./Germany R&D equation*

	RGK	XGK	CGK	IGK	PGK	GGK	FGK
RGK	1.0	0.184	0.394	0.345	0.022	0.384	−0.29
XGK		1.0	−0.168	−0.205	0.483	0.255	0.01
CGK			1.0	0.320	−0.123	0.097	0.46
IGK				1.0	−0.357	−0.267	−0.00
PGK					1.0	−0.276	−0.14
GGK						1.0	0.15
FGK							1.0

stimation

stimation of the full specification of the R&D equation gives the following
esult:

$$)LS\ RGK\ =\ -1.465 + 0.073XGK + 0.836^*CGK + 0.756^*IGK$$
$$(-1.254)\ (0.306)\qquad (2.507)\qquad\quad (2.245)$$
$$+\ 0.267PGK + 2.066^*GGK - 0.333^*FGK$$
$$(1.276)\qquad (2.897)\qquad (-3.168)$$
$$\bar{R}^2\ =\ 0.646\qquad F_{6,9}\ =\ 5.567^*\quad (10.5)$$

The results of the estimation are quite good, supporting a role for more of
he explanatory variables than in the single country equations. This suggests
nat controlling for industry-specific characteristics improves the estimation of
ne effects of the independent variables. The hypotheses of positive effects
n relative R&D of relative concentration, investment and growth are sup-
orted. The flow of funds/profit margin variable (PGK) is not significant
hough, as considered previously, it may be difficult to identify both a cash
ow and expected profit effect. The relative export variable is very insignifi-
ant though it has the predicted sign. If the equation is estimated with only
e expected profit variable GGK, and not PGK, the significance of XGK
creases (with a t-statistic of 1.429) but it remains insignificant. The results
f equation (10.5) reflect the simple correlations presented above, suggesting
at the model here may be adding little explanatory power over and above
ese correlations.

If XGK is omitted from the equation the following result is obtained:

$$LS\ RGK\ =\ -1.680 + 0.803^*CGK + 0.787^*IGK + 0.308^*PGK$$
$$(-1.888)\ (2.670)\qquad (2.576)\qquad\quad (2.019)$$
$$+\ 2.183^*GGK - 0.327^*FGK$$
$$(3.810)\qquad (-3.328)$$
$$\bar{R}^2\ =\ 0.678\qquad F_{5,10}\ =\ 7.325^*\quad (10.6)$$

he hypothesis of a positive effect of cash flow/profit margin is now
pported, implying that there is a separate role for cash flow and expected
ofit variables. Overall, the results indicate that there is a role for both
dustry structure and performance variables in determining R&D. The result
r concentration is particularly strong, since this type of cross-country study
ould control very well for technological opportunity, implying that concen-
ation has a strong positive effect, independent of its correlation with tech-
ological opportunity. This may imply positive effects of monopoly power
d/or of oligopolistic competition on R&D effort. The negative effect of
ltinationals is also interesting. The negative sign of FGK may indicate

that MNEs are importing technology from their parent companies. Howevei it could have the more serious implication that the presence of MNEs dis courages R&D by indigenous firms.

The results of the estimation of the relative R&D equation contrast wit' those of the individual country estimation. In the German equation export and technological opportunity were significant, while in the U.K. equatio these two variables and concentration were significant (and *PL* in the mor disaggregated analysis). In the relative R&D equation, technological oppoi tunity is not included in the specification and relative exports are not signif cant. All the remaining variables are significant, including those not found t have a role in any of the earlier equations – investment, expected profit an foreign participation.

The insignificance of the relative export variable is of particular concern given its significance in the earlier estimations and its role in the simultaneou system. Its insignificance may imply that U.K./German export compositio is sufficiently similar to make it impossible to distinguish any significar influence on R&D at this level of aggregation. Alternatively, it may be tha once industry-specific characteristics are more thoroughly normalised fo allowing the role of the other variables to be clearly estimated, exports hav no role. However, the two separate country analyses do eliminate tw particularly important industry characteristics in the estimation of R&L size and technological opportunity. The positive effect of exports on R&! in these separate country estimations may be due in part to the fact tha exports are reflecting product or industry characteristics that do not var very strongly across countries. Nevertheless, the separate country results als support the hypothesis that export markets allow firms to capture larg rents on specific assets such as R&D (Spencer and Brander 1983). Tł insignificance of exports here questions those results but, given the problen associated with the aggregation level, does not completely undermine it.

Further analysis of the role of exports, and of the failure of exports ι have a significant effect in the comparative study of Germany and the U.K would require comparison at a more disaggregated level with another countr or across a number of countries. This might help to demonstrate whether tł results are due to the level of aggregation, to the similarity of the tw countries studied, or to exports proxying product- or industry-specif characteristics.

10.3 Conclusions

This chapter has estimated the determinants of exports and R&D for the U.) and West Germany across sixteen manufacturing industries. The main purpo of this estimation was to undertake a comparative study with West Germai to gain further insights into the relationship between exports and R&D havi normalised for industry-specific characteristics. This estimation also allowed consideration of the effects of the aggregation level on the results obtained previously for the U.K.

The results in part supported the results of the more disaggregated study, in part questioned or failed to support some of the earlier results, in particular with respect to simultaneity. However, the small sample meant that little weight could be attached to the tests for simultaneity.

The estimation of relative exports reinforced the previous conclusions with respect to the positive and significant effect of the technology gap. Thus, the technology gap has been found to have an important effect on U.K. exports, whether across U.K. manufacturing industry alone or for U.K. exports relative to a major competitor. The only other significant effect on relative exports was that of technical and professional staff – a variable not found to be significant in the more disaggregated or individual country studies, though it was shown to have a negative effect on the change in exports and imports (Chapter 9). Thus, if the U.K. has a comparative advantage in this type of labour, it is important to note that trade would appear to be relatively declining in industries intensive in that type of labour. The individual export equations reinforced the conclusion of a positive role of R&D, though showing no significant effects of the technology gap or industry structure.

The R&D equations also reinforced some, but not all, of the earlier, more disaggregated results. The individual country equations both supported the conclusion of a positive effect of exports and of technological opportunity on R&D, and the U.K. equation confirmed the more disaggregated result for concentration. The equation for relative R&D not only reinforced most of the conclusions of the more disaggregated study but also demonstrated significant effects of investment and foreign participation and of both expected profit and the cash flow/profit margin variable. In a serious departure from the earlier results, however, the equation rejected any role of relative exports. It was suggested that this could be due to the level of aggregation, to similarity between the two countries or to exports reflecting general tradeability effects. Further analysis of this result with respect to exports would require more disaggregated data and a study of more countries.

Overall, the results in this chapter provide important additional information on the determinants of exports and R&D. The results partly add to, partly support, and partly question results obtained previously. They show both that the level of aggregation of the sample can have important effects on the results obtained and that the specification of equations across countries, or for one country only, can have important effects. It was not possible, though, to determine precisely the separate influences of the aggregation level and the cross-country estimation on the results obtained. The results suggest, however, that more information, or a more comprehensive view of the influences involved, can be obtained by analysing or specifying dependent variables in more than one way. The different U.K. results also suggest it is important to obtain fairly disaggregated data and to test the effects of a higher aggregation level. One potentially useful and interesting extension of the current analysis would be to estimate the model across a number of countries at a more disaggregated level. However, this would be difficult due to lack of data, in particular with respect to R&D.

CHAPTER 11

Summary and conclusions

This study has analysed various aspects of the relationship between exports and technology, both theoretically and empirically. This chapter presents a general summary and conclusions with respect to the main arguments and results.

General evidence on technological activity, trade performance and skill levels of the five main OECD countries was presented in Chapter 2. All five countries were shown to have high levels of R&D activity, and to have positive trade balances in the high technology industries. However, their relative positions had changed markedly over time – in particular that of Japan had improved, while that of the U.K. and, to some extent, of the U.S. had deteriorated. Chapter 3 went on to consider theoretical explanations of the potential role of R&D, skill and industry structure in determining trade performance. It was argued that the neo-technology theories, in combination with industrial structure variables, potentially offered a more comprehensive explanation of trade patterns than could human skills theories. However, it was suggested that the two sets of theories could be complementary in that they explained different aspects of trade. Nevertheless, acknowledgement of the role of innovation was seen to undermine the static nature of the neo-factor endowment theories. In addition to technology and skills, it was further argued that scale, investment and concentration may affect trade flows. Chapter 3 also discussed empirical evidence on the determinants of export composition and trade performance. Evidence was found that supported both neo-technology and human skills variables, though comparison across studies was difficult due to differences in choice and measurement of variables, countries and time periods.

Chapter 4 analysed in more depth the relationship between exports and technology. It was argued that, unlike skilled labour, R&D expenditure could not be treated strictly as an endowment. Two-way trade may exist between

163

competitors with similar R&D levels, in addition to trade arising due to gaps in R&D expenditure. However, it was suggested that there may be some flexible role for R&D 'endowments' in influencing industrial specialisation and exports, in combination with the effects of R&D working through both technology gaps and variety and scale effects. Chapter 4 then considered the role of other determinants of exports and specified an estimating equation for export composition. Export composition was seen as dependent on a group of technology, factor endowment and industry structure variables. In contrast to other analyses, both the technological level of an industry, and the gap between the technology level of domestic and foreign industries, were expected to have a positive effect on exports. It was further suggested that there would be a simultaneous relationship between exports and R&D. R&D expenditure should therefore be analysed, not only because of its potential role in U.K. export performance, but also because knowledge of its determinants was necessary for the export equation to be correctly specified and estimated.

Chapter 5 considered theoretical and empirical analyses of R&D. The Schumpeterian hypotheses with respect to innovation – based in particular on expected effects of firm size and market structure – were seen to represent a dynamic, disequilibrium approach. Positive effects of market structure were not only, or even mainly, related to advantages of a monopoly position but rather to the type of competitive forces operating within oligopolistic industries. This emphasis on market structure and competitive forces could be seen as complementary to those theories of innovation that stressed either demand factors or the scientific opportunity level of the industry. Empirical results were found to be varied, though technological opportunity had the most consistent positive effect on R&D. Positive effects of firm size and market structure had also been found in some studies, but not in others, so the evidence remained inconclusive. Demand variables had positive effects in some analyses, but the most appropriate measure to adopt was not clear. It was argued that further work was necessary to test the determinants of R&D at both firm and industry level, based on a clear specification of the expected relationships and on precise measurement of variables.

Chapter 6 considered an alternative analysis of the determinants of R&D, utilising the analysis of advertising decisions based on the Dorfman–Steiner conditions (Dorfman and Steiner 1954). These conditions could be reformulated by replacing advertising with R&D expenditure and by considering how and whether expected competitors' reactions would vary (Needham 1975). This failed to incorporate the possibilities that R&D would affect variable costs in addition to, or instead of, demand, and that the effective cost of R&D may vary by industry. The Dorfman–Steiner conditions were, therefore, extended to allow for these effects.

However, the Dorfman–Steiner approach was seen as limited because of the differences between R&D and advertising, in particular due to the greater uncertainty of both the output of R&D and its effects on demand. Nevertheless, it was argued that the model could be relevant where R&D resulted in small changes, while R&D directed at, or resulting in, large changes could be better analysed through a more general Schumpeterian approach. In establishing an estimating equation for R&D expenditure both approaches could be used. It was proposed that R&D intensity would depend on exports, concentration, technological opportunity, expected profit, investment, cash flow/profit margin and foreign participation. Exports represented a higher return to R&D and were expected to have a positive effect on R&D.

Chapter 7 presented the results of estimating the export equation by instrumental variables for the U.K. using more detailed R&D data than in any earlier U.K. studies. The level of R&D and the technology gap were found to have positive effects on exports. Skilled manual labour also had a positive effect while concentration had a negative effect. Hausman tests (Hausman 1978) rejected the hypothesis of no simultaneity. Heteroscedasticity was detected and adjusted for, leading to different results from those obtained if no adjustment were made. No role was found for the more traditional factor endowment variable – capital intensity – nor for technical and professional staff, investment or scale. The results, therefore, lent support to the neo-technology theory of trade, and partial support to the human skills theory, while indicating some role for industry structure. The determinants of import penetration and the net trade balance were also estimated. Net trade depended positively on R&D, while imports were positively related to both R&D intensity and skilled manual labour.

Chapter 8 presented the results of estimating the R&D equation. Hausman tests again supported the hypothesis of simultaneity. Exports were found to have a positive effect on R&D as did concentration, the profit margin, and technological opportunity. R&D was thus shown to depend on a group of variables reflecting inherent characteristics of the industry, and structural, performance and demand characteristics. Investment, expected profit and foreign participation had no significant effect. R&D was seen to be affected by a number of variables, hence it was argued that any theoretical analysis that focused exclusively on one variable would be misleading.

Chapter 9 estimated the change in export composition from 1972 to 1978. The results were poor but indicated negative effects of foreign participation and technical and professional staff, and a positive effect of growth in world demand. Superior results were obtained in estimating the change in imports and in the net trade balance, in part due to the better performance of the price variable. The results of the change in the net trade balance equation suggested that U.K. trade performance had relatively declined in R&D-

intensive industries, and was also negatively related to skilled manual labour, foreign participation and the change in relative prices. Thus, while R&D and skilled labour had positive effects on the level of exports, they were also areas where U.K. competitiveness was declining over time.

Chapter 10 reported the results of a comparative study of the U.K. and West Germany. This supported some, but not all, of the results of the more disaggregated study. The estimation of the relative export equation reinforced the conclusion of a positive and significant effect of the technology gap, and found a positive role for technical and professional staff. However, the individual export equations indicated a positive effect of R&D but not of the technology gap. The estimation of the relative R&D equation found no role for exports, but confirmed the effects of the other variables including those not significant for the U.K. alone — investment, expected profit and foreign participation. The individual R&D equations found a positive effect of exports. The hypothesis of no simultaneity was supported in the comparative study. It was suggested that this was due to the aggregation level which would result in biased instrumental variables estimates. The results of the comparative study provided additional information on the relationships being analysed, and indicated both the advantages of a cross-country study and the disadvantages of a relatively high aggregation level.

The results of the current study have shown that the neo-technology and neo-factor endowment theories can be distinguished. They demonstrate that U.K. export composition is dependent not only on the technology intensity level of manufacturing industry but also on the technology gap between the U.K. and competitors' industries. The results show that the human skills theory alone does not provide an explanation of U.K. exports, and that a variable commonly used to represent skilled labour endowments (technical and professional staff) has no influence. However, skilled labour does have a role, in the form of skilled manual labour. The neo-technology theories thus allow a more comprehensive picture of determinants of U.K. exports to be drawn and, by their nature, lead to expectation of, and contribute to an explanation of, changes over time.

The role of R&D and the analysis of the determinants of R&D is also of importance. The results have indicated that a number of factors influence R&D intensity. It is important to recognise the existence of all these factors not only in analysing, or deriving policy with respect to, manufacturing industry but also in the theoretical analysis of R&D. Many theories of R&D have focused on only one variable, or one inter-related group of variables. The results presented here suggest this is misleading.

These results also indicate that a number of complementary approaches may be required in analysing export composition and export performance. U.K. exports were analysed — in a cross-section — at a point in time, over time, and relative to another country. This does not necessarily involve conflicting results but produces a more comprehensive picture of the influences and relationships involved.

The current study has stressed the importance of a clear theoretical specification of the relationships and variables involved before empirical estimation. To differentiate the neo-technology and neo-factor endowment theories, precise specification and measurement of the variables involved is crucial. The influence of technology across industries was shown to operate through both the level of R&D and the gap between competitors' R&D. Failure to include both technology variables will, therefore, result in mis-specification. There will also be errors in variables if only crude categories of technology intensity are used. Similarly, human capital may have various in-fluences that cannot be captured in a single variable. Furthermore a simul-taneous relationship was shown to exist between technology and exports. This must cast doubt on the results of earlier studies which have not taken this into account, since OLS estimation will produce biased results. Similarly, the effects of failing to adjust for heteroscedasticity have been shown. Again, doubt must be cast on the results of those studies that have not tested or adjusted for the presence of heteroscedasticity.

The current study has emphasised, in particular, the ability of the neo-technology theory to offer a theoretical and empirical explanation of the relationships analysed. However, given the stress in neo-technology theory on dynamism and change, the question arises as to whether it can, in fact, be properly tested looking at, or only at, a point in time. The same point can be made with respect to Schumpeterian theories of R&D. It may be inappropriate to estimate cross-section relations for one year, since these will involve or reflect changing relationships. However, unless changes are expected to be very rapid, some information may be derived from analysing the relations existing at a point in time. It is then important that changes in these relationships are also analysed to consider whether these reinforce or contradict the relations observed for the levels. In contrast, in human skills trade theories, there is no conflict or contradiction in analysing levels alone.

This discussion highlights some of the limitations of the current study and, thus, also areas for future research. In order to consider the dynamic implications of these theories more fully, time-series analysis would provide a superior approach to taking the difference in a cross-section over two years. Alternatively, a case study approach could be adopted. This might allow more detailed information to be obtained on the variables involved and their change over time. An industry case study might also help to illuminate some of the dynamics of R&D competition. Analysis across a number of countries (rather than just relative to one country) at a relatively high level of disaggregation would also be both interesting and informative, though inevitably there would be data limitations. Further information on the relationships between technology and exports, and on the other determinants of these variables, may therefore be obtained by more detailed case study, cross-country or time-series analysis. This could extend and elaborate the results of the current analysis.

APPENDIX 1

Industry classifications and dummy variables

This Appendix sets out the industry classifications for the U.K. sample (Table A1.1) and for the foreign R&D categories and their correspondence with the U.K. industry categories (table A1.2). The classification of industries used for constructing dummy variables for capital and chemical goods, basic goods and consumer goods; for industries with concentration greater than 55 per cent; and for high, medium and low technology industries is also given (table A1.2).

Table A1.1. *Sample of U.K. manufacturing industries*

Num-ber	Industry	Minimum list heading	Capital, chemicals, basic and consumer goods dummies[a]	Concentration dummies[b]
1	Food	211–19	C	1
2	Drink	231–9	C	0
3	Tobacco	240	C	0
4	Petroleum products	262	B	0
5	Lubricating oils and greases	263	B	1
6	Inorganic chemicals	271.1	KC	0
7	Organic chemicals	271.2	KC	0
8	Pharmaceutical chemicals and preparations	272	KC	1
9	Paint	274	KC	1
10	Synthetic resins and plastics materials and synthetic rubber	276	KC	1
11	Fertilisers	278	KC	0

Table A1.1. *Continued*

Num-ber	Industry	Minimum list heading	Capital, chemicals, basic and consumer goods dummies[a]	Concentration dummies[b]
12	Pesticides	279.4	KC	0
13	Other chemicals	261, 271.3, 273, 275, 277, 279 except 279.4	KC	0
14	Iron and steel	311–13	B	0
15	Non-ferrous metals	321–3	B	0
16	Agricultural machinery	331	KC	1
17	Metal working machine tools	332	KC	1
18	Pumps, valves, compressors, hydraulic and pneumatic power equipment	333	KC	1
19	Industrial engines	334	KC	0
20	Textile machinery and accessories	335	KC	1
21	Construction and earth-moving equipment	336	KC	1
22	Mechanical handling equipment	337	KC	1
23	Industrial and process plant and constructional and fabricated steelwork, boilers and boilerhouse plant	341	KC	1
24	Other machinery and equipment	338, 339, 349	KC	1
25	Instrument engineering	351–4	KC	1
26	Electrical generating and transmission plant and other electrical machinery	361	KC	1
27	Insulated wires and cables	362	KC	0
28	Telephone and telegraph apparatus and equipment	363	KC	0
29	Electronic computers	366	KC	0
30	Electronic components	364	KC	1
31	Other electronic apparatus including broadcasting equipment, radio and radar	365, 367	KC	0

Table A1.1. *Continued*

Number	Industry	Minimum list heading	Capital, chemicals, basic and consumer goods dummies[a]	Concentration dummies[b]
32	Domestic electrical appliances	368	C	1
33	Miscellaneous electrical goods	369	KC	0
34	Wheeled tractors	380	KC	0
35	Motor vehicles	381, 382	KC	0
36	Aerospace equipment (including air cushion vehicles)	383	KC	0
37	Metal goods	390–9	B	1
38	Man-made fibres (staple fibre and continuous filament yarn)	411	KC	0
39	All other textile manu-factures and finishes	412–29	C	1
40	Leather, clothing and footwear	431–50	C	1
41	Bricks, cement, miscellane-ous building materials and abrasives	461, 464, 469	B	1
42	Pottery, china and glass	462, 463	B	0
43	Timber and furniture, etc.	471–9	C	1
44	Paper, paper products and board	481–4	B	1
45	Printing and publishing	485–9	C	1
46	Rubber and rubber products	491	B	1

[a]Where KC = capital and chemical goods, B = basic goods, C = consumer goods.
[b]Where industries with concentration ratios (in 1975) less than 55 per cent = 1, those greater than 55 per cent = 0.
Source: *Industrial Research and Development Expenditure and Employment*, 1978, *Business Monitor* MO14, London, HMSO, 1980; *Report on the Census of Production* 1974 and 1975, London, HMSO.

The technology dummies are set out in table A1.2. The eighteen foreign R&D categories were ranked by average R&D intensity (i.e. by the variable FR) in 1973 and 1975. They were initially split into three groups of six industries. This resulted in two industries being in the medium technology group — stone, clay and glass, and paper and printing — even though their

R&D intensity was close to that of the low technology group. They were therefore allocated to the latter group. The dummies were then applied to the U.K. industry groups by the correspondence indicated in table A1.2. However, this led to two main anomalies: computers were ranked as medium technology since they are included in machinery, and wheeled tractors in high technology since they are included in motor vehicles. Computers were therefore allocated a high technology dummy, tractors a low technology dummy.

Table A1.2. *Foreign R&D categories and their correspondence with the U.K. industry categories[a]*

	Foreign R&D categories	U.K. industry numbers	High, medium and low technology dummies[b]
1	Electrical machinery	26, 27, 32, 33	H
2	Electronic equipment and components	28, 30, 31	H
3	Chemicals	6, 7, 9, 10, 11, 12, 13	M
4	Drugs	8	H
5	Petroleum refining	4, 5	L
6	Aerospace	36	H
7	Motor vehicles	34, 35	H
8	Ferrous metals	14	L
9	Non-ferrous metals	15	M
10	Fabricated metal products	37	L
11	Instruments	25	H
12	Machinery	16, 17, 18, 19, 20, 21, 22, 23, 24, 29	M
13	Food, drink and tobacco	1, 2, 3	L
14	Textiles, footwear and leather	38, 39, 40	L
15	Rubber and plastic products	46	M
16	Stone, clay, glass	41, 42	L
17	Paper and printing	44, 45	L
18	Wood, cork and furniture	43	L

[a] Derived from a correspondence table provided by the Department of Industry.
[b] Where H = high technology, M = medium technology, L = low technology.

Data and construction of data series for the U.K. sample of forty-six industries

This Appendix describes in more detail the data used in estimating equations for the disaggregated U.K. sample for forty-six industries. The sources and construction of data series are set out. A complete list of data sources is given after the References.

Exports, imports and gross output

Constant price data on exports, imports and gross output, with 1975 as the base year, were purchased from the Department of Industry for internal use in the Department of Economics, Bristol University. This data had been disaggregated to the level of ninety industries according to the Disaggregated Information System (DIS). A correspondence table between the DIS and MLH categories, provided by the Department of Industry, was used to group the data into the industry categories used, as set out in Appendix 1. Some of the DIS categories had to be split up further to match the industry groupings of the current price MLH data to the constant data, to get constant price estimates for industry groups 4, 5, 12, 13 and 35 (as set out in table A1.1). Current price export and import data were obtained from *Business Monitor* M10 1978 and 1974. This does not include MLH 342 — small arms — and so an estimate of this was made for the constant price group that included it, and it was excluded from the sample. The current price data for 1972 do not contain disaggregated information on MLH 279.4, 271.1, 271.2 and 474. These were estimated from U.K. trade statistics, from the *Annual Statement of the Overseas Trade of the U.K.*, using a SITC/SIC correspondence table provided for these groups by the Department of Industry. Current price gross output data were taken from the Census of Production.

U.K. R&D

U.K. R&D data were obtained from the Department of Industry. After excluding ships and marine engines, and other manufacturing, forty-six industry groups remained. As with the export, import and gross output data, MLH 342 was excluded from industry group 24, using value-added data on MLH 342 to estimate its R&D. It was assumed its R&D/value-added ratio was the same as the average for group 24, and an estimate of its R&D thus obtained.

The R&D data were adjusted to include R&D carried out within industrial sectors, financed by public corporations and research associations. This was obtained from *Business Monitor* MO14 1975 and *Studies in Official Statistics No 27,* 1972. A pro rata allocation of this expenditure relative to industries' private R&D was used to disaggregate the data for the following industry groups: 1, 2, 3, 5, 6, 7, 11, 12, 13, 22, 23, 44 and 45. For the category electronic components and apparatus including telecommunications, it was assumed that half should be allocated to telecommunications, group 28, and a quarter each to groups 30 and 31. The same procedures were adopted for both the 1972 and 1975 data.

U.K. value-added data

Value-added data were taken from various Censuses of Production. However, only data for net output existed for 1972. This differs from value-added by the cost of non-industrial services. This was estimated for 1972 by calculating the ratio of non-industrial services to net output in another year, and using this ratio to estimate non-industrial services for 1972. Assuming non-industrial service costs vary less over the cycle than net output does, and since net output in 1973 and 1975 may have been, respectively, high and low, 1974 data were used to estimate this variable for 1972. Thus, the ratio of non-industrial services to net output in 1974 was used to estimate non-industrial services as a proportion of net output in 1972. 1972 value-added could then be estimated.

Foreign R&D and value-added

Foreign R&D data were obtained for 1973 and 1975 from the OECD *International Statistical Years 1973* and *1975,* for the industry groups set out in table A1.2. Value-added data were obtained from the *U.N. Yearbook of Industrial Statistics,* 1973 and 1975. Data on foreign R&D are available disaggregated to nineteen industry groups. However, lack of R&D and/or value-added data for various countries for the ships category means that this observation must be omitted from the analysis. Data on the remaining groups are used to calculate *FR* and FR_5. These variables are disaggregated to the level of the U.K. R&D data by applying the same foreign R&D/value-added ratio to all the industries it includes. For example, the single foreign ratio for mechanical engineering is applied to all the U.K. mechanical engineering groups. This procedure inevitably introduces spurious variation into the analysis. To take a simple example, if there are two U.K. industries with R&D/value-added ratios represented by *a* and *b*, and two foreign industries with ratios α and β, the data available on foreign R&D will be the ratio $(\alpha + \beta)/2 = \delta$. If it is the case that $a > b$ and $\alpha > \beta$, then a measure of the technology gap $(a - \delta)$ will be biased upwards, the measure of the gap $(b - \delta)$ will be biased downwards. Thus, this will affect the slope of the coefficient on the technology gap, unless the two effects cancel out, in which case it will only increase the standard error. Even in this simple example it cannot be predicted whether the slope of the relationship will increase or decrease. When looking at ten groups rather than two, this will be more difficult. This is also true with respect to the technological opportunity variable *FR*. Thus, while the coefficients of FR_5 and *FR* may be biased either way, their standard errors will be definitely greater than if more disaggregated data were available.

The data sets on foreign R&D and foreign value-added were not complete and adjustments had therefore to be made to the data as described in the following paragraphs.

For the foreign categories 1 and 2, and 3 and 4, German R&D and value-added data were not disaggregated, nor were French value-added data. The average of the R&D/value-added ratios for the U.S. and Japan were calculated for each category — a_1 and a_2 — and the average of both categories — a_t. The German average of both categories — a_g — was also calculated. The R&D/value-added ratio for category 1 was estimated from the product $a_1 \div a_t) \times a_g$. The R&D and value-added values could then be calculated. This procedure was repeated for groups 2, 3 and 4, and similarly for the French value-added estimates. For group 18, German gross output data were used to estimate value-added. The average German and U.S. R&D/value-added ratios were then used as above to calculate Japan's R&D and France's value-added, both of which had included other manufacturing in group 18.

Gross output data, obtained from the *U.N. Yearbook of Industrial Statistics*, were used where possible to estimate missing value-added data. The OECD *International Statistical Year* provides a concordance between the International Standard Industrial Classification used by the U.N. and the OECD industry groups. Estimates of German value-added data, using gross output data, were made from groups 10, 11, 12, 17 and 18. Estimates of Japan's value-added for group 13 were derived from gross output. The average value-added ratios for the U.S., Japan and France were used to estimate German value-added for groups 8 and 9, and the ratios for the U.S. and Japan to estimate French and German value-added for group 7. Japan, U.S. and German ratios were used to estimate French value-added for groups 11 and 12.

Aerospace data were based on the U.S. alone. There were no French value-added data and no Japanese R&D data. It was considered that aerospace was one industry, in particular, where the U.S., followed by the U.K., was clearly in advance of the other three countries. The technology gap between U.K. and U.S. R&D was therefore the crucial one. The proportion of aerospace value-added to total transport value-added for the U.S. in 1972 (U.S. Census of Manufactures 1972) was used to estimate the 1973 and 1975 U.S. aerospace value-added from total transport value-added in those years.

In constructing the variables FR and FR_5 the sum of the four countries' R&D relative to the sum of their value-added was calculated. Current U.S. dollar exchange rates were used for Japan, France and Germany, derived from *International Financial Statistics* for 1973 and from the OECD for 1975 (OECD 1979). The following local currency exchange rates per US dollar were used:

	1973	1975	
Japan	269.2	297.8	yen
West Germany	2.597	2.461	marks
France	4.401	4.286	francs

Purchasing power parity rates were calculated but, since the same rates had to be applied to R&D and value-added and as this had little effect on the variables FR and FR_5, the data were not adjusted.

Skilled labour and total employment

The skilled labour data – used by Smith *et al.* (1982) – were obtained from the Department of Industry. They had been derived from the OPCS Census 1971, GB, Economic Activity Part IV, tables 33 and 34. The classification professional and technical workers' includes workers in the health professions, teachers at all levels, engineers, technologists, chemists, physical and biological scientists, accountants, company secretaries, surveyors, architect and town planners. Skilled workers are defined as those in socio-economic groups 8 (skilled manual workers with the status of foreman) and 9 (skilled manual workers). The data did not include food, drink and tobacco, or MLH 261, 262, 263, 396, 433 and 474. These data were constructed from the 1971 Census. MLH 271 was not disaggregated. It was assumed that skilled labour was in the same proportions in 271.1, 271.2 and 271.3. It was a sumed 279.4 had the same proportion of skilled labour in 279 as output. However, once R&D employment was estimated this indicated that the estimate for professional and technical staff in 279.4 was too low, so it was assumed 279.4's proportion of these staff was the same as its proportion of 279's R&D, i.e. 30 per cent.

Data on scientists and engineers employed in R&D were obtained from *Studies in Official Statistics*, No. 27, table 16 for 1972 for thirty-one product groups. These data were disaggregated to the sample level of forty-six industries by assuming R&D employment was proportional to R&D expenditure. These employees were then subtracted from the estimate of technical and professional staff to obtain the skilled labour variable *TP*.

Data on total employment for 1971 and 1975 were obtained from the Census of Production 1971 and 1975.

Concentration ratios

The five-firm sales concentration ratio was derived from the Census of Production 1975. MLHs' individual concentration ratios were aggregated to the sample for forty-six industry groups by weighting the ratios by the share of total sales of each MLH in the total sales of the industry groups and adding.

Investment and capital stock

Investment data were obtained for the period 1971–6 from various Censuses of Production. Since capital stock data were at constant 1975 prices, a price index for the investment data was necessary. This was derived from the *Monthly Digest of Statistics*, No. 393, 1978, and No. 381, 1977. An implicit index of fixed capital expenditure was obtained for eleven industry groups, with 1975 as the base year. The index was spliced with an index with 1970 as the base year to obtain an index that included 1971 and 1972. The 'other manufacturing' index was applied to industry groups 41, 43 and 46.

Gross capital stock data by MLH constructed by R. Allard were made available by the Office of Fair Trading. These were applied to the forty-six industry groups for the period 1971–6. Iron and steel data were not available, so estimates made by Armstrong (1979) were used. These estimates took 1970 as the base year, so iron and steel investment was also calculated at 1970 prices.

Scale economies

The scale economy measure used Hufbauer's estimate of scale elasticities (Hufbauer 1970) multiplied by an estimate of minimum efficient scale (MES). A correspondence table had to be drawn up between the SITC(R) and the

U.K. SIC, since the scale elasticities were given by SITC categories. This is shown in table A2.1.

Table A2.1. *Assumed correspondence between SITC(R), SIC and sample industry groups*[a]

Industry group	Minimum List Heading	Standard International Trade Classification (Revised)
1	211–29	421, 013, 032, 046–8, 053, 055, 061–2, 691
2	232, 239	111, 112
3	240	122
4	262	332
5	263	332
6	271.1	513, 514
7	271.2	512
8	272	561
9	274	533
10	276	531, 581, 231.2
11	278	561
12	279.4	599
13	271, 273, 275, 279 (not 279.4)	332, 521, 532, 551, 553, 571, 599
14	311–13	671–9
15	321–3	682–9
16	331	712, 714, 718, 719
17	332	715
18	333	719
19	334	691, 711
20	335	717
21	336	712, 714, 718, 719
22	337	719
23	341	691, 711
24	338, 339, 349	712, 714, 718, 719
25	351–4	861–4
26	361	722
27	362	723
28	363	724, 726
29	366	714
30	364	729

Table A2.1. *Continued*

Industry group	Minimum List Heading	Standard International Trade Classification (Revised)
31	365, 367	724, 726
32	368	725
33	369	729
34	380	732–3
35	381, 382	732–3
36	383	734
37	390–9	681, 692–8, 897
38	411	266
39	412–19, 421–2, 429	651–7
40	431–3, 441–9, 450	611–13, 831, 841–2, 851
41	461, 464, 469	661–3
42	462–3	664–6, 812
43	471–9	242, 631–3, 812
44	481–4	251, 641–2, 892
45	485–9	251, 641–2, 892
46	491	621, 629

[a]Based on: Correspondence table in Armstrong (1974); 1968 Census of Production; United Nations Statistical Papers Series M no. 38, 'Commodity Series for the Standard International Trade Classification, Revised', New York, 1963.

Where more than one elasticity applied to one industry group the elasticities were summed, weighted by the share of U.K. trade of the relevant SITC category to total trade for that product group. These data were taken from the *Annual Statement of the Overseas Trade of the U.K. 1970*. Where one elasticity applied to more than one industry group the same elasticity was used in each case.

Minimum efficient scale was proxied by the average size of plant in the top 50 per cent of net output divided by total net output. Similar measures have been used in a number of studies (for example, Wolter 1977; Caves 1981). The data were obtained from the Census of Production Industry Reports 1975. The 1–19 employment plant size class was omitted, since these plants are specialised and cannot necessarily be compared with larger plants producing different output. Minimum efficient scale (MES) was calculated as follows. The midpoint class net output was divided by the number of plants in that class to give average plant size. This average was used to estimate the number of plants in that part of the midpoint class in the top 50 per cent of net output. The number of plants in the top 50 per cent of net output could then be calculated. The average plant size in the top 50 per cent of net output was then divided by total net output to give a measure of MES. The individual MLH estimates of MES were then aggregated into the sample industry groups using net output as weights.

Cash flow/profit margin

The cash flow/profit margin variable (*PL*) is measured as value-added minus wages and salaries, divided by value-added. The data are taken from various Censuses of Production. The adjustments to the 1972 value-added data have been discussed above. The 1972 wage data do not include employers' national insurance (NI) contributions. Data on total employers' NI contributions in 1972 were obtained from the *National Income and Expenditure Accounts 1965–1975*. It was assumed that NI contributions were distributed in the same proportions in 1972 as in 1973. These NI estimates were then added to the wages and salaries data for 1972.

Foreign participation

The proportion of sales by foreign-owned firms in total sales was derived from data in the Census of Production 1968. This gave information on foreign participation for 1963 and 1968. The data set was incomplete since data for many MLHs were withheld for confidentiality reasons. Where data existed for 1963 but not for 1968 the same foreign to total sales ratio was used for 1968. Where data existed for part of an industry group or MLH these were used to estimate the remainder of the group. There was incomplete information for twenty-two industry groups, i.e. industry groups 3, 4, 11, 14, 15, 19, 20, 22–4, 26–31, 33–6, 40, 45. MLHs 278 and 383 were reported as having insignificant (i.e. less than 1 per cent) foreign participation. Estimates of 0.25 per cent of sales were applied to these. Tobacco, MLH 240, was estimated by using data for foreign participation in order III from the Census of Production, 1971, 1973, 1975. Foreign participation had grown over this period from 11 to 14 per cent. It was assumed that in 1968 the ratio of foreign-owned sales to total sales for order III was 8 per cent. This gave an estimated ratio for tobacco alone of 19.6 per cent.

Growth of world demand

The growth of world demand was proxied by the change in the weighted sum of the industrial production index, base year 1975, between 1972 and 1978. The index was obtained from the *U.N. Yearbook of Industrial*

Statistics for the following countries: Canada, Italy, Japan, Sweden, the U.K., the U.S. and West Germany. These countries were chosen both because they constitute a major part of the OECD and also because of the quality and existence of the appropriate statistics. The weighted sum of the indices for each industry in each country in 1975 was derived by using gross output for each industry in each country in 1975 as weights. The industry categories used in the International Standard Industrial Classification were applied to the current sample industry groups using the CSO concordance between the national and international SICs. Where one category applied to more than one of the sample industry groups the same growth rate was assumed to apply to each group.

Where there was no industry gross output data available, the share of a country's 1975 GDP in the sum of all countries' GDP was used as a weight. This was done for Italy and Germany for ISIC categories 351, 352, 3522, 353, 354, 383, 3833, 384, 3841 and 3843, and for Italy alone for ISIC categories 361, 362, 369, 382 and 3825.

Where industrial production indices were not sufficiently disaggregated it was assumed they were the same for each constituent ISIC category. Where the categories were too disaggregated they were added using gross output weights. This was necessary for some categories for all countries.

Data and construction of data series for the comparative study of the U.K. and West Germany

The level of aggregation of the comparative study of the U.K. and West Germany was determined by the level of aggregation of the German R&D data. This was at a level of sixteen industries, excluding ships and other manufacturing as in the more disaggregated U.K. study. The German data categories combine electrical machinery with electronic equipment and components, and chemicals with drugs; there are hence sixteen industries rather than the eighteen industries used to calculate *FR* (Appendixes 1 and 2).

Table A3.1 sets out the assumed correspondence between the OECD industry groups, the International Standard Industrial Classification (ISIC), the Standard International Trade Classification (R2) and the German Industrial Classification SYPRO.

West German Data

Exports

Data on West German exports 1978 in U.S. dollars were obtained from the OECD *Trade by Commodities, Series C 1978* and aggregated to the level of the OECD R&D categories using the correspondence set out in table A3.1. The exchange rate of the pound for the dollar in 1978 was taken as 1.919 pounds sterling equal to one U.S. dollar (*International Financial Statistics 1978*).

R&D and value-added

R&D data were obtained from the OECD *International Statistical Year 1975*, and value-added data from the *U.N. Yearbook of Industrial Statistics 1975* and the *Statistisches Jahrbuch* 1975–8. The 1975 exchange rates used were

Table A3.1. *Assumed correspondence between the OECD R&D categories, ISIC, SITC (R2) and SYPRO*

OECD R&D categories	ISIC	SITC(R2)	SYPRO
1 Electrical machinery, electronic equipment and components	383	77, 761–2, 764	36
2 Chemicals and drugs	351, 352	53–9, 882	24, 40
3 Petroleum refining	353, 354	32, 33	22
4 Aerospace	3845	792	35
5 Motor vehicles	3843	781–4	33
6 Ferrous metals	371	67	27, 29, 3011
7 Non-ferrous metals	372	68	282
8 Fabricated metal products	381	69, 81	{ 3015, 3021, 3025, 3030, 31, 38
9 Instruments	385	87, 881, 885	37
10 Machinery	382	71–75	32, 50
11 Food, drink and tobacco	31	01–09, 11, 12, 21–2, 29, 41–3	68, 69
12 Textiles, footwear and leather	32	26, 65	61–64
13 Rubber and plastic products	355, 356	23, 62, 893	58, 59
14 Stone, clay, glass	36	66 (not 667), 273, 277–8	25, 51, 52
15 Paper and printing	341, 342	25, 64, 892	55–7
16 Wood, cork and furniture	33	24, 63, 82	53, 54

Sources: OECD *International Statistical Year 1975*; OECD *Concordance between SITC (R1) and ISIC Classifications 1979*: U.N. Standard International Trade Classification, Revision 2; *Schwerpunktmässige Zuordnung von SYPRO-Nummern Zu ISIC-Position, 1982*

2.461 marks to the U.S. dollar, and 5.4663 marks to one pound sterling (OECD 1979).

Investment, wages and salaries, gross output

Data on investment for 1974 and 1975, wages and salaries for 1972 to 1974, and gross output for 1978 were taken from the *U.N. Yearbook of Industrial Statistics* (various issues). The 1975 and 1978 exchange rates used were the same as for exports and R&D. Where ratios were used no exchange rate conversion was necessary. The rate of growth of gross output for 1968 to

1974 was proxied by the change in the industrial production index, also taken from the *U.N. Yearbook of Industrial Statistics*. The indices were aggregated using gross output as weights.

Capital stock

Capital stock data for 1974 and 1975 were obtained from estimates of the value of fixed assets in German manufacturing industry for 1978, in the *Monthly Report of the Deutsche Bundesbank 1981*, vol. 33, no. 11, pp. 24–5. The values were deflated using an implicit price deflator index of GDP for manufacturing industries with 1975 as the base year, obtained from the *U.N. Yearbook of National Account Statistics 1979*, vol. 2, table 108. The implicit price deflator was used to express 1974 investment in 1975 prices. Where no data for fixed assets were given, estimates were made using the average investment/capital ratio for 1974 and 1975 of a similar industry group. Group 4 was estimated using the group 5 investment capital ratio, and group 9 using an average of groups 1 and 10. Tobacco and leather were estimated using food and drink, and textiles and clothing ratios respectively. Groups 3, 13 and 15 were estimated using the average investment/capital stock ratios of those industries for which data initially existed.

Concentration ratio

Data for the six-firm sales concentration ratio, 1970, were obtained from the *Bericht des Bundeskartellamtes über seine Tätigkeit in Jahre 1973*. The concentration ratios were aggregated from the SYPRO classification to the OECD classification using 1970 sales, obtained from the *Statistisches Jahrbuch 1973*. Where ratios did not exist, the ratio from the most recent preceding year was used. For SYPRO groups 24, 50, 3015, 3021 and 3030 no data existed. The concentration ratios of groups 40 and 32 were applied to 24 and 50 respectively, and an average of 3011 and 3025 to 3015, 3021 and 3030.

Sales by foreign-owned companies

Data on sales by foreign-owned companies were obtained from the *Monthly Report of the Deutsche Bundesbank 1981*, vol. 33, no. 10, p. 50. The data was for 1978. Data on sales for 1978 were obtained from the *Statistiches Jahrbuch 1981*. Estimates were made for industry groups 4 and 7 using the foreign sales ratios of groups 5 and 6 respectively. Similarly, food and drink ratios were used to estimate tobacco. Groups 15 and 16 were estimated using the average ratios for all industry groups.

U.K. data

The U.K. data were obtained by aggregating the data used for the more disaggregated sample, using the correspondence given in table A1.2. The concentration ratio and minimum efficient scale were aggregated using output and net output weights respectively. The scale elasticity was aggregated using trade weights derived from the *Annual Statement of the Overseas Trade of the U.K. 1970*. In calculating the relative U.K./German variables FGK and PGK no deflators were used, since the data on deflators did not vary across industries. Any difference could therefore affect the constant only.

Inconsistency of the OLS estimators

This Appendix analyses the inconsistency of the OLS estimators in the simultaneous system estimated in this work.

If OLS is used to estimate an equation from a simultaneous system, the parameter estimates will be biased and inconsistent. In general, two-stage least squares or instrumental variables estimates are also biased but they are consistent (see, for example, Intriligator 1978). The hypothesis of no simultaneity can be tested with a Hausman test (Hausman 1978) as explained in Annexe 7.2. If there is simultaneity present, it is helpful to show that the OLS estimator is an inconsistent estimator and to consider whether it will over- or under-estimate the true parameter value. This would be useful in interpreting the empirical literature.

The simultaneous model presented in section 7.1 can be re-expressed as follows:

$$y_1 = y_2\gamma_1 + X_1\beta_1 + \epsilon_1 \tag{A4.1}$$

$$y_2 = y_1\gamma_2 + X_2\beta_2 + \epsilon_2 \tag{A4.2}$$

where X_1, X_2 are matrices of exogenous variables and y_1 and y_2 are the endogenous variables. In this model, it is expected that $\gamma_1 > 0$ and $\gamma_2 > 0$.

Following Intriligator (1978, section 11.3), the matrix Z is defined to include all the data on explanatory variables from equation (A4.2), whether endogenous or exogenous:

$$Z = \left(y_1 \mid X_2 \right) \tag{A4.3}$$

and δ is a vector that summarises all the coefficients to be estimated in the equation:

$$\delta = \left(\frac{\gamma_2}{\beta_2} \right) \tag{A4.4}$$

The OLS estimator is then:

$$\hat{\delta}_{OLS} = (Z'A)^{-1}Z'y. \tag{A4.5}$$

$Z'Z$ has the form:

$$\begin{pmatrix} y_1'y_1 & \vdots & y_1'X_2 \\ \hline X_2y_1 & \vdots & X_2'X_2 \end{pmatrix} \tag{A4.6}$$

Substituting $Z\delta + \epsilon_2$ for y_2 in (A4.5) and taking expectations gives:

$$E(\hat{\delta}) = \delta + E((Z'Z)^{-1}Z'\epsilon_2) \tag{A4.7}$$

Z includes y_1 which is not independent of the stochastic disturbance terms. ϵ_2; thus the OLS estimators are biased. In the probability limit they are inconsistent:

$$\text{plim}\,(\hat{\delta}) = \delta + \text{plim}\left(\frac{1}{n}Z'Z\right)^{-1}\left(\frac{1}{n}Z'\epsilon_2\right) \tag{A4.8}$$

To consider whether $\hat{\gamma}_2$ is an under- or over-estimate of γ_2, it is necessary to find the product of the first row of $(Z'Z)^{-1}$ and $Z'\epsilon_2$. However, $(2 \ldots n)$ elements of $Z'\epsilon_2$ are zero; thus plim $Z'\epsilon_2$ is equivalent to plim $y_1\epsilon_2$. Substituting (A4.2) into (A4.1):

$$y_1 = \frac{1}{(1 - \gamma_1\gamma_2)} (\gamma_1(X_2\beta_2 + \epsilon_2) + X_1\beta_1 + \epsilon_1) \tag{A4.9}$$

Assuming X_1, X_2 are uncorrelated with the errors, plim $y_1\epsilon_2$ can be calculated:

$$\text{plim}\,y_1\epsilon_2 = \frac{1}{(1 - \gamma_1\gamma_2)} (\gamma_1\sigma_{\epsilon_2}^2 + \sigma_{\epsilon_2\epsilon_1}) \tag{A4.10}$$

$(Z'Z)^{-1}$ can be re-expressed using the formula for partitioned matrices (Johnston 1978, p. 93):

$$\begin{aligned} (Z'Z)^{-1} &= (y_1'y_1 - y_1'X_2(X_2'X_2)^{-1}X_2'y_1)^{-1} \\ &= (y_1'(y_1 - X_2(X_2'X_2)^{-1})X_2'y_1)^{-1} \\ &= (y_1'\,M\,y_1)^{-1} \end{aligned} \tag{A4.11}$$

where:

$$M = (I - X_2(X_2'X_2)^{-1}X_2') \tag{A4.12}$$

$(y_1'\,M\,y_1)^{-1}$ is positive since M is positive definite and idempotent. If the reduced form estimate of y_1 is expressed as:

$$y_1 = X_2\pi_2 + \eta \tag{A4.13}$$

then

$$\hat{\pi}_2 = (X_2'X_2)^{-1}X_2'y_1 \tag{A4.14}$$

and

$$\hat{\eta} = y_1 - X_2(X_2'X_2)^{-1}X_2'y_1 \tag{A4.15}$$

(A4.11) can then be expressed as:

$$
\begin{aligned}
(y_1'My_1)^{-1} &= ((X_2\pi_2 + \eta)'M(X_2\pi_2 + \eta))^{-1} \\
&= (\eta'M\eta)^{-1} \\
&= (\Sigma\hat{\eta}^2)^{-1} \tag{A4.16}
\end{aligned}
$$

Substituting (A4.10) and (A4.16) into the expression for the plim (A4.8) gives:

$$\text{plim}(\hat{\delta}) = \delta + \frac{1}{(1-\gamma_1\gamma_2)} \frac{(\gamma_1\sigma_{\epsilon_2}^2 + \sigma_{\epsilon_2\epsilon_1}^2)}{\sigma_\eta^2} \tag{A4.17}$$

This is, in effect, the plim of $\hat{\gamma}_2$, since $(2\ldots n)$ elements of $Z'\epsilon_2$, from equation (A4.8), are zero. Whether this is an under- or over-estimate depends on $\sigma_{\epsilon_2\epsilon_1}$ and $\gamma_1\gamma_2$. The expected sign of $\sigma_{\epsilon_2\epsilon_1}$ is unknown. It would have to be negative and greater than $\gamma_1\sigma_{\epsilon_2}^2$ to result in an under-estimate. If $\gamma_1\gamma_2 > 1$, there will be an under-estimate. Both γ_1 and γ_2 are expected to be positive but there is no expectation as to whether either will be greater than 1. If only one of the two is greater than 1 there may still be an over-estimate. Hence, if the effects of γ_1 and γ_2 are not so strong as to make $\gamma_1\gamma_2 > 1$ the bias will be positive if the rest of the expression is positive. The expected direction of bias on γ_1 and γ_2 will be the same, equations (A4.1) and (A4.2) are symmetrical.

Notes

2. Technological competitiveness and export performance in the U.S., Japan, West Germany, U.K. and France

1. Recent estimates suggest R&D represents 40% of the total innovation cost (Kamin *et al.* 1982). This will vary by industry and over time.

3. Neo-factor endowment and neo-technology theories of trade

1. Leamer and Bowen (1981) criticise the methodology of studies such as Baldwin's (1971) and Harkness' (1978), since a legitimate test of the Heckscher–Ohlin theorem requires independent measures of trade, factor intensities and factor abundance. Thus, 'an analysis such as Harkness' which uses measures of only two of these concepts can be used to infer the third concept, but cannot be said to be a test of the model.'

5. Research and development spending – theories and evidence

1. This focus on R&D reflects, in part, the rise in professional R&D since the 1940s, owing to increasing technological complexity of research, increased scale and increased specialisation of scientific work (Freeman 1974).

6. A model of the determinants of R&D intensity

1. If $Q = X + D$, where $X =$ exports and $D =$ domestic demand, then

$$\eta_R = \left(\frac{\mathrm{d}X}{\mathrm{d}R} + \frac{\mathrm{d}D}{\mathrm{d}R} \right) \frac{R}{X + D},$$

which can be re-expressed as

$$\eta_R = \eta_{XR} \frac{X}{Q} + \eta_{DR} \frac{D}{Q}$$

Thus the relative shares of exports and domestic demand act as weights on the two elasticities.

7. Estimation of the composition of U.K. manufactured exports, 1978

1. Chapter 8 reports the results of the R&D equation.
2. This may be preferable to a linear form since, at different levels of the independent variables, absolute changes may have different effects while proportionate changes may be similar. In particular, this might be true of the R&D variable; the same absolute increase in R&D intensity may have more effect on exports at lower R&D levels, than where large amounts of R&D are already being applied.
3. Appendix 1 gives details of the industry classification. Appendix 2 gives further details on data and data construction.
4. The U.S. is the largest R&D spending country, and this measure of R&D will give more weight to the U.S., which may be justified if the U.S. is, on average, more technologically advanced than the other three countries are.
5. This is the scale elasticity coefficient from a logarithmic regression of the value-added per employee for a given size class of plants on the average number employed per establishment in the given size class.
6. FL is included as the effect of multinationals on exports is tested below.
7. Regressing the squared residuals from equation (1): (i) on the independent variables from the equation, NR^2 is 11.868 where χ^2_8 is 15.507 at the 5% significance level, and (ii) on all the independent variables in the model, NR^2 is 15.210 where χ^2_{11} is 19.675. Regressing the squared residuals on estimated X_8, NR^2 is again insignificant, suggesting that the logarithmic transformation is acceptable.
8. OLS $X_8 = 3.369^* + 0.255^*R_s + 0.548^*\hat{R}_s - 0.329^*FR_s + 0.901^*HS$
   (3.189)   (2.258)   (2.887)   (−2.589)   (3.647)

   $- 0.468^*C_s - 14.564SM$
   (−2.279)   (−1.497)

   This is a stronger rejection than that for the full specification of the export equation and underlines the fact that estimation by OLS will result in biased estimates.
9. Regressing the squared residuals from equation (4) on all the independent variables from equation (1), NR^2 is 16.790, χ^2_{11} is 19.675.
10. The following result was obtained for the Hausman test:

    OLS $X_8 = 3.317^* + 0.248^*R_s + 0.445^*\hat{R}_s - 0.229^*FR + 0.796^*HS - 0.518^*C_s$
    (3.094)   (2.169)   (2.478)   (−2.087)   (3.309)   (−2.513)

    With respect to homoscedasticity, regressing the squared residuals on 11 independent variables, NR^2 is 15.934, χ^2_{11} is 19.675.
11. A dummy variable was similarly constructed for food, drink and tobacco. This also failed to reject the hypothesis that food, drink and tobacco are similar in behaviour to the other observations.

8. Estimation of the R&D intensity of U.K. manufacturing industry, 1975

1. If equation (1) is re-estimated using exports from an earlier year, 1972, the results are similar. The coefficient on exports 1972 is smaller but still positive and significant. The use of exports from 1978 in estimating the simultaneous system is not, therefore, resulting in the measurement of a spurious relationship that disappears when lagged exports are used.

2. One solution to this problem is to do a cross-country study. Results for a comparative study of the U.K. and West Germany are given in Chapter 10.
3. Equation (1) was re-estimated with *GL* calculated for 1971–4, and for 1972–4. Its significance fell.
4. Given the uneven nature of investment expenditure, this variable was re-calculated for an average of four years (1972 to 1975) and equation (1) re-estimated. The variable was still negative, slightly less significant and with a smaller coefficient.
5. Regressing the squared residuals from equation (1) on all the independent variables in the system, NR^2 is 16.488 where χ^2_{11} is 19.675.

9. U.K. trade performance 1972–8

1. The three clear outliers in the import equation are food, lubricating oils and greases, and fertilisers. The square root of the ratio of the mean square error of the rest of the observations to the mean square error of these three observations is used as the weight for these observations. Its value is 0.3898.
2. For equation (7), table 9.7, there is one, fertilisers, which is weighted by the square root of the ratio of the mean square error of the other observations to its mean square error, giving a weight of 0.3739.

10. Export performance and R&D effort of the U.K. and West Germany – a comparative study

1. Tests of the hypothesis of homoscedasticity fail to reject the hypothesis for the equations presented in this chapter. This is, however, a quite weak result and highlights some of the weaknesses of the test used. The test regresses the squared residuals on any set of independent variables. NR^2 is compared with χ^2_{r-1} where N is the number of observations, and r, the regressors. Thus, at the extreme, even if R^2 is one, if sufficient variables are included – ten or more – χ^2 will be greater than sixteen and fail to reject the hypothesis.
2. All variables are measured in logarithms.

References

Acquino, A. (1978), 'Intra-industry Trade and Inter-industry Specialization as Concurrent Sources of International Trade in Manufactures', *Weltwirtschaftliches Archiv*, Band 114, pp. 175–95.

Acquino, A. (1981), 'Changes Over Time in the Pattern of Comparative Advantage in Manufactured Goods', *European Economic Review*, vol. 15, pp. 41–62.

Adams, W.J. (1970), 'Firm Size and Research Activity: France and the United States', *Quarterly Journal of Economics*, vol. 84, pp. 386–409.

Advisory Council for Applied Research and Development (1978), *Industrial Innovation*, London, HMSO.

ACARD (Advisory Council for Applied Research and Development)(1980), *R&D for Public Purchasing*, London, HMSO.

Ahlström, G. (1982), *Engineers and Industrial Growth*, London, Croom Helm.

Aho, C.M. and Rosen, H.F. (1980), 'Trends in Technology-Intensive Trade with Special Reference to U.S. Competitiveness', OECD, Science and Technology Indicators Conference, Paris, mimeo.

Allen, G.C. (1981), 'Industrial Policy and Innovation in Japan', in Carter, C. (ed.) *Industrial Policy and Innovation*, Joint Studies in Public Policy, no. 3, London, Heinemann.

Arrow, K. (1962), 'Economic Welfare and the Allocation of Resources for Invention', in Nelson, R.R. (ed.), *The Rate and Direction of Inventive Activity*, Princeton University Press.

Balassa, B. (1979), 'The Changing Pattern of Comparative Advantage in Manufactured Goods', *Review of Economics and Statistics*, vol. 61, no. 2, pp. 259–66.

Baldwin, R.E. (1971), 'Determinants of the Commodity Structure of U.S. Trade', *American Economic Review*, vol. 61, no. 1, pp. 126–46.

Baldwin, R.E. (1972), 'Determinants of the Commodity Structure of U.S. Trade: Reply', *American Economic Review*, vol. 62, p. 465.

Baldwin, R.E. (1979), 'Determinants of Trade and Foreign Investment: Further Evidence', *Review of Economics and Statistics*, vol. 61, no. 1, pp. 40–8.

192

Barker, T.S. (1977), 'International Trade and Economic Growth: an Alternative to the Neo-classical Approach', *Cambridge Journal of Economics*, vol. 1, no. 2, pp. 151–72.

Blackaby, F. (ed.)(1978), *De-industrialisation*, London, Heinemann Educational Books.

Blaug, M. (1963), 'A Survey of the Theory of Process Innovation', *Economica*, vol. 30, no. 117, pp. 13–32.

Bosworth, D.L. (1978), 'The Rate of Obsolescence of Technical Knowledge – A Note', *Journal of Industrial Economics*, vol. 26, no. 3, pp. 273–9.

Bosworth, D.L. (1981), 'The Demand for Qualified Scientists and Engineers', *Applied Economics*, vol. 13, no. 4, pp. 411–29.

Bound, J., Cummins, C., Griliches, Z., Hall, B., and Jaffee, A. (1982), 'Who does R&D and Who Patents?', Harvard Discussion Paper no. 913, July.

Buxton, A.J. (1975), 'The Process of Technical Change in UK Manufacturing', *Applied Economics*, vol. 7, pp. 53–71.

Cable, J. (1972), 'Market Structure, Advertising Policy and Intermarket Differences in Advertising Intensity' in Cowling, K. (ed.), *Market Structure and Corporate Behaviour*, London and Basingstoke, The Macmillan Press Ltd.

Cable, V. and Rebelo, I. (1980), 'Britain's Pattern of Specialisation in Manufactured Goods with Developing Countries and Trade Protection', World Bank Staff Working Paper no. 425, October.

Caves, R.E. (1981), 'Intra-Industry Trade and Market Structure in the Industrial Countries', *Oxford Economic Papers*, vol. 33, no. 2, pp. 203–23.

Caves, R.E. and Khalilzadeh-Shirazi, J. (1977), 'International Trade and Industrial Organisation: some Statistical Evidence', in Jacquemin, A.P. and de Jong, H.W. (eds.), *Welfare Aspects of Industrial Markets*, Leiden, Martinus Nijhoff Social Sciences Division.

Caves, R.E. and Porter, M.E. (1978), 'Market Structure, Oligopoly and Stability of Market Shares', *Journal of Industrial Economics*, vol. 26, June, pp. 289–313.

Caves, R.E., Porter, M.E. and Spence, A.M. with Scott, J.T. (1980), *Competition in the Open Economy*, Cambridge, Massachusetts, Harvard University Press.

Comanor, W.S. (1967), 'Market Structure, Product Differentiation and Industrial Research', *Quarterly Journal of Economics*, vol. 81, no. 4, pp. 639–57.

Cowling, K. (1972), 'Optimality in Firms' Advertising Policies: an Empirical Analysis' in Cowling, K. (ed.), *Market Structure and Corporate Behaviour*, London and Basingstoke, The Macmillan Press Ltd.

Cowling, K., Cable, J., Kelly, M. and McGuinness, T. (1975), *Advertising and Economic Behaviour*, London and Basingstoke, The Macmillan Press Ltd.

Cowling, K. and Cubbin, J. (1971), 'Price, Quality and Advertising Competition: An Econometric Investigation of the United Kingdom Car Market', *Economica*, vol. 38, no. 152, pp. 378–94.

Cowling, K. and Waterson, M. (1976), 'Price–Cost Margins and Market Structure', *Economica*, vol. 43, pp. 267–74.

Cowling, K., Stoneman, P., Cubbin, J., Cable, J., Hall, G., Domberger, S. and Dutton, P. (1980), *Mergers and Economic Performance*, Cambridge, Cambridge University Press.

Daly, A. (1981), 'Industrial Policies and Innovation: The Machine Tool Industry', NIESR Discussion Paper no. 39.

Das, S.P. (1982), 'Economies of Scale, Imperfect Competition and the Pattern of Trade', *Economic Journal*, vol. 92, no. 367, pp. 684–93.

Davidson, W.H. (1979), 'Factor Endowment, Innovation and International Trade Theory', *Kyklos*, vol. 32, no. 4, pp. 764–74.

Davies, S. (1979), *The Diffusion of Process Innovations*, Cambridge, Cambridge University Press.

Dehez, P. and Jacquemin, A. (1975), 'A Note on Advertising Policy Under Uncertainty and Dynamic Conditions', *Journal of Industrial Economics*, vol. 24, no. 1, pp. 73–8.

Demsetz, H. (1969), 'Information and Efficiency: Another Viewpoint', *Journal of Law and Economics*, vol. 12, pp. 1–22.

Dixit, A. and Norman, V. (1980), *Theory of International Trade*, Welwyn Garden City, Cambridge University Press/Nisbet.

Dorfman, R. and Steiner, P.O. (1954), 'Optimal Advertising and Optimal Quality', *American Economic Review*, vol. 44, no. 5, pp. 826–36.

Dosi, G. and Soete, L. (1983), 'Technology Gaps and Cost-Based Adjustment: Some Explorations on the Determinants of International Competitiveness', *Metroeconomica*, vol. 35, no. 3.

Drèze, J. (1960), 'Quelques Reflections Sereines sur l'Adaptation de l'Industrie Belge au Marche Common', *Comptes Rendus des Travaux de la Société Royale d'Economic Politique de Belgique*, no. 275.

Dunning, J.H. (1979), 'The U.K.'s International Direct Investment Position in the mid-1970s', *Lloyds Bank Review*, no. 132, April, pp. 1–22.

Eads, G.C. (1980), 'Regulation and Technical Change: Some Largely Unexplored Influences', *American Economic Review*, papers and proceedings, vol. 70, no. 2, pp. 50–4.

Ethier, W.J. (1979), 'Internationally Decreasing Costs and World Trade', *Journal of International Economics*, vol. 9, pp. 1–24.

Farber, S. (1981), 'Buyer Market Structure and R&D Effort: A Simultaneous Equations Model', *Review of Economics and Statistics*, vol. 63, no. 3, pp. 336–45.

Finger, J.M. (1975), 'A New View of the Product Cycle Theory', *Weltwirtschaftliches Archiv*, Band 3, vol. 1, pp. 79–99.

Fisher, F.M. and Temin, P. (1973), 'Returns to Scale in Research and Development: What Does the Schumpeterian Hypothesis Imply?', *Journal of Political Economy*, vol. 81, Jan./Feb., pp. 56–70.

Freeman, C. (1971), 'The Role of Small Firms in Innovation in the United Kingdom since 1945', Committee of Inquiry on Small Firms, Research Report no. 6, London.

Freeman, C. (1974), *The Economics of Industrial Innovation*, Penguin Books Ltd., Harmondsworth, Middlesex.

Freeman, C. (1978), 'Technical Innovation and British Trade Performance', in Blackaby, F. (ed.), *De-industrialisation*, NIESR, London, Heinemann Educational Books Ltd.

Globerman, S. (1972), 'The Empirical Relationships Between R&D and Industrial Growth in Canada', *Applied Economics*, vol. 4, pp. 181–95.

Globerman, S. (1973), 'Market Structure and R&D in Canadian Manufacturing Industries', *Quarterly Review of Economics and Business*, vol. 13, pp. 59–67.

Goodman, B. and Ceyhun, F. (1976), 'US Export Performance in Manu-facturing Industries: An Empirical Investigation', *Weltwirtschafliches Archiv*, Band 112, pp. 525–55.

Grabowski, H.G. (1968), 'The Determinants of Industrial Research and Development: A Study of the Chemical, Drugs and Petroleum Industries', *Journal of Political Economy*, vol. 76, Jan. Feb., pp. 292–306.

Grabowski, H.G. and Baxter, N.D. (1973), 'Rivalry in Industrial Research and Development: An Empirical Study', *Journal of Industrial Economics*, vol. 21, no. 3, pp. 209–35.

Griliches, Z. (1958), 'Research Costs and Social Returns: Hybrid Corn and Related Innovations', *Journal of Political Economy*, October, pp. 419–31.

Griliches, Z. (1979), 'Issues in Assessing the Contribution of Research and Development to Productivity Growth', *Bell Journal of Economics*, vol. 10, no. 1, pp. 92–116.

Griliches, Z. (1980), 'R&D and the Productivity Slowdown', *American Economic Review*, vol. 70, no. 2, pp. 343–8.

Grubel, H.G. and Lloyd, P.J. (1975), *Intra-Industry Trade*, London and Basingstoke, The Macmillan Press Ltd.

Gruber, W.H., Mehta, D. and Vernon, R. (1967), 'International Trade and International Investment of United States Industries', *Journal of Political Economy*, vol. 75, no. 1, pp. 20–37.

Gruber, W.H. and Vernon, R. (1970), 'The Technology Factor in a World Trade Matrix', in Vernon, R. (ed.), *The Technology Factor in International Trade*, New York, NBER.

Gustafson, W.E. (1962), *R&D: Essays on the Economics of Research and Development*, New York, Random House.

Hamberg, D. (1966), *R&D: Essays on the Economics of Research and De-velopment*, New York, Random House.

Hansen, K.M., Moller, K. and Strandskov, J. (1983), 'On the Relationship between R&D and International Competitiveness in the case of Denmark 1970–1980', Directorate for Science, Technology and Industry, OECD, mimeo.

Harkness, J. (1978), 'Factor Abundance and Comparative Advantage', *American Economic Review*, vol. 68, no. 5, pp. 784–800.

Harvey, A.C. (1981), *The Econometric Analysis of Time Series*, Oxford, P. Allen.

Hatzichronoglou, T. (1980), 'Les Échanges Internationaux des Produits de Haute Intensité de Recherche-developpement', OECD, Directorate of Science, Technology and Industry, Science and Technology Indicators Conference, 15–19 September, Paris, mimeo.

Hausman, J.A. (1978), 'Specification Tests in Econometrics', *Econometrica*, vol. 46, no. 6, pp. 1251–71.

Heller, P.S. (1976), 'Factor Endowment Change and Comparative Advantage: The Case of Japan, 1956–1969', *Review of Economics and Statistics*, vol. 58, no. 3, pp. 283–92.

Hirsch, S. (1965), 'The United States Electronics Industry in International Trade', *National Institute Economic Review*, November.

Hirsch, S. (1974), 'Capital or Technology? Confronting the Neo-Factor Proportions and Neo-Technology Accounts of International Trade', *Weltwirtschaftliches Archiv*, Band 110, pp. 535–63.

Hirschey, R.C. and Caves, R.E. (1981), 'Research and Transfer of Technology by Multinational Enterprise', *Oxford Bulletin of Economics and Statistics*, vol. 43, no. 2, pp. 115–30.

Hood, N. and Young, S. (1979), *The Economics of Multinational Enterprise*, London and New York, Longman Inc.

Horn, E.J. (1977), 'International Trade and Technological Innovation: the German Position vis-à-vis other Developed Market Economies', in Stroetmann, K. (ed.), *Innovation, Economic Change and Technology Policies*, Basel and Stuttgart, Birkhauser Verlag.

Horowitz, I. (1970), 'A Note on Advertising and Uncertainty', *Journal of Industrial Economics*, vol. 19, no. 2, pp. 151–60.

Horwitz, P. (1979), 'Direct Government Funding of Research and Development: Intended and Unintended Effects on Industrial Innovation', in Hill, C.T. and Utterback, J.M. (eds.), *Technological Innovation for a Dynamic Economy*, New York, Pergamon Press.

Hufbauer, G.C. (1966), *Synthetic Materials and the Theory of International Trade*, London, Gerald Duckworth and Co. Ltd.

Hufbauer, G.C. (1970), 'The Impact of National Characteristics and Technology on the Commodity Composition of Trade in Manufactured Goods', in Vernon, R. (ed.), *The Technology Factor in International Trade*, New York, NBER.

Intriligator, M.D. (1978), *Econometric Models, Techniques and Applications*, Amsterdam, North-Holland Publishing Co.

Japanese Journal of Trade and Industry (1983), no. 1.

Jewkes, J., Sawers, D. and Stillerman, R. (1960), *The Sources of Invention*, London, Macmillan & Co. Ltd.

Johnson, H.G. (1970), 'The State of Theory in Relation to the Empirical Analysis', in Vernon, R. (ed.), *The Technology Factor in International Trade*, New York, NBER.

Johnson, H.G. (1975), *Technology and Economic Interdependence*, London and Basingstoke, The Macmillan Press Ltd.

Johnston, J. (1978), *Econometric Methods*, New York, McGraw-Hill.

Kaldor, M. (1980), 'Technical Change in the Defence Industry', in Pavitt, K. (ed.), *Technical Innovation and British Economic Performance*, London and Basingstoke, The Macmillan Press Ltd.

Kaldor, N. (1957), 'A Model of Economic Growth', *Economic Journal*, vol. 67, Dec., pp. 591–624.

Kaldor, N. (1961), 'Capital Accumulation and Economic Growth', in Lutz, F.A. and Hague, D.C. (eds.), *The Theory of Capital*, St. Martin's Press.

Kamien, M.I. and Schwartz, N.L. (1975), 'Market Structure and Innovation – a Survey', *Journal of Economic Literature*, vol. 13, pp. 1–37.

Kamien, M.I. and Schwartz, N.L. (1976), 'On the Degree of Rivalry for Maximum Innovative Activity', *Quarterly Journal of Economics*, vol. 90, pp. 245–60.

Kamien, M.I. and Schwartz, N.L. (1982), *Market Structure and Innovation*, Cambridge, Cambridge University Press.

Kamin, J.Y., Bijaoui, I. and Horesh, R. (1982), 'Some Determinants of Cost Distribution in the Process of Technological Innovation', *Research Policy*, vol. 2.

Katrak, H. (1973), 'Human Skills, R&D and Scale Economies in the Exports of the United Kingdom and the United States', *Oxford Economic Papers*, vol. 25, no. 3, pp. 337–60.

Katrak, H. (1982), 'Labour Skills, R&D and Capital Requirements in the International Trade and Investment of the United Kingdom 1968–1978', *National Institute Economic Review*, no. 101, August, pp. 38–47.

Keesing, D.B. (1965), 'Labour Skills and International Trade: Evaluating Many Trade Flows with a Single Measuring Device', *Review of Economics and Statistics*, vol. 47, no. 3, pp. 287–94.

Keesing, D.B. (1967), 'The Impact of Research and Development on United States Trade', *Journal of Political Economy*, vol. 75, no. 1, pp. 38–48.

Keesing, D.B. (1971), 'Different Countries' Labour Skill Coefficients and the Skill Intensity of International Trade Flows', *Journal of International Economics*, vol. 1, no. 4, pp. 443–52.

Kelly, T.M. (1970), 'The Influences of Firm Size and Market Structure on the Research Efforts of Large Multiple-Product Firms', Ph.D. Dissertation, Oklahoma State University.

Kennedy, C. and Thirlwall, A.P. (1972), 'Surveys in Applied Economics: Technical Progress', *Economic Journal*, vol. 82, March, pp. 11–72.

Krugman, P.R. (1979a), 'A Model of Innovation, Technology Transfer and the World Distribution of Income', *Journal of Political Economy*, vol. 87, no. 2, pp. 253–66.

Krugman, P.R. (1979b), 'Increasing Returns, Monopolistic Competition and International Trade', *Journal of International Economics*, vol. 9, pp. 469–79.

Krugman, P.R. (1980), 'Scale Economies, Product Differentiation and the Pattern of Trade', *American Economic Review*, vol. 70, no. 5, pp. 950–9.

Krugman, P.R. (1981), 'Intra-industry Specialization and the Gains from Trade', *Journal of Political Economy*, vol. 89, no. 5, pp. 959–73.

Lary, H.B. (1968), *Imports of Manufactures from the Less Developed Countries*, New York, NBER.

Leamer, E.E. (1980), 'The Leontief Paradox, Reconsidered', *Journal of Political Economy*, vol. 88, no. 3, pp. 495–503.

Leamer, E.E. and Bowen, H.P. (1981), 'Cross-Section Tests of the Heckscher–Ohlin Theorem: Comment', *American Economic Review*, vol. 71, no. 5, pp. 1040–3.

Leech, D. and Stoneman, P. (1976), 'An Application of Random Coefficient Regression: The Case of R&D Expenditure and Market Structure', Warwick Economic Research Papers no. 91, July.

Leffler, K. (1981), 'Industry Equilibrium in New Product Research and Development: A Simple Approach', *Economic Inquiry*, vol. 19, no. 1, pp. 60–76.

Leontief, W.W. (1953), 'Domestic Production and Foreign Trade: The American Capital Position Re-examined', *Proceedings of the American Philosophical Society*, Sept.

Leontief, W.W. (1956), 'Factor Proportions and the Structure of American Trade: Further Theoretical and Empirical Analysis', *Review of Economics and Statistics*, vol. 38, Nov., pp. 392–7.

Linder, S.B. (1961), *An Essay on Trade and Transformation*, New York, Wiley.

Little, B. (1979), 'New Technology and the Role of Marketing', in Baker, M.

(ed.), *Industrial Innovation, Technology Policy and Diffusion*, London and Basingstoke, Macmillan.

Lyons, B.R. (1983), 'International Trade in Manufactured Products: UK Manufacturing's Trade with the World and the EEC', University of Cambridge, mimeo.

Maddala, G.S. (1977), *Econometrics*, Tokyo, McGraw-Hill Kogakusha Ltd.

Majumdar, B.A. (1979), 'Innovations and International Trade: An Industry Study of Dynamic Competitive Advantage', *Kyklos*, vol. 32, no. 3, pp. 559–70.

Mansfield, E. (1968), *Industrial Research and Technological Innovation: An Econometric Analysis*, New York, Norton & Company Inc.

Mansfield, E. (1980), 'Basic Research and Productivity Increase in Manufacturing', *American Economic Review*, vol. 70, no. 5, pp. 863–73.

Mansfield, E., Rapoport, J., Romeo, A., Wagner, S. and Beardsley, G. (1977), 'Social and Private Rates of Return from Industrial Innovations', *Quarterly Journal of Economics*, vol. 91, pp. 222–40.

Mansfield, E., Rapoport, J., Schnee, J., Wagner, S. and Homburger, M. (1971), *Research and Innovation in the Modern Corporation*, London and Basingstoke, The Macmillan Press Ltd.

Mansfield, E. and Romeo, A. (1980), 'Technology Transfer to Overseas Subsidiaries by US Based Firms', *Quarterly Journal of Economics*, vol. 95, pp. 737–80.

Mansfield, E., Romeo, A. and Wagner, S. (1979), 'Foreign Trade and US Research and Development', *Review of Economics and Statistics*, vol. 61, no. 1, pp. 49–57.

Mansfield, E., Teece, D. and Romeo, A. (1979), 'Overseas Research and Development by US Based Firms', *Economica*, vol. 46, pp. 187–96.

Markham, J.W. (1965), 'Market Structure, Business Conduct and Innovation', *American Economic Review*, vol. 55, no. 2, pp. 323–32.

Markusen, J.R. (1981), 'Trade and the Gains from Trade with Imperfect Competition', *Journal of International Economics*, vol. 11, no. 4, pp. 531–51.

Matthews, R.C.O. (1973), 'Foreign Trade and British Economic Growth', *Scottish Journal of Political Economy*, vol. 20, no. 2, November, pp. 192–209.

McEachern, W.A. and Romeo, A.A. (1978), 'Stockholder Control, Uncertainty and the Allocation of Resources to Research and Development', *Journal of Industrial Economics*, vol. 26, no. 4, pp. 349–61.

McLean, I.W. and Round, D.K. (1978), 'Research and Product Innovation in Australian Manufacturing Industries', *Journal of Industrial Economics*, vol. 27, no. 1, pp. 1–12.

Mueller, D.C. and Tilton, J.E. (1969), 'Research and Development Costs as a Barrier to Entry', *Canadian Journal of Economics*, vol. 2, no. 4, pp. 570–9.

Myrdal, G. (1957), *Economic Theory and Under-developed Regions*, London, Duckworth.

Nadiri, M.I. and Schankerman, M.A. (1981), 'Technical Change, Returns to Scale, and the Productivity Slowdown', *American Economic Review*, papers and proceedings, vol. 71, no. 2, pp. 314–19.

National Economic Development Council, Manpower Services Commission (1984), *Competence and Competition – Training and Education in the*

Federal Republic of Germany, the United States and Japan, National Economic Development Office, London, HMSO.

Needham, D. (1975), 'Market Structure and Firms' R&D Behaviour', *Journal of Industrial Economics*, vol. 23, no. 4, pp. 241–55.

Nelson, R.R. (1980), 'Technical Advances and Productivity Growth: Retrospect, Prospect and Policy Issues', in Leveson, I. and Wheeler, J. (eds.), *Western Economies in Transition: Structural Change and Adjustment Policies in Industrial Countries*, London, Croom Helm.

Nelson, R.R. and Winter, S.G. (1977), 'In Search of Useful Theory of Innovation', in Stroetman, K. (ed.), *Innovation, Economic Change and Technology Policies*, Basel and Stuttgart, Birkhauser Verlag.

Nelson, R.R. and Winter, S.G. (1978), 'Forces Generating and Limiting Concentration under Schumpeterian Competition', *Bell Journal of Economics*, vol. 9, no. 2, pp. 524–48.

Nerlove, M. and Arrow, K. (1962), 'Optimal Advertising Policy under Dynamic Conditions', *Economica*, vol. 29, pp. 129–42.

Nordhaus, W.D. (1969), *Invention, Growth and Welfare*, Cambridge, Massachusetts and London, England, The MIT Press.

Norris, K. and Vaizey, J. (1973), *The Economics of Research and Technology*, London, George Allen and Unwin Ltd.

OECD (1975), *Patterns of Resources Devoted to Research and Experimental Development in the OECD Area 1963–1971*, Paris, OECD.

OECD (1976), *The Measurement of Scientific and Technical Activities*, Paris, OECD.

OECD (1979), *Trends in Industrial R&D in Selected OECD Member Countries 1967–1975*, Paris, OECD.

OECD (1980), *Technical Change and Economic Policy*, Paris, OECD.

OECD (1983), 'International Trade in High Technology Products: an Empirical Approach', Paris, mimeo.

OECD (1984a), 'Recent Trends in R&D Resources in OECD Member Countries', DSTI/SPR/84.45, Paris, mimeo.

OECD (1984b), 'Indicators of the Technological Position and Performance in OECD Member Countries During the Seventies', DSTI/SPR/84.43, Paris, mimeo.

OECD (1984c), 'Indicators of Government Financial Support for Industry-related R&D', DSTI/SPR/84.47, Paris, mimeo.

OECD (1984d), 'Specialisation and Competitiveness in Manufacturing Industries of High, Medium and Low R&D Intensity: General Trends', DSTI/SPR/84.49, Paris, mimeo.

Pagoulatos, E. and Sorensen. R. (1976), 'Domestic Market Structure and International Trade: An Empirical Analysis', *Quarterly Review of Economics and Business*, vol. 16, no.1, pp. 45–59.

Panić, M. and Joyce, P.L. (1980), 'UK Manufacturing Industry: International Integration and Trade Performance', *Bank of England Quarterly Bulletin*, vol. 20. June, pp. 42–55.

Parker, J.E.S. (1978), *The Economics of Innovation*, London and New York, Longman.

Pavitt, K. (1981), 'Technology in British Industry: a Suitable Case for Improvement', in Carter, C. (ed.), *Industrial Policy and Innovation*, London, Heinemann.

Pavitt, K. and Soete, L. (1980), 'Innovative Activities and Export Shares: Some Comparisons between Industries and Countries', in Pavitt, K. (ed.), *Technical Innovation and British Economic Performance*, London and Basingstoke, The Macmillan Press Ltd.

Posner, M.V. (1961), 'International Trade and Technical Change', *Oxford Economic Papers*, vol. 13, no. 3, pp. 323–44.

Prais, S.J. (1981), 'Vocational Qualifications of the Labour Force in Britain and Germany', *National Institute Economic Review*, no. 98, November.

Rosenberg, J.B. (1976), 'Research and Market Share: A Re-appraisal of the Schumpeter Hypothesis', *Journal of Industrial Economics*, vol. 25, no. 2, pp. 101–12.

Rosenberg, N. (1974), 'Science, Invention and Economic Growth', *Economic Journal*, vol. 84, March, pp. 90–108.

Roskamp, K.W. and McMeekin, G.C. (1968), 'Factor Proportions, Human Capital and Foreign Trade: The Case of West Germany Reconsidered', *Quarterly Journal of Economics*, vol. 82, no. 1, pp. 152–60.

Rothwell, R. (1979), 'The Relationship between Technical Change and Economic Performance in Mechanical Engineering: Some Evidence', in Baker, M. (ed.), *Industrial Innovation, Technology Policy and Diffusion*, London and Basingstoke, Macmillan.

Rothwell, R. (1980), 'Non-Price Factors in the Export Competitiveness of Agricultural Engineering Products', Science and Technology Indicators Conference, Paris, OECD.

Rothwell, R. and Teubal, M. (1977), 'Sappho Revisited: A Re-appraisal of The Sappho Data', in Stroetmann, K.A. (ed.), *Innovation, Economic Change and Technology Policies*, Basel and Stuttgart, Birkhauser Verlag.

Saunders, C. (1978), *Engineering in Britain, West Germany and France*, Sussex European Papers no. 3.

Scherer, F.M. (1965), 'Firm Size, Market Structure, Opportunity and the Output of Patented Inventions', *American Economic Review*, vol. 55, no. 5, pp. 1097–1125.

Scherer, F.M. (1967), 'Market Structure and the Employment of Scientists and Engineers', *American Economic Review*, vol. 57, pp. 524–31.

Scherer, F.M. (1982), 'Demand-Pull and Technological Invention: Schmookler Revisited', *Journal of Industrial Economics*, vol. 30, no. 3, pp. 225–37.

Schmalensee, R. (1979), 'Market Structure, Durability and Quality: a Selective Survey', *Economic Inquiry*, vol. 17, April, pp. 177–96.

Schmookler, J. (1962), 'Economic Sources of Inventive Activity', *Journal of Economic History*, vol. 22, March, pp. 1–20.

Schmookler, J. (1966), *Invention and Economic Growth*, Cambridge, Massachusetts, Harvard University Press.

Schott, K. (1976), 'Investment in Private Industrial Research and Development in Britain', *Journal of Industrial Economics*, vol. 25, no. 2, pp. 81–100.

Schott, K. (1978), 'The Relations Between Industrial Research and Development and Factor Demands', *Economic Journal*, vol. 88, March, pp. 85–106.

Schott, K. (1981), *Industrial Innovation in the United Kingdom, Canada and the United States*, London, British North America Committee.

Schumpeter, J.A. (1976), *Capitalism, Socialism and Democracy* (5th edition), London, Allen and Unwin.

Shaw, J.A. and Leet, D.R. (1973), 'Research and Development and Productivity Change in the US, 1948–1968', *Journal of Industrial Economics*, vol. 22, no. 2, pp. 153–5.

Sheshinski, E. (1976), 'Price, Quality and Quantity Regulation in Monopoly Situations', *Economica*, vol. 43, no. 170, pp. 127–37.

Shonfield, A. (1981), 'Innovation: Does Government Have a Role?', in Carter, C. (ed.), *Industrial Policy and Innovation*, Joint Studies in Public Policy, no. 3, London, Heinemann.

Shrieves, R.E. (1978), 'Market Structure and Innovation: A New Perspective', *Journal of Industrial Economics*, vol. 26, no. 4, pp. 329–47.

Shubik, M. with Levitan, R. (1980), *Market Structure and Behaviour*, Cambridge, Massachusetts, Harvard University Press.

Singh, A. (1977), 'UK Industry and the World Economy: a Case of De-industrialisation?', *Cambridge Journal of Economics*, vol. 1, no. 2, pp. 113–36.

Smith, S.R., White, G.M., Owen, N.C. and Hill, M.R. (1982), 'UK Trade in Manufacturing: The Pattern of Specialisation During the 1970s', Departments of Industry and Trade Government Economic Service Working Paper no. 56, London.

Smyth, D.J., Samuels, J.M. and Tzoannos, J. (1972), 'Patents, Profitability, Liquidity and Firm Size', *Applied Economics*, vol. 4, pp. 77–86.

Soete, L.L.G. (1979), 'Firm Size and Inventive Activity: the Evidence Reconsidered', *European Economic Review*, vol. 12, pp. 319–40.

Soete, L.L.G. (1980), 'The Impact of Technological Innovation on International Trade Patterns: The Evidence Reconsidered', OECD, Science and Technology Indicators Conference, 15–19 September, Paris, mimeo.

Soete, L.L.G. (1981), 'A General Test of Technological Gap Trade Theory', *Weltwirtschaftliches Archiv*, Band 117, no. 4, pp. 638–59.

Solo, R. (1966), 'The Capacity to Assimilate an Advanced Technology', *American Economic Review*, Papers and Proceedings, vol. 56, May, pp. 91–7.

Solomon, R.F. and Ingham, K.P. (1977), 'Discriminating between MNC Subsidiaries and Indigenous Companies: A Comparative Analysis of the British Mechanical Engineering Industry', *Oxford Bulletin of Economics and Statistics*, vol. 39, pp. 127–38.

Spence, A.M. (1975), 'Monopoly, Quality and Regulation', *Bell Journal of Economics*, vol. 6, no. 2, pp. 417–29.

Spencer, B.J. and Brander, J.A. (1983), 'International R&D Rivalry and Industrial Strategy', *Review of Economic Studies*, no. 163, pp. 707–22.

Stern, R.M. and Maskus, K.E. (1981), 'Determinants of the Structure of US Foreign Trade, 1958–76', *Journal of International Economics*, vol. 11, no. 2, pp. 207–24.

Stoneman, P. (1979), 'Patenting Activity: A Re-evaluation of the Influence of Demand Pressures', *Journal of Industrial Economics*, vol. 27, no. 4, pp. 385–401.

Stoneman, P. (1983), *The Economic Analysis of Technological Change*, New York, Oxford University Press.

Stout, D. (1981), 'The Case for Government Support of R&D and Innovation', in Carter, C. (ed.), *Industrial Policy and Innovation*, Joint Studies in Public Policy, no. 3, London, Heinemann.

Stroetmann, K.A. (1979), 'Innovation in Small and Medium-sized Industrial Firms – a German Perspective', in Baker, M.J. (ed.), *Industrial Innovation*, London and Basingstoke, Macmillan.

Sveikauskas, L. (1983), 'Science and Technology in United States Foreign Trade', *Economic Journal*, vol. 93, no. 371, pp. 542–54.

Swan, P.L. (1970), 'Market Structure and Technological Progress: the Influence of Monopoly on Product Innovation', *Quarterly Journal of Economics*, vol. 84, no. 4, pp. 627–38.

Sylos-Labini, P. (1969), *Oligopoly and Technical Progress*, Cambridge, Massachusetts, Harvard University Press.

Taylor, C.T. and Silberston, Z.A. (1973), *The Economic Impact of the Patent System*, University of Cambridge, Department of Applied Economics, Monograph 23, Cambridge University Press.

Terleckyj, N.E. (1980), 'What do R&D Numbers Tell us about Technological Change?', *American Economic Review*, Papers and Proceedings, vol. 70, no. 2, pp. 55–61.

Thatcher, A.R. (1978), 'Labour Supply and Employment Trends', in Blackaby, F. (ed.), *De-industrialisation*, London, Heinemann Educational Books.

Utterback, J.M. (1979a), 'The Dynamics of Product and Process Innovation in Industry', in Hill, C.C.T. and Utterback, J.M. (eds.), *Technological Innovation for a Dynamic Economy*, New York, Pergamon Press.

Utterback, J.M. (1979b), 'Product and Process Innovation in a Changing Competitive Environment', in Baker, M.J. (ed.), *Industrial Innovation*, London and Basingstoke, Macmillan.

Utton, M. and Morgan, E. (1983), *Concentration and Foreign Trade*, Cambridge, Cambridge University Press.

Vernon, R. (1966), 'International Investment and International Trade in the Product Cycle', *Quarterly Journal of Economics*, vol. 80, no. 2, pp. 190–207.

Walker, W.B. (1979), *Industrial Innovation and International Trading Performance*, Greenwich, Connecticut, JAI Press Inc.

Weiser, L. and Jay, K. (1972), 'Determinants of the Commodity Structure of US Trade: Comment', *American Economic Review*, vol. 62 (June), pp. 459–64.

Wells, L.T. Jnr. (1969), 'Test of a Product Cycle Model of International Trade: US Exports of Consumer Durables', *Quarterly Journal of Economics*, vol. 83, no. 1, pp. 152–162.

White, G.M. (1981), 'The Adoption and Transfer of Technology and the Role of Government', in Carter, C. (ed.), *Industrial Policy and Innovation*, Joint Studies in Public Policy no. 3, London, Heinemann.

White, L.J. (1974), 'Industrial Organisation and International Trade: Some Theoretical Considerations', *American Economic Review*, vol. 64, no. 6, pp. 1013–20.

Williamson, O.E. (1965), 'Innovation and Market Structure', *Journal of Political Economy*, vol. 73, pp. 67–73.

Wilson, R.W. (1977), 'The Effect of Technological Environment and Product Rivalry on R&D Effort and Licensing of Inventions', *Review of Economics and Statistics*, vol. 59, no. 2, pp. 171–8.

Winters, L.A. (1981), *An Econometric Model of the Export Sector*, Cambridge

Studies in Applied Econometrics: 4, Cambridge, Cambridge University Press.

Wolter, F. (1977), 'Factor Proportions, Technology and West German Industry's International Trade Patterns', *Weltwirtschaftliches Archiv*, Band 113, pp. 250–67.

Data and data classification sources

I would like to thank the Department of Industry for making available data on exports, imports and gross output at constant prices; research and development expenditures; skilled manual labour and professional and technical staff; and the Office of Fair Trading for making available data on capital stock, prepared by R. Allard. I would like to thank the OECD for making data available from the OECD/STIU data bank.

Annual Statement of the Overseas Trade of the United Kingdom, vol. 1, Summary Tables of Imports and Exports, 1970, 1972, London, HMSO.

Armstrong, A. (ed.), 1974, *Structural Change in the British Economy 1948–1968*, Department of Applied Economics, University of Cambridge, Chapman and Hall.

Armstrong, A.G. (1979), 'Capital Stock in UK Manufacturing Industry: Disaggregated Estimates 1947–1976', in Patterson, K.D. and Schott, K. (eds.), *The Measurement of Capital*, London and Basingstoke, The Macmillan Press Ltd.

Bericht des Bundeskartellamtes über seine Tätigkeit in Jahre 1973.

Census 1971, Great Britain, Economic Activity Part IV (10 per cent sample), Office of Population, Censuses and Surveys, London, HMSO, 1975.

Commodity Indices for the Standard International Trade Classification, Revised, United Nations Statistical Papers, Series M, no. 38, vol. 1, New York, 1963.

Concordance between SITC (R1) and ISIC Classifications, Paris, OECD, 1979.

Hufbauer, C.G. (1970), 'The Impact of National Characteristics and Technology on the Commodity Composition of Trade in Manufactured Goods', in Vernon, R. (ed.), *The Technology Factor in International Trade*, New York, NBER.

Indexes to the International Standard Industrial Classification of All Economic Activities, United Nations Statistical Papers, Series M, no. 4, rev. 2, add. 1, New York, 1971.

Industrial Research and Development Expenditure and Employment, 1975, *Business Monitor* M014, London HMSO, 1979.

Industrial Research and Development Expenditure and Employment, 1978, *Business Monitor* M014, London, HMSO, 1980.

International Financial Statistics 1973, yearbook, Washington D.C., International Monetary Fund.

International Financial Statistics, 1978, yearbook, Washington D.C. International Monetary Fund.

International Statistical Year 1973, Paris, OECD, 1977.

International Statistical Year 1975, Paris, OECD, 1979.

Monthly Digest of Statistics, no. 381, 1977, London, HMSO.

Monthly Digest of Statistics, no. 393, 1978, London, HMSO.

Monthly Report of the Deutsche Bundesbank, 1981, vol. 33, no. 10.

Monthly Report of the Deutsche Bundesbank, 1981, vol. 33, no. 11.

National Income and Expenditure Accounts 1965–1975, CSO, London, HMSO, 1976.

OECD (1979), *Trends in R&D in Selected OECD Member Countries 1967–1975*, Paris, OECD.

Overseas Trade Analysed in Terms of Industries, 1974, *Business Monitor* BM10, London, HMSO.

Overseas Trade Analysed in Terms of Industries, 1978, *Business Monitor* BM10, London, HMSO.

Report on the Census of Production 1968, 158 Summary Tables: Enterprise Analyses, London, HMSO.

Report on the Census of Production, Business Monitor PA1002, 1971–1973, 1976, 1978, Summary Tables, London, HMSO.

Report on the Census of Production 1974 and 1975, *Business Monitor* PA1002, vol. 1, Summary Tables, Establishment Analyses, vol. 2, Summary Tables, Enterprise Analysis, London, HMSO.

Report on the Census of Production 1975, *Business Monitors* PA211–PA491, London, HMSO.

Research and Development Expenditure and Employment 1972, CSO Studies in Official Statistics no. 27, London, HMSO, 1976.

Schwerpunktmässige Zuordnung von SYPRO-Nummern zu ISIC-Positionen 1982, Wiesbaden Statistisches Bundesamt.

Standard International Trade Classification Revision 2, Statistical Papers, Series M, no. 34/rev. 2, United Nations, New York, 1975.

Statistisches Jahrbuch, 1973, 1975, 1976, 1977, 1978, 1979, Wiesbaden Statistisches Bundesamt.

Trade by Commodities Market Summaries: Exports Jan–Dec 1978. Series C. Statistics of Foreign Trade, OECD, Paris.

US Census of Manufactures, 1972, U.S. Department of Commerce, Bureau of the Census, Washington D.C.

Yearbook of Industrial Statistics, vol. 1, 1972–1975, 1978, New York, United Nations.

Yearbook of National Account Statistics, 1979, vol. 2, United Nations, New York.

Index of Authors

General Index